Welcome to Montpellier!

PUBLISHING
Collection Directors and Authors: Dominique AUZIAS and Jean-Paul LABOURDETTE
Responsables for Publishing: Tristan CUCHE

Authors: Marc BASTIDE, Anne-Charlotte ERIAU, Tatiana TISSOT, Annie FAYON, Manon JACQUEMIN, Gil MARTIN, Alain MARTINEZ, Marie Christine HARANT, Annabelle ARBONVILLE, Elodie ROUX, Nicolas MAZET, Jean-Paul LABOURDETTE, Dominique AUZIAS and alter

Publishing Director: Stéphan SZEREMETA
Publishing Team: François TOURNIE, Jeff BUCHE, Grégoire DECONIHOUT, Perrine GALAZKA, Patrick MARINGE, Caroline MICHELOT, Morgane VESLIN, Pierre-Yves SOUCHET

STUDIO
Studio Manager: Sophie LECHERTIER assisted by Romain AUDREN
Layout: Julie BORDES, Élodie CLAVIER, Sandrine MECKING, Delphine PAGANO, Laurie PILLOIS, Hugues RENAULT
Pictures Management and Mapping: Audrey LALOY

WEB
Web Technical Director: Lionel CAZAUMAYOU
Web Management and Development: Jean-Marc REYMUND assisted by Florian FAZER, Anthony GUYOT, Cédric MAILLOUX, Christophe PERREAU

PUBLICITY TEAM
Web and Sales Director: Olivier AZPIROZ
Local Publicity Responsible: Michel GRANSEIGNE
Assistant: Victor CORREIA
Customer Relationship Management: Vimla MEETTOO

NATIONAL PUBLICITY TEAM
National Publicity Responsible: Aurélien MILTENBERGER assisted by Sandra RUFFIEUX

Advertising Managers: Caroline AUBRY, Perrine DE CARNE MARCEIN, Caroline GENTELET, Stéphanie MORRIS, Caroline PREAU, Sacha GOURAND, Carla ZUNIGA, Florian MEYBERGER

INTERNATIONAL PUBLICITY TEAM
Director: Karine VIROT assisted by Elise CADIOU
Advertising Managers: Romain COLLYER, Camille ESMIEU, and Guillaume LABOUREUR

CIRCULATION AND PROMOTION
Sales Promotion Director: Bénédicte MOULET assisted by Aissatou DIOP and Alicia FILANKEMBO
Sales Manager: Jean-Pierre GHEZ assisted by Nathalie GONCALVES
Press-Sponsors Partnership Management: Jean-Mary MARCHAL

ADMINISTRATION
Chairman: Jean-Paul LABOURDETTE
Financial Director: Gérard BRODIN
Human Resources Director: Dina BOURDEAU assisted by Léa BENARD, Sandra MORAIS
Information Technology Manager: Pascal LE GOFF
Accounting: Nicolas FESQUET assisted by Jeannine DEMIRDJIAN, Oumy DIOUF, Christelle MANEBARD
Collection: Fabien BONNAN assisted by Sandra BRIJLALL
Switchboard: Jehanne AOUMEUR

PETIT FUTE BEST OF MONTPELLIER 2015
Dominique Auzias founded Le Petit Futé.
Published by Les Nouvelles Editions de l'Université
18 rue des Volontaires - 75015 Paris.
Tel: + 33 (0)1 53 69 70 00 - Fax +33 (0)1 42 73 15 24
Internet: www.petitfute.uk.com
SAS with a capital of € 1000000 -
RC PARIS B 309 769 966
Cover: Marc Rigaud © Fotolia
Printed by: IMPRIMERIE CHIRAT -
42540 Saint-Just-la-Pendue - 14110 Condé-sur-Noireau
ISBN: 9782746975941

To contact us by email, family name (lowercase)
followed by @petitfute.com
Send an e-mail to the editor: info@petitfute.com

Today 8th city of France, Montpellier continues its vertiginous development. More young than its Languedoc neighbors as far as history is concerned, it is however the figurehead of the region, by its incredible dynamism. Montpellier is young, thanks to its population, which in particular has a large number of students present here. The Entertainment and the festival, the frank good humour of the south, contribute to the construction of unforgettable memories. City side, the facilities have increased these recent years, and urbanism and architecture are strongly turned to a thought-out modernism. The existence of the largest pedestrian centre of France and urban requirements in terms of sustainable development are showing it. All this results in a beautiful harmony and the old buildings in the centre, many of them dating from the Middle Ages live side by side with the most modern architectural achievements, whose some are signed by the greatest names of architecture. The dynamism is also cultural, and the number of festivals and events taking place in Montpellier is simply breathtaking. But do not panic! Petit Futé is there to guide you through the mass of what to see and do. Montpellier is also and especially the sun, which shines here with insolence (more than 300 days of sunshine per year), and the sea close by. Everything is there to make you spend pleasant holidays, and you can easily enjoy the city and take a dip in the same day. inland Getaways will also delight lovers of wild and preserved nature, For, whether towards Camargue, the stretches of Languedoc vineyards or the foothills of the Cévennes, we are very quickly out of Montpellier and the magic of the landscapes is immediately required.

Certifié PEFC
Ce produit est issu de forêts gérées durablement et de sources contrôlées.
pefc-france.org

DIGITAL VERSION FOR FREE
See page 39

Contents

Restaurants

High Budget	12
Medium Budget	16
Small Budget	22
Specialities	23
World Cuisine	23
Fast Food & Delivery	26
Gourmet Escapes	28

Accommodation

Hotels	32
Hostel	37
Camping	37
Guesthouses	38
Cottages	38
Other Accommodation	40

Having Fun Going Out

Bars – Coffeehouses	42
Clubs – Nightclubs	46
Shows	46

Sports & Leisures

Air Sports	50
Individual Sports	50
Water Sports	52

Shopping Fashion Gifts

Jewellery – Clocks	54
Good Tips	54
Gifts	55
Shopping Centres	57
Naughty – Sex	58
Art Galleries	58
Games & Toys	60
Bookshops	61
Fashion Clothes	62
Multimedia – Picture – Sound	62
Music	63

Grourmet Products Wines

Coffee – Tea – Herbal Tea	66
Delicatessen	66
Cheese Shops – Dairies	68
Markets – Covered Markets	69
Breads – Cakes	
Chocolates – Ice Creams	70
Fish - Seafood	72
Local products	72
Products Of The World	73
Caterers	74
Wines & Spirits	74

Beauty & Wellness

Hairdressers	80
Relaxation & Body Shape	81

Home Decor Garden

Outdoor Arrangements	84
Tableware	84
Antique Dealers	84
Arts & Crafts	85
Do-It-Yourself – Gardening	85
Decoration	86

Tours Points of Interest

Tourist Offices	98
Guides Tours	98
Monuments & Buildings	102
Religious Buildings	104
Museums	105
Urban Sites	107
Parcs & Gardens	108
Nature Sites	110
Theme Parks	113
Animals – Aquariums	113

Services

Administrations – Public Services	88
Banks – Insurances	88
Culture	90
Teaching	90
Real Estate	93
Wedding & receptions	95
Business Services	95

Travel Tourism Transport

Travel Agencies	116
Transport	116
Vehicle Rentals	120

Champ de Mars garden of Montpellier

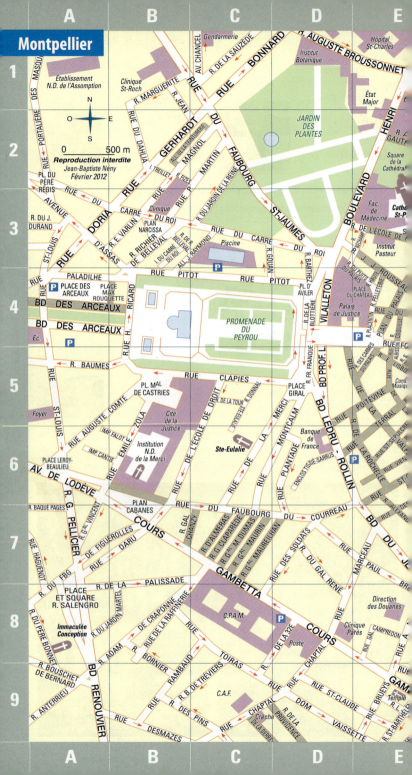

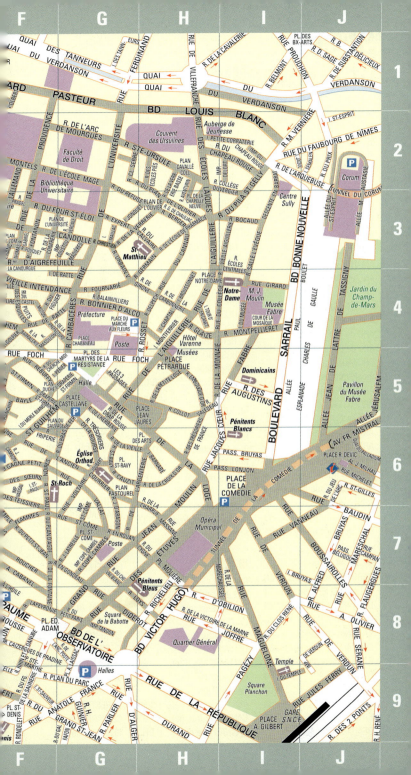

Streets of Montpellier

A

ABBÉ M. MONTELS (rue de l')........E2/G2
ADAM (place Ed.)......G8
AIGREFEUILLE (rue d')F4/G4
AIGUILLERIE (rue de l')........H4/H3
ALBISSON (rue).......E5
ALGER (rue d')........H8/H9
ALMÉRAS (rue d').....C7
AMANDIER (rue de l')...E5
ANCIEN COURRIER (rue de l')..........G6
ANTERRIEU (rue)......A9
ARAGON (rue J.)...G6/G7
ARC de MOURGUES (rue de l')..........G2
ARCEAUX (boulevard des).....A4/B4
ARCEAUX (place des)...A4
ARGENTERIE (rue de l')..........H7/H6
ARQUEBUSE (rue de l')I2/J3
ARTS (place des)......H5
ASSAS (avenue d')..A3/B4
ASTRUC (rue).........E4
AUGUSTINS (rue des)....I5
AUSTASIE (allée M.)..J3/J2
AVENTURIN (rue).....H3
AVILER (place d')......D4

B

BABOTTE (square de la). G8
BALAINVILLIERS (rue)... G4
BALANCES (rue des) .E7/E6
BAQUÉ PAGÈS (rue) A6
BARNABE (impasse) ... H6
BARRALERIE (rue la) .F4/G4
BARRAT (descente en)...I3
BARTHEZ (rue)..... D3/D4
BAUDIN (rue)........I6/J7
BAUMES (rue) A5/B5
BAYLE (rue du)........F5
BEAUX-ARTS (place des) .I1
BÉCHAMP (rue) B3
BELLEVAL (rue de)...B3/C3
BELMONT (rue).........I1
BERGER (rue).........H3
BLANC (boulevard Louis).... H2/I2
BLOTTIÈRE (rue de la) .. D4
BOCAUD (rue) I3
BONNARD (rue).....C2/C1
BONNE NOUVELLE (boulevard) I4/I3
BONNIER D'ALCO (rue) G4/H4
BORNIER (rue)........ B8
BOULET (allée Paul)....I4
BOUSCHET de BERNARD (rue)...A8/A9
BOUSSAIROLLES (rue) I6/J7
BRAS de FER (rue du) G6/G5
BROUSSE (rue Paul)..D7/E7
BROUSSONNET (impasse)............. H4
BROUSSONNET (rue Auguste).......D1/E1
BRUEYS (rue)......D9/E9
BRUN (impasse)...... E6
BRUYAS (impasse)......I7
BRUYAS (passage)......I6
BRUYAS (rue Alfred).. I7/J7
BURGUES (impasse).... F2

C

CABANEL (rue Alexandre) E6/E7
CABANES (plan)....... B6
CAIZERGUES de PRADINE (rue)....F8/G8
CALVAIRE (rue du) H3
CAMBACÉRÈS (rue) G4
CAMBON (rue J.) F6
CAMPREDON (rue Général) D8/E8
CANDOLLE (rue de) ..F3/G3
CANNAU (rue du) ... H4/H3
CANOURGUE (place de la)F4
CANOURGUE (rue de la) . E4
CANTIE (impasse) ...A6/B6
CARBONNERIE (rue de la) H4
CARDINAL de CABRIÈRES (rue du) ..E1/E3
CARMES du PALAIS (rue des) D5
CARRÉ du ROI (impasse du) B4/B3
CARRÉ du ROI (rue du) A3/B3
CASTEL-MOTON (rue) F4/G4
CASTELLANE (place) ... G5
CASTELNAU (rue de) . F5/F6
CASTILLON (rue) F8
CASTRIES (place Maréchal de).... B5
CATHEDRALE (square de la) E2
CAUZIT (rue) G6/H6
CAVALERIE (rue de la) H1/I1
CAVALLÉ COLL (plan)... H2
CHABANEAU (place)... G4
CHAMP-DE-MARS (jardin du) J4
CHANCEL (Av.)........ C1
CHANZY (rue Général)B7/C7
CHAPEAU ROUGE (impasse du) I2
CHAPEAU ROUGE (rue du) H2/I2
CHAPELLE NEUVE (place de la).......... H3
CHAPTAL (impasse) H4
CHAPTAL (rue)........ C9
CHARANCY (rue) F2
CHARRUE (rue de la) ... H6
CHATEAU (place du) ... D4
CHAULIAC (rue G. de)... H3
CHERCHE-MIDI (rue du) . G5
CHEVAL VERT (rue du)E8/F9
CHRESTIEN (rue) G3
CLAPARÈDE (rue G.)... C7
CLAPIES (rue) C5

CLÉMENCEAU (avenue G.) F9
CLOS RENÉ (rue du).....I8
CŒUR (rue Jacques) H6/H5
COLBERT
(rue Joachim) F2/F1
COLLÈGE (rue du) H4
COLLÈGE DUVERGIER
(rue) H3/I3
COLLOT (rue).........H5
COMEDIE (place de la)..H6
COMÉDIE
(tunnel de la) H7/I6
COMTE (rue Auguste) A6/B5
CONFRERIE (rue de la)..G3
COPÉ-CAMBES (impasse)G7
COPÉ-CAMBES (rue) ...G7
COQUILLE (rue) E4
CORRATERIE ST-GERMAIN
(rue de la) F3
CORUM (tunnel du) J3
COSTE FRÈGE (rue) ..E4/E3
COUSTOU (impasse) ...G3
CRAPONNE
(rue Adam de) B8
CROIX D'OR (rue de la) H6
CYGNE (rue du) H7

■ D ■

DAHLIA (rue du).......B2
DARU (rue)............B7
DÉLICIEUX (rue B.).....J1
DELPECH (rue).........H4
DESMAZES (rue) B9
2 PONTS (rue des).....J9
DEVIC (place rue).....J6
DIDEROT (rue) G7/H8
DIGEON (rue S.).......E5
DOM VAISSETTE (rue)C9/D9
DONNAL (rue) C5
DORIA (rue) A4/B3
DRAPERIE ST-FIRMIN
(impasse)............G5
DUCHÉ (plan).........G5
DUMAS (rue Général M.) C7
DURAND (rue du J.)....A3
DURAND (rue) G9/H9

■ E ■

ÉCOLE de DROIT
(rue de l').........B6/C5
ÉCOLE de MÉDECINE
(rue de l')..........D3/E3
ÉCOLE de PHARMACIE
(rue de l')............H3
ÉCOLE MAGE
(rue de l').........G2/G3
ÉCOLES CENTRALES
(rue des) I4
ECOLES LAÏQUES
(rue des) H2/H3
ECOLES PIÈS
(rue des) H3/H2
EMBOUQUE D'OR (rue)..H5
EN GONDEAU (rue).....G7
EN ROUAN (rue) G7/H7
ENCLOS
TISSIÉ-SARRUS D6
EPEISSES (rue d').....E5
ESTELLE (rue)........F8
ETUVES (rue des)...G8/H7
EXPERT (rue) G3

■ F ■

FABRE (rue)..........I5
FAFON (rue du Général) . G9
FALOT (impasse) B6
FAUBOURG de FIGUEROLLES
(rue du) A7/B7
FAUBOURG de NÎMES
(rue du) I2/J2
FAUBOURG du COURREAU
(rue du) C6/D6
FAUBOURG ST-JAUMES
(rue du) C1/D3
FERDINAND (rue) ..G2/H1
FERRY (rue Jules) ...I9/J8
FIGUIER (rue du) G4
FIZES (rue).........B3/C3
FLAUGERGUES (rue)..J8/J7
FOCH (rue)........E4/E5
FONTAINE (rue de la) G7/G8
FONTANON (rue) F3/G3
FOUQUET (rue).....F3/G3
FOUR des FLAMMES
(rue du) E7/G6
FOUR ST-ÉLOI (rue du)..G3
FOURNARIÉ (rue) G4
FRANCE (rue Anatole)F9/G8
FRANQUE (rue Fr.)....D5
FRIPERIE (rue) F6

■ G ■

GABRIEL (rue) F3
GAGNE-PETIT (rue du)F6/G6
GALAVIEILLE (rue) E9
GAMBETTA (cours)...B7/C7
GAULLE
(esplanade Charles de) ..I5
GAUTIER (rue A.) E2
GERBE (impasse de la) . C9
GERHARDT (rue) B3/C2
GERMAIN (rue).....H4/H3
GILBERT (place A.)......I9
GIRAL (place) D5
GIRARD (rue) I4
GIRAUDIN (rue Louise) . . E9
GIRONE (rue de).......H4
GLAIZE (rue).........H4
GOUAN (rue) C3/C4
GRAND ST-JEAN
(rue du) F9/G9
GRAND-RUE
JEAN MOULIN G7/H6
GUINIER (rue H.).......G9
GUIRAUD (rue) E9

■ H ■

HAGUENOT (rue) A7
HAUTE (rue)..........D4
HERBERIE (rue de l') ...G5
HÔTEL de VILLE
(rue de l')............F4
HUGO
(boulevard Victor)...H8/H7
HUILE (rue de l').......E5

■ J ■

JAOUL (impasse) I2
JAURÈS (place Jean) ...H5
JEAN (rue) B2
JÉRUSALEM (allée) J5
JEU de L'ARC (rue du) ..J6
JEU de PAUME
(boulevard du) D7/F8
JOFFRE (rue) H8/I8
JONQUET (impasse). G3/H3
JOUBERT (rue).........G6

■ L ■

LAISSAC (place A.).....G8
LALLEMAND (rue) ...F3/F2

LAPEYRONIE (rue) . . . F8/G8
LATREILLE (rue J.) G7
LATTRE de TASSIGNY
(allée Jean de) J5/J4
LEBOUX (impasse) F2
LEDRU-ROLLIN
(boulevard) D5/D6
LEROY-BEAULIEU (place) A6
LIONNET (impasse) F2
LISBONNE (rue E.) E5
LODÈVE (avenue de) . . . A6
LOGE (rue de la) G5/H6
LONJON (passage) . . . H6/I6
LOYS (rue) H7/H8

■ M ■

MAGNOL (rue) B3/C2
MAGUELONE (rue) I7/I8
MAILLAC (impasse) G3
MARCEAU (rue) D8/D7
MARCHÉ AUX FLEURS
(place du) G4
MARÉCHAUSSÉE
(rue de la) I7/I8
MARESCHAL (rue) . . J8/J7
MARGUERITE (rue) . .B2/B1
MARTEL
(rue du jardin) B8/B7
MARTIN (rue P.) B3/C2
MARTYRS de LA
RÉSISTANCE (place des) G5
MASSANE (rue) H7
MASSILLON (rue) G4
MAUREILHAN
(rue Général) C7
MAURIN (rue Général) . . C7
MERCI (rue de la) . . . C6/D5
MERLE BLANC (I. du) F5/G5
MICHEL (rue A.) E8
MICHELET (rue) J6
MILHAU (allée J.) J6
MISTRAL (avenue Fr.) J6/J5
MONNAIE (rue de la) . . . H5
MONTCALM (rue) . . . C6/D5
MONTFERRIER
(impasse) H5
MONTGOLFIER (rue) . .F5/F4
MONTPELLIERET (rue) . . .I4
MOSAÏQUE (cour de la) . .I4
MOULIN À L'HUILE
(impasse du) F7

MULTIPLANTS
(impasse des) F6/F7
MULTIPLANTS
(rue des) E6/F6
MUSÉE (impasse du) I4

■ N ■

NARCISSA (plan) B3
NOTRE-DAME (place) . . H4

■ O ■

OBILION (rue d') H7/I8
OBSERVATOIRE
(boulevard de l') G8
OLIVIER (rue A.) I8/J8
OM (plan de l') F3

■ P ■

PAGÉZY (rue) H9/I8
PALADILHE (rue) . . . A4/B4
PALAIS (plan du) E4
PALAIS des GUILHEM
(rue du) E4/F4
PALISSADE (rue de la) . . B7
PALLADIUM (quai du) . . . J6
PARAN (impasse) E6
PARLIER (rue) G9
PASTEUR (boulevard) F1/G2
PASTOUREL (plan) G6
PELLETERIE (rue) . . . D4/E4
PELLICIER (rue G.) . . A6/A7
PÈRE BONNET (rue du) . A8
PÈRE RÉGIS (rue du) . . A2
PERIER (impasse) G5
PETIT PARIS (rue du) . . . G8
PETIT SCEL (rue du) F5
PETIT ST-JEAN
(rue du) F7/G7
PETITE CORRATERIE
(impasse) H2/I2
PETITE LOGE
(rue de la) H5
PÉTRARQUE (place) H5
PHILIPPY (rue) F5
PILA ST-GÉLLY
(rue du) H3/I3
PINS (rue des) B9/C9
PISTOLET (rue) F4
PITOT (rue) B4/C4
PLACENTIN (rue) D4

PLAN D'AGDE
(rue du) G6/G7
PLAN de L'OLIVIER
(rue du) H3
PLAN du PARC (rue) G8
PLANCHON (square) I8
PLANTADE (rue) C6/D6
POITEVINE (rue) D5/E5
PORTALIÈRE DES MASQUES
(rue de la) A2/A1
POSTE
(rue de l'Ancienne) G8
PRADEL (rue) F3
PRÉFECTURE (rue de la) . G4
PREMIER 1ER
(place Albert) F1
PRIX (rue du) J3/J2
PROUDHON (rue) I1
PROVIDENCE (rue de la) . D9
PUITS des ESQUILLES
(rue) F4
PUITS du PALAIS
(rue du) D4
PUITS du TEMPLE
(rue du) F6/F7

■ Q – R ■

IV (boulevard Henri) . .D3/E1
RAFFINERIE
(rue de la) B8/B7
RAMBAUD (rue) B9/C8
RANC (rue) F3
RANCHIN (rue) F5
RATTE (impasse de) G4
RATTE (rue de) F4/G4
RAYMOND (allée J.) . .B4/C3
REBUFFY (rue) F5/G5
REFUGE (rue du) . . . G3/H3
REINE
(rue du jardin de la) . .C3/C2
RENE (rue du Général) . D7
RENÉ (rue H.) J9
RENOUVIER
(boulevard) A8/B9
RÉPUBLIQUE
(rue de la) H8/I9
REY (rue) E6
RHIN ET DANUBE
(rue) F8/G8
RICARD (rue H.) B5/B4
RICHELIEU (rue) H8/H7

Botanical garden of Montpellier.
© STÉPHANE SAVIGNARD

RICHIER de BELLEVAL
(rue) B3
ROCHELLE (rue de la) D5/E6
RONDELET (rue). F9
ROSSET (rue). H5/H4
ROUCHER (rue) E6/E7
ROUCHER (rue) F7/G7
ROUSSEAU (rue J. J.) D3/E4

S

SAGE (rue D.). I1/J1
SALENGRO
(place et square rue) . . . A7
SALLE L'EVÊQUE (rue) . I4/I3
SARRAIL (boulevard) . . I6/I4
SAUNERIE (rue
du faubourg de la). . . F9/G8
SAUVAGE (plan du). G5
SAUZÈDE (rue de la) C1
SEMALEN (impasse) I2
SÉRANE (rue). J8
SERRE (rue Cl.) . . . H3/H2
SŒURS NOIRES
(rue des) F6/G6
SOLDATS (rue des) . C7/D7
ST-BARTHÉLÉMY (rue). . E9
ST-CLAUDE (rue) . . . D8/D9
ST-CÔME (impasse). . . . G6
ST-CÔME (place) G7
ST-CÔME (rue). G7
ST-DENIS (place) F9
ST-ESPRIT (allée du) . . . J3
ST-ESPRIT (impasse) . . . J2
ST-FIRMIN (rue). F5
ST-GILLES (rue) J6
ST-GUILHEM (rue) . . .D6/E6
ST-LOUIS (rue). A5/A6
ST-PAUL (rue) G6
ST-PIERRE (place) E3
ST-PIERRE (rue). F3/F4
ST-RAVY (place). G6
ST-RAVY (rue) G6
ST-SAUVEUR
(impasse). G8/G9
ST-SÉPULCRE (rue) . . E6/E5
STE-ANNE (rue) F5/F6
STE-CROIX (rue). F4
STE-MARTHE (P.) F8/G8
STE-URSULE (rue) H2
SUBSTANTION (rue de). . J1

T

TANDON (impasse). G8
TANNEURS
(impasse des) G1/H1
TANNEURS (quai des) F1/G1
TEINTURERIE
(allée de la) B2/C2
TEISSIERS (rue des). .F6/G6
TEMPLE (impasse du) . . .I8
TERRAL (rue). D6/E5
THOMAS (rue). F4/F3
TOIRAS (rue) C8
TOUR D' EN CANET
(impasse). H4
TOUR STE-EULALIE
(rue de la) C5
TREILLET (impasse) . .B2/B3
TRENTE DEUX 32ᴱ
(rue de la) C8/D8
TRÉSORIERS de FRANCE
(rue des) H6/H5
TRÉSORIERS
de LA BOURSE (rue). G5/G6
TRÉVIERS (rue B. de) B9/C8
3 PASSAGES (les). G5

U

UNIVERSITÉ (plan de l') . G3
UNIVERSITÉ
(rue de l'). G4/G2
URBAIN V (rue). G3/G4

V – Z

VALEDEAU (rue) H5
VALFÈRE (rue de la) . .D5/E6
VALLAT (rue) G6
VANNEAU (rue). I7/I6
VARLIN (rue E.) B3
VASSAL (impasse) F6
VERDANSON (quai du) H1/I2
VERDUN (impasse de) I8/J8
VERDUN (rue de) I8/J8
VERNIÈRE (rue M.) I2
VERRERIE (rue de la) G3/H3
VERRERIE BASSE
(rue de la) H3
VESTIAIRE (rue du). F4
VICTOIRE de LA MARNE
(rue de la) H8
VIEILLE (rue de la) . . G6/H6
VIEILLE AIGUILLERIE
(rue) H4/I3
VIEILLE INTENDANCE
(rue) F4/G4
VIEN (rue) E6
VILALLETON
(boulevard Prof. L.) . D5/D4
VILLEFRANCHE
(rue de) H1/H2
VINCENT
(rue Général) A7/B6
VOLTAIRE (rue). G6
ZOLA (rue Emile) . . .B6/B5

Restaurants

High Budget	→ 12
Medium Budget	→ 16
Small Budget	→ 22
Specialities	→ 23
World Cuisine	→ 23
Fast Food & Delivery	→ 26
Gourmet Escapes	→ 28

High Budget

■ LE CINQ
5, boulevard des Arceaux
☎ + 33 (0) 4 67 58 31 30
www.restaurantlecinq.com
restolecinq@gmail.com

Open all year. Monday to Friday for lunch; Thursday to Saturday for dinner. Booking advised. À la carte: Around €35. Daily special: €13. Terrace.

It is at the foot of the aqueduct of the Arceaux that Le Cinq stands, not far from the Esplanade du Peyrou. Stéphane and his team designed the place carefully and the result is a room with contemporary volumes, simple and elegant, with white, chocolate – brown and black colours. The service is professional and the cooking is fine, creative and changes regularly. You can taste the homemade fried foie gras and stewed apples rhubarb, followed by the dish: squid and Iberian chorizo with pesto. Dishes are creative, the control and storage is available. For dessert still, beautiful discoveries such as the homemade salted butter caramel. Recommended.

■ LA DILIGENCE
Place Pétrarque
☎ + 33 (0) 4 67 66 12 21
www.la-diligence.com
info@la-diligence.com

Open all year. Monday to Saturday for dinner; Tuesday to Friday for lunch. Menu from 38 € to 65 €. Lunch menu: 18 € (starter and main course or main course and dessert; 23 € for starter + main course + dessert).

Walking through the doors of Diligence, you will curiously discover a typical architecture of Montpellier with over six centuries of history. The velvet Bordeaux chairs gives the room a pleasant ancient French style setting. From the entrance, you will discover a whiskey cellar with over 200 bottles. Chef Laurent Riflade invites you to discover a traditional cuisine that changes with seasons. The lunch menu offers a delicious appetizer of avocado and tomato, a tasty fish soup and a fillet of swordfish. For dessert, you will have a chocolate tart. All you have to do is delight the taste buds. In the evening, La Diligence offers three menus: the discovery menu which opens with a crab cream soup, an oven dish of beans and flaked crab with scallions. Continue with fish to savour thick slices of cod, fried endive caramelized with honey and for meat, a piglet's rib, braised in beer. For dessert, the «delicious burger» (brioche in sugar, stuffed cakes, carpaccio of mango and lemon verbena) cornet is a refinement of flavours. The gourmet menu is a variation around duck and the tasting menu brings together all the dishes in a trilogy, accompanied by a glass of wine.

■ LA FACTORY
598, avenue Raymond Dugrand
☎ + 33 (0) 4 67 20 20 60
http://lafactory-restaurant.com
lafactorymontpellier@gmail.com

Open all year. Low season: Monday to Friday for lunch and dinner. High season: Monday to Saturday. Booking is essential. À la carte: Around €30. Groups welcome. Terrace.

It is an original decor of industrial style, Cédric the chef prepares a refined and inventive cuisine. On the menu: tomato Pan con and Black ventrèche bacon from Bigorre as starter; Salmon carpaccio of Norway in Gravlax, small tip of Wasabi and cream mounted on candied lemons or large prawns, vegetables Chop Suey and creamy risotto or asparagus. The desserts are not left out, and guests can enjoy a pineapple gazpacho and its granite flower hibiscus or the famous destructured lemon tart of the chef. The hotel also has a fine wine list.

■ LES GOURMANDS
40, avenue Saint-Lazare
☎ + 33 (0) 4 67 72 82 76
www.lesgourmands.com

Open all year. Tuesday to Saturday for lunch and dinner. Except Saturday for lunch. Booking advised. Menu from €32 to €45. Lunch menu: €15. Wine by the glass. Daily menu: €15 (only for lunch, except public holidays). Chèque Restaurant.

The chefs Patrice and Carlos welcome you in their culinary universe, undoubtedly one of the best tables of Montpellier. The setting is neat and consists of three dining rooms, the first tinged with red, the two others open to the outside through large windows. The cuisine is inventive and refined, and the menu explores a large range of dishes and flavours. As a starter scallops roast, fresh citrus tartare and vinaigrette turmeric- passion; we also recommend tasting the dishes using the excellent homemade foie gras. For the dishes, black Bigorre pork with chanterelles, juice reduced to the shavings of foie gras or hazelnuts of lamb roasted in the oven and its drippings shortbread, Parmesan and olive condiment. As for the dessert, crispy tulip with orange, muddle of seasonal fruit, creamy lime and Yuzu sorbet will make somebody happy. The address offers good value for money given the quality of food served.

■ LE JARDIN DES SENS
11, avenue Saint-Lazare
✆ + 33 (0) 4 99 58 38 38
www.jardindessens.com
Closed from January 2nd to January 7th. Open Monday to Saturday for dinner from 7.30pm to 9.30pm; Tuesday and Thursday to Saturday for lunch from 12.30pm to 2pm. Closed weekly: Sunday, Monday for lunch and Wednesday for lunch. Menu from €90 to €184. À la carte: Around €170. Children's menu: €32. Lunch menu: €49 (Tuesday, Thursday and Friday). Wine by the glass. Groups welcome. Terrace.
The exemplary table of Montpellier and the Mediterranean over the past twenty years and the quality of the facility has not been disproved. The cuisine of the Pourcel brothers is exported to Shanghai, but here it takes root and continues today to evolve and reinvent itself. A large glass cube as a room open to the outside and into a garden with many Mediterranean species, distinguished decoration successfully blends the contemporary art and natural space, the place open to the imagination and already makes our senses alert. Then this is the myriad of flavors offered by the two leaders, a whole creative cuisine of contrasts and alliances, excellent products and rich and complex preparations. For starters, you can discover the duo langoustines: tartar with sweet lemon and caviar Osetra and roasted orange flavor, warm vinaigrette with spices, fresh mango. For the main dish: fillets roasted pigeons, pastilla with offal curry, fried quarter pears, pigeon broth with bitter cocoa; or travel around the lamb: squared & roasted, crispy shoulder with sesame, kefta with lime, potatoes with dried fruits, lamb broth with curry coconut carrot with orange. The sommelier chooses a glass of wine in agreement with each dish, a gourmet adventure made of finesse and harmony.

■ L'ALLIANCE DES PLAISIRS
8 bis, rue du Petit-Saint-Jean
✆ + 33 (0) 4 34 26 50 94
www.lalliancedesplaisirs.fr
contact@lalliancedesplaisirs.fr
Open all year. Monday to Saturday for dinner from 7.30pm to 11pm. Booking advised. Set menu at €48. À la carte: Around €40. Wine by the glass.
A native of Florensac, the young chef Vincent Valat was trained at the hotel school of Saint-Chely-d'Apcher in Lozère. After working for the Pourcel brothers (where he met his wife, Audrey Ginestet) and a chef at l'Insensé (where he obtained a bib), he goained his autonomy with Audrey by opening this property. In the kitchen, the focus is on a small menu, but controlled and highly refined. Laminated eggplant and roasted farmer cabecou, asparagus and grilled lobster tails, bisque emulsion as starter; roasted scallops in butter, braised endive with orange and coriander, cream of carrot leaves and chorizo emulsion to continue. The chef is full of taste and creativity and offers us a personal and interesting cuisine. The place also organizes cooking classes, which has some success.

■ L'ARTICHAUT
15 bis, rue Saint-Firmin
✆ + 33 (0) 4 67 91 86
www.artichaut-restaurant.fr
Open all year. Tuesday to Saturday for lunch from 12pm to 2pm and for dinner from 7.30pm to 9.30pm; Sunday for lunch. Menu from €31 to €35. Lunch menu: €18.
In a setting that is both simple and chic, dressed in contemporary art paintings (including stylized artichokes of the local painter Jerome Dacher) and furniture worthy of the greatest designers, Laura and Sebastian (a new chef who comes from Vichy and has worked in the biggest restaurants; Lasserre, Petrus …) welcome you to visit this cool little street downtown. In fine weather, some metal and anise pedestal tables unfold in the alley and promise a relaxed meal, away from Montpellier sun, friendly but sometimes a little violent in summer. On the menu is a succession of mainly Mediterranean dishes made with fresh and seasonal produce. Also, you may enjoy couteaux à la plancha, small linguine mackerel fillet with shell juice, both delicious. In the evening, a more sophisticated menu with burrata cream of artichoke, crusted lamb fillet Cevennes mashed olive and onions. For dessert, the flavours are still in the spotlight: we work with mango, pineapple, rhubarb and raspberry. A restaurant taken over in a beautiful way! We especially appreciate the small street where the school is located, quiet and away from the major tourist areas. Be careful however and think to book, especially at night: if the street seems almost confidential L'Artichaut is one of the best addresses circulating within Montpellier gourmets and sometimes it is complete. It is rightly so, because it is very well deserved.

Restaurants of the Jean Jaurès square.

HIGH BUDGET

■ LE PASSIONNÉ
12, rue Aristide Olivier
✆ + 33 (0) 4 34 11 55 71
www.retaurant-lepassionne.fr
Open all year. Closed from July 30th to August 22nd. Monday to Saturday for dinner; Tuesday and Thursday to Saturday for lunch. Booking is essential. Menu from €35 to €45. Lunch menu: €18 (starter, main course, desert). Chèque Restaurant.

This restaurant is a great success. The decor is modern and comfortable, the plant walls aerates the space in a pleasant way and it is inviting for relaxarion. The chief Wilfredo Halsdorf welcomes you to his table and offers a neat and refined cuisine inspired by the culinary traditions of southern Europe. Smoked salmon by the chef on a shortbread of parmesan grannysmith apples, and on the plate are fillet duckling with vegetables & frozen beetroot juice. The desserts are made in fine style also e.g the crispy cocoa cylinder, coffee mousse with Mexican chocolate... Everything will be washed down with a delicious white Domaine d'Archimbaud in organic farming, the four stones.

■ LE PASTIS
3, rue du Terral
Carré Sainte Anne
✆ + 33 (0) 4 67 66 37 26
www.pastis-restaurant.com
Open Tuesday to Saturday for lunch and dinner. Booking is essential. Menu from €36.50 to €48. Lunch menu: €25 (starter/main course or main course/dessert, dumardi at Friday). Wine by the glass. Terrace.

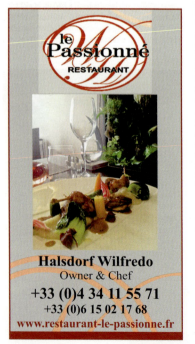

In the narrow streets of Sainte Anne district, in the heart of Montpellier, Pastis is a lovely place with a gastro bistro atmosphere. The small room is tastefully decorated, tha tables are wooden and the terrace opens in the morning with the first sun rays. In the kitchen, Daniel Lutrand takes things in hand. Spiritual son of Michel Bras, he exudes a Mediterranean-inspired cuisine but also introduces in his dishes exotic flavors, to suit all tastes. Chicken eggplant laquered with Thai pepper; or whiting line mediterranean juice, nasturtium, leeks wand and black soybeans. Note, the original concept of the surprise menu, the chef makes you discover the kitchen through produce directly purchased from the market. As for wines, Jean-Philippe Life takes over, and offers a nice wine list of the region and elsewhere.

■ LE PETIT JARDIN
20, rue Jean-Jacques-Rousseau
✆ + 33 (0) 4 67 60 78 78
www.petit-jardin.com
contact@petit-jardin.com
Closed 15 Christmas Days at the beginning of January. Open Tuesday to Sunday for lunch from 12pm and for dinner from 7.30pm. Closed on Monday and Sunday for dinner from October 15th to May 15th. À la carte: Around €60 (dish from €20 to €30 on average). Daily special: €18 (Dish of the market, weekday lunchtime only). Wine by the glass.

If you wander through the narrow streets of old Montpellier, on the side of the Botanical Gardens, you may pass by this little paradise, without doubt of the enchanting setting hidden on the other side. Here, the staffs are all dressed in black, and guide you to the chic and contemporary room, after taking off your coat. The home is formal, but still very friendly, and the dining room is bright, with large windows opening onto a lovely terrace and a beautiful garden. The view is overlooking Saint Peter's Cathedral and the Faculty of Medicine, between the trees. For dishes, the chef Damian Martin showcases seasonal produce. We loved the skate wings in rosemary butter, with salsify: it melts in the mouth. The menu offers both seafood dishes (bouillabaisse, Scallops shells) than meat (veal sweetbreads with mushrooms, beef tenderloin Aubrac). Note that the wine list is particularly good and a formula for small gourmet dishes (from 7 euros a plate and 5 euros a glass of wine), very friendly, is offered nightly at the bar in a second room. During the week, you can also enjoy a dish of fresh market dsih at €18 lunch (ballotine guinea onTuesday, tournedos of veal head gribiche sauce on Thursday, and fish in bouillabaisse way on Friday ...). Vegetarian and gluten free dishes are also available. This beautiful place is also a beautiful place for groups, and it is not uncommon to see corporate chic meals here or even wedding meals. Good taste in every sense of the word: all together an elegant, refined and charming setting, and a cuisine and service in perfect harmony.

■ RESTAURANT CELLIER-MOREL
La Maison de la Lozère
27, rue de l'Aiguillerie
✆ + 33 (0) 4 67 66 46 36
www.celliermorel.com
contact@celliermorel.com
Qualité Tourisme label. Sud de France. Open on Monday, Wednesday and Saturday from 8pm to 9.30pm; Tuesday,

Thursday and Friday from 12pm to 1.30pm and from 8pm to 9.30pm. Booking advised. Menu from €33 to €87. Lunch menu: €33. Wine by the glass. American Express. Groups welcome. Terrace.

For the past twenty years now, the Cellier-Morel restaurant has earned a solid reputation in Montpellier. Between constant creative research and solid attachment to the values of the regional culinary traditions, this restaurant is primarily based on the quality of prepared food, carefully found at local producers. Authenticity therefore, the rest is the audacity and sensitivity of Éric Cellier the chef that highlight the whole. As starter: fried scallops caviar lemon patchoï grilled emulsion of cimes pepper. For the suckling pig dish cooked at low temperature, Jerusalem artichoke, vegetables with vinegar and grilled, reduced juice; the unmissable in the year beef fillet crust of foie gras or lobster with Maury. For dessert, beautiful mixtures such as the crunchy cinnamon aniseed ice cream lemon meringue with rosemary. The innovation; a cellar on 80 m^2 where you can discover the wines of Languedoc and elsewhere.

■ **RESTAURANT LE 360 –**
GOLF DE MONTPELLIER MASSANE
Domaine de Massane
BAILLARGUES
℘ + 33 (0) 4 67 87 87 87
www.massane.com

Open all year. Monday to Friday and public holidays for lunch from 12pm to 2.30pm and for dinner from 7.45pm to 9.15pm; the weekend from 12pm to 3.30pm. Every day from 12pm to 9.30pm, Tapas in Bar Lounge. Booking advised. Menu from €18 to €36. À la carte: Around €35. Children's menu: €9.90. Salads from €12.50, burger from €11.30, pasta from €12.80. American Express, Diners Club, Chèque Restaurant. Groups welcome. Garden. Terrace. Shop.

The panoramic view which has given its name to the restaurant, overlooks the golf. The room and the terrace welcomes you in a very pleasant setting. The chef Eric Virely prepares a cuisine with flavours of the south, made of salad-meals, griddled fish, grilled meat, burgers... On the often renewed menu, you will find paved salmon with pistou; whole cuttlefish; Pepper burger; as For the rest: Charolais beef tartar chopped with a knife with condiments; grilled steak with shallot confit; steak butler butter, race Simmental (240 g); heart of rump with green pepper, race Simmental(200 g); andouillette grilled with mustard. The dessert menu is equally attractive: apple tart, salted butter caramel ice cream; fresh fruit swim & its sorbet; pineapple carpaccio and coconut sorbet; crème brûlée with vanilla from Madagascar; iced nougat & dried fruits; chocolate cake, English cream & vanilla ice cream. Finally, the wine list includes carefully selected wines from the region.

■ **LE TRIDENT**
Port de Plaisance
1, rue de l'Etang-de l'Or
CARNON
℘ + 33 (0) 4 67 50 92 57
www.restaurant-trident.fr
contact@restaurant-trident.fr

Open all year. Monday to Saturday for dinner; Wednesday to Sunday for lunch. Booking advised. Menu from €26 to €31. Children's menu: €10. Daily special: €20.

The restaurant is open since the beginning of 2012 and has satisfied the gastronomic offer of Carnon. The restaurants of the coast are sometimes tourist traps, but you are in a place where we respect the guest and good cooking. After his career in Michel Rostand in Paris (2 star) and in Emmanuel Renaud at Megève (3 star), the young chef Christophe Legros treats the passers-by in Carnon. You can taste the snail millefeuille, emulsion of fennel, or the mussel soup with curry and its crunchy vegetables as a starter. For the rest: roasted prawns, crushed fingerling, honey and sesame or thick slices of cod and its creamy risotto with herbs. The fish are served according to the catch of the day and the smoked salmon in the kitchen. The desserts, to be ordered at the beginning of the meal, are homemade: toasted brioche, roasted pineapple and its pineapple sorbet, or mirliton with citrus fruits and grapefruit sorbet. An address that continues its beautiful establishment and which continues to become popular. Recommended.

HIGH BUDGET

■ **LE DOMAINE DE SORIECH**
Chemin de Soriech
Avenue de Boirargues
LATTES
✆ + 33 (0) 4 67 15 19 15
www.domaine-de-soriech.fr
michel.loustau@domaine-de-soriech.fr
Open Tuesday to Saturday for lunch and dinner; Sunday for lunch. Menu from €43 to €55. Children's menu: €18.50. Lunch menu: €32. Garden. Terrace.
A large wood dominated by large trees, a large establishment which is at the bend of a narrow path: everything in this enchanting place exudes mystery... The magician who reigns in this place is called Michel Lousteau. A great character of gastronomy in Montpellier for over 30 years, he expresses his powers of charm in his cuisine based on products from his native land (the Southwest) and those of his region of adoption. Then, try, depending on the mood of the chef or the seasons, with his duck foie gras from the Landes which he prepares in the form of terrine and serves it accompanied by a marbled prunes with old Armagnac. You will also enjoy a crab with smoked salmon mixed with the bush of chêvre and toasted hazelnuts. As dish, a delicious lobster medallion cooked in its herb broth or roast of monkfish grilled and served in escalopes. For dessert, it will be difficult to choose between hull of white chocolate, apricot mousse or a sorbet with muscat. The dishes change regularly, are always surprising and of very high quality. Undoubtedly one of the very best addresses of the region.

■ **LE MAZERAND**
CD172
Mas de Causse
LATTES
✆ + 33 (0) 4 67 64 82 10
www.le-mazerand.com
info@le-mazerand.com
Open Tuesday to Saturday for dinner; Tuesday to Friday and Sunday for lunch. Closed on Monday, Saturday for lunch and Sunday for dinner. Menu from €31 to €68. Children's menu: €13. Groups welcome. Terrace.
In an old winery of the seventeenth century, the Mazerand brothers welcome you to their table to help you discover a gourmet cuisine between the sea and scrubland. The decor is modern while respecting the identity of the place and the service is attentive and very considerate. The chef, Jacques offers a passionate, modern and inventive cuisine, but mindful of the values of yesteryear, precise but enriched with creative fantasy that always surprises. His cooking bases its refinement on the quality and authenticity of products, offering some wonderful discoveries. For Starters, the plate of tapas will make you discover the best of the menu in portions. For the main dish, lobster ravioli with vegetables, topped with grated truffles; or complicity of the Iberian pig and bull, plucked for the first or gardianne broth for the second. For dessert, nothing beats a good chocolate therapy: shortbread and chocolate praline covered with a creamy caramel, thin sheets of crunchy dark chocolate, grand cru trend, Maralumi plantation of the house. As for wine, it is Christian who will guide you through the wine cellar of the hotel.

■ **LES CAVES PASSENT À TABLE**
3040, route de Mende
MONTFERRIER-SUR-LEZ
✆ + 33 (0) 4 99 61 02 65
www.lescavespassentatable.com
Open all year. Low season: Monday to Saturday for lunch; Thursday to Saturday. High season: Monday to Saturday for lunch and dinner. Menu from €20 to €56. Lunch menu: €17. Terrace. Shop.
The address of Lionel Seux, formerly of Pastis, today restaurateur- wine merchant is worth visiting in more than one way. In an atmosphere of cellar with bottles and portraits of the winemakers on display, you can eat in a stylish mezzanine bistro decor. In the lunch menu, a back from the market cuisine, the chef Guillaume Leclere offers his best with as starter, just snakés salmon dice, then a calf's head to carrot mayonnaise with capers finally a roasted pineapple vanilla verbena crumble with cocoa. In the only drink of organic wines, for example the Highlands of Gilles Azam, tasty limouxin wine. A reference address of north Montpellier.

Medium Budget

■ **L'ACOLYTE**
1, rue des Trésoriers de France
✆ + 33 (0) 4 67 66 03 43
www.lacolyte.fr
Open all year. Monday to Saturday for dinner from 6.30pm to 1am. Booking advised. À la carte: Around €30. Wine by the glass. Tapas from €8, dish for dinner around €18. Terrace.
This trendy bar restaurant wine bar, with *afterwork* atmosphere, offers a bistro cuisine declined in evening dishes or French tapas, if you are a little hungry. Here, the tapas are of high quality! The crispy cheese, the big plate of shredded ham with truffles, Bouzigues oysters, skewers of small octopuses... Tapas that rather look like starters, good and copious hence the high prices. The place has a beautiful floor, very cosy: you will enjoy a glass of wine or a cocktail from the Acolytet sitting on comfortable armchairs, in a pretty setting. Here, you will meet people in costume and youth in their thirties with dynamic appearance. As for the service, it is fast, pleasant but sometimes not so much satisfying.

MEDIUM BUDGET

■ **LES BAINS DE MONTPELLIER**
6, rue Richelieu
✆ + 33 (0) 4 67 60 70 87
www.les-bains-de-montpellier.com
Open all year. Monday to Saturday for lunch and dinner. Booking advised. À la carte: Around €40. Lunch menu: €26.90. Set menu for lunch: €26.90. Set menu for dinner: €36.90. Baby chairs. Terrace.
Les Bains is a unique place in Montpellier. Just 50 metres away from the comedy, its patio, palm trees and its small fountain. In autumn 2012, a coat of paint was added. The decor is chic and always of good taste, armchairs, mauves or raspberry, small lamps, pendants... The celebrities and the politcians flock here. The quality of the cuisine is clearly improved with its hot meals, the dish of les Bains, salad, skewers of salmon, courgette spaghetti, taboulé with coriander (€15) or its antipasti meal. Daily specials also: bream à la plancha with basmati rice and vegetables in the wok. Delicious!

■ **CAFE LEON – RESTAURANT AGRICOLE**
12, rue du Plan-d'Agde
✆ + 33 (0) 4 67 60 56 83
Open Monday to Saturday from 6.30pm to 11pm. Booking advised. Menu from €21 to €26. Lunch menu: €12.50. Wine by the glass. Chèque Restaurant. Groups welcome. Terrace.
Settled in a rustic décor, this agricultural restaurant offers cooked and raw meats and other specialties, with the added bonus of a friendly atmosphere. The service is extremely fast and friendly, and the waitresses wriggle with zeal between tables. The Sirloin steak with shallot is tender to perfection, with the delicious potatoes, and the cheese plate is generous, with good slice of bleu d'auvergne, Cantal and goat's cheese. The produce selected by the owner, Gigi, are good because she gets her supplies exclusively from breeders-butchers. If you have forgotten the names of the parts of beef, a board will make you recall them! The speciality that we highly recommend is the meat of the Salers breed but the card also offers snails, frogs' legs or salads. You can taste these dishes during summer on the small terrace or in the patio which is also heated in winter. Significant detail: a variety of wines are available by the glass. An address to remember; endeavour to reserve!

■ **LES BISTRONOMES**
22, place du Nombre-d'Or
✆ + 33 (0) 4 67 83 28 67
lesbistronomes@gmail.com
Open all year. Continuous service. Monday to Saturday from 8am to 11pm. Booking advised. Menu from €15 to €19 (for dinner à la carte). Lunch menu: €11.50. Wine by the glass. Chèque Restaurant. Terrace.
Alicia and Arnaud (former chefs in great Parisian breweries) have taken over this little restaurant in the heart of Antigone, in the neighbourhood of the golden number. The first originality of Bistronome (contraction of bistro and gastronomy) is a non-stop 8h/23h service, and the second is that, Arnaud heartily cooks tasty and flavour cuisine.

12, rue du Plan d'Agde - 34000 Montpellier
Tél. 04 67 60 56 83 - www.lecafeleon.com

The menu changes every season (guarantee of quality, as it is proves that everything is homemade) and has a limited number of dishes. You may, depending on the inspiration of Arnaud enjoy a beef fillet with homemade potato croquettes or mashed potatoes, decorated with a thin layer of tapenade, or a bagel and wolf portion with a ratatouille. Discover also the best-selling Italian beef tartare, pesto, pine nuts and parmesan. Finally savour a chocolate cake with a scoop of salted butter caramel. Do not also miss when they are on the menu: a duck in orange sauce and a very delicious French toast (old style). It is delicious and cheap, we do not ask for anything better! And besides, to crown everything, service and hospitality are adorable.

■ LE BOCAL
136, avenue de Toulouse
✆ + 33 (0) 4 67 65 71 73
Open Monday to Friday for lunch (last sitting at 1.30pm); Tuesday to Saturday for dinner (last sitting at 10.30pm). Menu from €22 to €35. À la carte: Around €30. Children's menu: €13. Daily special: €8 (only for lunch). Terrace.
The Bocal looks like a haven of peace on avenue de Toulouse. Gourmets appreciate the inventive cuisine, which changes with the seasons, as well as the cosy and refined atmosphere. In summer, a large patio replaces the two indoor rooms. For the dishes, you have the choice between traditional dishes like-, salmon, steak – or more original like a piece of veal with apricots, the tagine way, pasta with foie gras or a skewer of Scallops. With a little luck, you will be entitled to appetisers in a jar. For dessert, the chocolate is deliciously melting. An Zen address, quiet, where the reception is discreet and very friendly. Practical and nice: the house allows you to take along your own bottle of wine if it is not finished on site!

■ O'COING
2, place de Strasbourg ✆ + 33 (0) 4 67 64 01 88
www.o-coing.com - ocoing@ggzingueurs.com
Open all year. Monday to Friday for lunch; Thursday to Saturday for dinner. Booking advised. Menu from €22 to €26 (for dinner). Daily special for lunch: starter main course at €9.90 - or main dish and dessert at €12.90 and fixed rate formula supplement at €14.90. Wine by the glass. For dinner menu options from €15. Chèque Restaurant. Theme parties second Wednesday of each month.
At Ô'Coing, it is actually the GG Zingueurs (that is Gregory and William) that hold the table, located at the corner of the place de Strasbourg and rue du Général-Riu, next to the station. Both having left the Saint-Chély-d'Apcher hotel school, in Lozère, here the friendliness and good food are the targeted objectives since the opening of this restaurant, and the success they have earned so far prove them right! On the table, you will encounter beautiful meat: a board of meats of Aubrac and the Aubrac steak. For dessert: the chocolate cake. Seasonal dishes are finely prepared with vegetables from the Mauguio market gardening. To accompany let's mention: the Agentier Vintage, of the Argentier Estate and the 50/50 Vintage of Anne gros. In short a great corner!

■ COM À LA MAISON
49, rue de L'Aiguillerie ✆ + 33 (0) 4 67 60 67 40
Open Tuesday to Saturday for lunch and dinner. Set menu at €25. Lunch menu: €12. Daily special: €9.
Anne and Medhi welcome you in the small long room, with stone walls and metal ornaments (such as around the counter) or a lovely shaded terrace and Michel, the chef, offers a menu that blends bothe flavors from around the world and traditional cuisine. Only fresh and quality products tasted here and salads as well as cooked dishes, are excellent. So you can enjoy a chicken breast, a lamb shank or beef fillet in duo with pepper. For dessert, it will be a tarte Tatin, or a pink grapefruit with hints of pepper. Note also that the wine will look in the regional wines and some of Corsica or Bouches du Rhône references.

■ FOLIA – CHÂTEAU DE FLAUGERGUES
1744, avenue Albert-Einstein
Quartier Le Millénaire
✆ + 33 (0) 4 99 52 66 37
www.flaugergues.com
folia@flaugergues.com

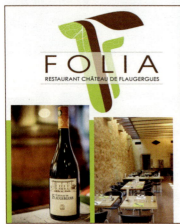

Château de Flaugergues
1744, avenue Albert Einstein
Le Millénaire - 34000 MONTPELLIER
✆ 04 99 526 635
www.flaugergues.com

Open Monday to Friday for lunch from 11.30am to 2.30pm. Booking advised. Menu from €18.50 to €20.50. Daily special: €15. Wine by the glass. Garden. Terrace.

This restaurant, open at lunchtime, is located in one of the prettiest places in Montpellier: the castle of Flaugergues. This is one of those houses built in the late seventeenth century in Montpellier campaign,»madness» – hence the name of the restaurant! Behind this address: a combination between the owners of the place and the regional promising young chef Thierry Alix. The proof is indeed in the pudding, as they say in cuisine... Marie and Pierre de Colbert renovated stone by stone a half collapsed old cellar to transform it into large and modern fine room to welcome his customers. A pleasant terrace is sheltered by plane trees and overlooks the courtyard. The cuisine is a real treat, the chef uses the vegetables and meat with lots of taste: fried leeks to paprika and tartare of tomatoes to dill; mix beef duck with juice of rosemary; and finally: a duo of cakes with one compote of red fruits. The wines of Flaugergues are largely honoured here, but the wines of Pays d'Oc did not say their last word! And then, why not head to the gardens and the castle, a way of extending the festivities with a digestive stroll through this beautiful site?

■ **CHEZ FRAMBOIZE**
41, rue de la Valfère
✆ + 33 (0) 4 67 56 90 23
Open all year. Monday to Saturday for lunch and dinner. À la carte: Around €20.

Julie (aka Framboize), the daughter is in the kitchen. Annick, the mom (lovely) is at the service. They opened a small restaurant in the Sainte Anne district. A good taste, simple decor, untreated wood, stone, concrete countertop, indirect lighting and a lively atmosphere but still freindly. Julie offers a very creative market cuisine: pastilla with Oriental Chicken, pot-au-feu of duck, and amazing delicious of skewers sépion with chorizo. For dessert, a sublime lemon cheesecake with raspberry coulis, all homemade of course, are always tastefully presented and led by Annick and her big sincere smile, always paying attention to its customers. The food is very good and in a cozy atmosphere but not a prude, and it's still a pretty nice point, either on the plate or on the reception.

■ **LE SALEYA**
4, place du Marché-aux-Fleurs
✆ + 33 (0) 4 67 60 53 92
Open Monday to Saturday. Menu from €12.90 to €25 (salad meal €14). Children's menu: €8.50.

Open from February to November, the Saleya is a small restaurant where one is serve only on the terrace under the plane trees of place du marché of flowers. Also plan, for that matter, to go on a sunny day. It will be worth it, because the place is charming and the food of good quality. Note however that if you want to eat indoors, the bosses of the Saleya get along very well with those of the Café de la Mer, right next door, where you can eventually sit and get served. Fresh produce are used here and hearty and many salads are available as well as some hot food of good quality, such as this confit veal shoulder with mashed vegetables in season. In Saleya, you will not be disappointed by either the place or the plate. Nor by the right (special mention to Armelle, a sacred character, the Chief waitress, with a humor and formidable efficiency!) natural, services full of "peps". There is therefore no reason to deprive yourself!

■ **LA SENTINELLE**
17, rue de la Cavalerie
✆ + 33 (0) 4 67 04 51 27
Open all year. Wednesday to Monday for lunch; Wednesday to Sunday for dinner. Booking advised. Menu from €14 to €32 (for dinner 24 and €32). Daily special: €9.80. Activities. Evenings large, €3 half-time of Rugby, gay.

Some steps away from the place des Beaux-Arts, Christophe Lapouge, a figure of catering facilities in Montpellier, warmly welcomes guests in his small local bistro, embellished with stone walls and a beautiful crackling fireplace. You feel at home! The cuisine is inventive: the combination of flavours is honoured. Also, you can choose between stuffed sweetbreads, fried piece of Aubrac from the north, prawns with cumbava. The house will offer quality wines to discover; Roc des Anges and its carignan, the extraordinary estate of the Tours de Raynaud, with the tasting of whiskeys of captain Hadock, Loch Lomond. Original evenings on request.

■ **LA SENTINELLE**
17, rue de la Cavalerie
✆ + 33 (0) 4 67 04 51 27
Open all year. Wednesday to Monday for lunch; Wednesday to Sunday for dinner. Booking advised. Menu from €14 to €32 (for dinner 24 and €32). Daily special: €9.80. Activities. Evenings large, €3 half-time of Rugby, gay.

Some steps away from the place des Beaux-Arts, Christophe Lapouge, a figure of catering facilities in Montpellier, warmly welcomes guests in his small local bistro, embellished with stone walls and a beautiful crackling fireplace. You feel at home! The cuisine is inventive: the combination of flavours is honoured. Also, you can choose between stuffed sweetbreads, fried piece of Aubrac from the north, prawns with cumbava. The house will offer quality wines to discover; Roc des Anges and its carignan, the extraordinary estate of the Tours de Raynaud, with the tasting of whiskeys of captain Hadock, Loch Lomond. Original evenings on request.

■ **LA SUITE DES BAINS**
6 bis, rue Richelieu
✆ + 33 (0) 4 67 66 08 94
lasuitedesbains@gmail.com
Open all year. Monday and Saturday for dinner from 6pm to 1am; Tuesday to Friday for lunch from 12pm to 2.30pm and for dinner from 6pm to 1am. Set menu at €14.90 (only at lunchtime). À la carte: Around €15. Wine by the glass: from €2.50.

Decorations made of wrought iron and lamps, a kitsch on the bar. Here, a bistro-type fine cuisine is served, added to this offer a wide range of homemade tapas. It goes from the most classic: squid or cuttlefish à la plancha, pan con tomato, Patatas Bravas, Iberian ham, tortillas or chicken croquettes, to the most original: samosas of duck or monkfish sweets.

Here, the fresh produce is king and the chef Damien, gets his fish at the Sète wet market and its shells with cheerful Oyster, a famous fish shop in Montpellier, while its fruits and vegetables come from the vegetable producers of Mauguio. Steaks, sea bream, sea bass and couteaux are made à la plancha, and the homemade tapas. We enjoy and the team is a nice one, which always helps. Enjoyment is quickly established here and the hotel regularly organises kitsch evenings and other quirky activities. Also, we come here to have fun! The purpose for this restaurant lies in its wine list, offering a range of carefully selected references.

■ **LE VIEUX FOUR**
59, rue de l'Aiguillerie
✆ + 33 (0) 4 67 60 55 95
www.levieuxfour.fr
contact@levieuxfour.fr
Open all year. Closed three weeks in July. Thursday to Tuesday for dinner from 7: 30 pm to 10: 30 pm; for dinner. Closed on Wednesday. Set menu at €28. À la carte: Around €30. Children's menu: €12. Terrace.
With more thirty-five years of profession, Vieux Four is an institution in Montpellier. Located at the bottom of rue de l'Aiguillerie, it is immediately noticeable with its small cosy wooden terrace. The interior is beautiful: old stones, wooden tables, candles, fireplace… It is in a warm and intimate setting that Aurélie and Cyril therefore welcome their guests. The house specialities, unchanged since the beginning, are grilled meat… with wood fire please! As a starter, you will be tempted by the Saint-Marcellin cheese with grilled bacon, duck breast or the beef rib for two! The sweet touch is brought by the dismantled lemon tart and its biscuits with citrus fruits, made by Aurelie the pastry chef. To accompany all this, fine wine from the region, including excellent estate of the Madeleine in Marseillan.

■ **VILLA 29**
29, avenue de l'Ecole-d'Agriculture
✆ + 33 (0) 4 67 91 07 97
www.villa29.fr
decor.accord@orange.fr
Open on Monday and Tuesday for lunch; Wednesday to Saturday for lunch and dinner. Dishes from €13 to €19. Wine by the glass.
The sign is not necessarily discovered at first glance but the place is good! This small restaurant with a sober and chic interior is worth seeing. Alain, who had some great times at Pizz'Agri, gave cover almost opposite. White seats, a simple black and white decor brightened by green walls, place calls for calm and has a pleasant intimacy. For the dishes, excellent food served generously like a plate of El Canardo (gizzards, foie gras, smoked duck), a suggestion: scallops à la plancha… In the summer, tuna and swordfish a la plancha, tapas… For good appetites, we can only advise a burger from the variety: traditional (100% Charolais), Rossini (foie gras), Basque (chorizzo, bell pepper and cheese), vegetarian… a beautiful menu of Pic Saint-Loup particularly rosy. A beautiful carte with some amber rum with some outdated references. Gourmand Rhum for dessert.

■ **DUCOS RESTAURANT**
Allées de l'Europe
JUVIGNAC
✆ + 33 (0) 4 67 45 38 33 / + 33 (0) 6 99 52 22 27
www.maitresrestaurateurs.com/ducos34
ducosrestaurant@gmail.com
Open all year. Tuesday to Friday for lunch and dinner; Saturday for dinner; Sunday for lunch. Booking advised. Menu from €21 to €29. À la carte between €10 and €30. Children's menu: €12. Daily special: €12. Chèque Restaurant. Groups welcome. Take-away.
Brice Ducos (maître restaurateur in France) is the chef of the Ducos restaurant, formerly the owner of the Grange de Celleneuve. Contemporary decor; a water fountain in one corner and an open kitchen on the restaurant. Affordable menus with local cuisine. The chef prepares surprising dishes like the just snaked scallops and breaded camembert with camembert ice cream (ice cream made by a craftsman). The homemade foie gras is remarkable and the whole bar is representative of the slate. The wine list is extensive and the service is friendly.

■ **LE BISTROT D'ARIANE**
5, rue des Chevaliers-de-Malte
Port Ariane
LATTES
✆ + 33 (0) 4 67 20 01 27
www.bistrot-ariane.fr
lebistrotdariane@free.fr
Booking advised. Menu from €22 to €34. À la carte: Around €40. Wine by the glass. Menu at €22 (for lunch and dinner every day except Saturday Sunday public holidays). American Express, Holiday voucher, Chèque Restaurant. Groups welcome. Terrace. Take-away.
Near the Lattes port, Bistrot d'Ariane has a very pleasant setting. The large bay windows let in beautiful light and it is with a greatpleasure that you will immerse in the atmosphere that reigns here. Caroline and Christian intend to make this place a friendly space, between bouchon lyonnais and parisian brasserie. The Masters of the place decorated the room with their findings, sharing their passion for flea market and travelling. As for their second passion, namely oenology, it will not displease you. The couple opens their cellar and offers some 300 wine references, representing more than 120 properties. In the

+33 (0)4 67 60 55 95

WWW.LEVIEUXFOUR.FR

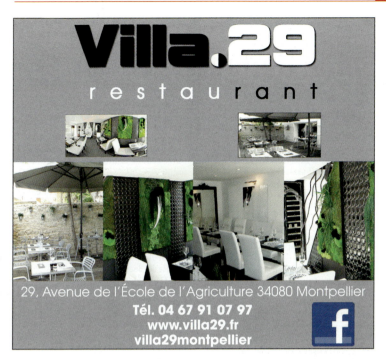

kitchen the chef Denis Roubaud proposes specialities with original and refined touches. Pea soup and lobster, truffles and shellfish as starters, monkfish with the creamy risotto or scallops pasta with squid ink for the dish. For dessert preparations are also tasty. On weekdays the market menu will allow you to discover this table at €19.50.

■ **BRASSERIE LE CAZ**
1, boulevard Maréchal-Foch
PALAVAS-LES-FLOTS
✆ + 33 (0) 4 67 68 00 01
www.casinopalavas.com
Open all year. Wednesday to Sunday for lunch and dinner. Closed late 11.30pm, instead of 10.30pm Friday for dinner and Saturday for dinner. Booking advised. Set menu at €27. Daily special: €9.90. American Express, Holiday voucher, Chèque Restaurant. Valet.
Opposite the marina of Palavas, the restaurant of the casino offers you to taste a sunny cuisine in a design and elegant setting open onto the sea. The main advantage of this place is also to be in calmness and comfort. In the kitchen, the young chef prepares dishes of high quality including grilled cuttlefish ratatouille and basil, a duck breast on the Roman ravioli skin crème with mushrooms or finally, beef burger. We leave very satisfied!

■ **LA CHAPELLE**
110, rue des Anémones
VILLENEUVE-LÈS-MAGUELONE
✆ + 33 (0) 4 67 07 95 80
Open all year. Sunday to Wednesday for lunch from 11.45am to 2pm; Thursday to Saturday for lunch from 11.45am to 2pm and for dinner from 7pm to 10pm. Menu from €12 to €25. Children's menu: €8. Lunch menu: €12. Wine by the glass. Chèque Restaurant. Garden. Terrace.
The place, undoubtedly, is original! A pretty chapel converted into a restaurant and a very secular enthusiasm to quickly make your mouth full with water. The outdoor setting is to be tried if the weather is nice, the small garden is very calming. Olivier the chef prepares Catalan specialities – suquet des peix (fish bouillabaisse and shellfish), chorizo cuttlefish à la plancha, guinea fowl with lobster... Several grills are offered (including bull), pata negra fillet with espelette pepper is also a safe bet. For dessert, chocolate cake and rum babas will delight the most unrepentant gourmets.

Find all our best deals and good addresses on our website www.petitfute.uk.com

Small Budget

■ LE COMPTOIR DU CLAPAS
2, rue de l'Ancien Courrier
✆ + 33 (0) 4 67 60 59 95

Open all year. Low season: Monday to Saturday from 9am to 7pm. High season: Tuesday to Friday from 9am to 10pm. À la carte: Around €20. Children's menu: €7.90. Lunch menu: €9.90. Wine by the glass. Starters from €3.90, dessert from €3, La Clapassade at €12. Terrace.

From the outside, the place does not seem like much. However if you open the door you will find a brasserie decor in this small bistro restaurant that is also a tearoom. This Friendly and simple address offers familiar dishes at moderate prices. The welcome is friendly; the service attentive and fast. This restaurant is the only establishment in Montpellier to serve the famous Clapassade elected specialty of Montpellier! For the record, the city had no emblematic dish, the authorities had the idea to create one from scratch in 2011, on competition. The winner: a lamb stew with olives, flavored with licorice and honey. If this product has not been able to impose the proposed Clapassade Comptoir is a treat. Go for the taste! If, however, the Clapassade does not appeal to you, you always find excellent homemade traditional dishes of stew to the huge salad, unpretentious, tasty and at very affordable rates at the Clapas desk. And, a brasserie spirit in the old establishment, which is more copious.

■ FLORIDA KAFÉ
23, rue du Chio
Port Marianne
✆ + 33 (0) 9 83 79 81 16

Open daily for lunch and dinner. Lunch menu: €12.

In Port Marianne, this address was opened in late 2013. It offers a terrace overlooking the Jacques Cœur pond and a modern and clear decor that a lot of regulars already enjoy. At noon the menu at 12 € wins all the votes. Starters are is at will, hot main course at choice and dessert at will also. The cuisine is traditional and simple, made with fresh vegetables, in a fish dish of the day a la plancha, unilateral salmon and duck. The desserts are the of the same simple and at will like the starters: tarte tatin, tiramisu, and other Catalan cream fudge. In the evening, the place is gradually transformed into the after work during the aperitif. From19: 00 to 20: 00 tapas are offered and friends meet after work on the terrace around a palette of more than twenty tapas. Among these, one can enjoy sardines escabeche of Pata Negra, roasted bell peppers, tapenade. Also note: and a small wine list which showcases the best wines of our region. A musical atmosphere. In short, a somewhat unusual address that a real success.

■ LE KOEUR
22, rue Jacques Coeur
✆ + 33 (0) 4 67 66 47 76

Open all year. Monday to Saturday from 8.30am to 7.30pm. Menu from €13.90 to €15. Daily special: €11. Terrace.

Koeur, in rue Jacques Cœur stretches out its terrace in the (modest) shade of a big palm tree. It is both a tea room, bar and restaurant and its originality is five different daily specials (pork tenderloin with ceps, tagine of grouper, ravioli with ham and roquefort...) and also is the «the Koeur specials» with its ten tartars and carpaccios meat and fish. Beef tartar the Indian way, served with sautéed potatoes and salad. In the afternoon the chocolates from Guadeloupe and teas from China. If you want to continue the travel the library of the five continents is opposite.

■ LE SPOT
6, place des Beaux-Arts
✆ + 33 (0) 4 67 04 46 39
spot.lespot@gmail.com

Open all year. Monday to Saturday for lunch and dinner. Daily menu (stater and main course) from €11 to €13 for lunch. Daily special: €11. Wine by the glass. Menu at €16, €18 and €21. Beers from €2 to €5. Wine by the glass from €2.50 to €5. Chèque Restaurant. Terrace.

On the place des Beaux-Arts, Spot offers a beautiful terrace and a trendy interior, with beautiful stone walls. Before sitting on the comfortable seat covered with cushions, throw a glance into the kitchen, separated from the restaurant by a transparent window to see the cooks bustle! At noon, there is a choice between dishes of 11 to 21 euros, and in the evening tapas, at 4euros a cup is add to the menu. The house prepares delicious tagines of beef, chicken and lamb. Vegetables are fondant, just like the meat, a delight. We recommend as starter, the carrot soup with curry coconut. The only problem, at noon, is that the address may be taken by a storm! Stress rises in kitchens, and you must take this patiently before being served... People are in a hurry, fold up to another address or come early! The evening is fortunately much more relaxed.

■ LA TOMATE
6, rue du Four-des-Flammes
✆ + 33 (0) 4 67 60 49 38
www.la-tomate.fr
restaurant@la-tomate.fr

Open every day. Lunch menus: €9.50 and €10.50. For dinner from €15.50 to €27.50. Children's menu: €8.90. Daily special: €8.50.

The restaurant recently celebrated its 45 years and the chef has 25 years in the house. This is obviously a Montpellier institution, the big fireplace, paneling and checkered tablecloths sees the best eaters on a budget. The dish of the day, alone, is already rich and on the classic carte: devilled eggs, the chef's terrine, herring fillets in salads or grated carrot vinaigrette as starter; homemade cassoulet with duck confit, trout with almonds, frog legs or monkfish tail with parsley for the dish. On the four menus, we also find: charcuteries, quail in vineyard (tomato and red wine sauce), fish soup, frog legs, or the mysterious Nelly pie.

Everything is homemade and it shows! The dessert menu does has it; chocolate cake, creme caramel, lemon pie, cheese and fruit coulis or charlotte with Fishery has a taste of authenticity.

Specialities

■ LE PESCATOR
23, place du Nombre-d'Or
✆ + 33 (0) 4 67 13 29 16 / + 33 (0) 6 03 98 98 34
Open all year. 7 days a week for lunch and dinner. Booking advised. Menu from €20 to €30. Lunch menu: €15. Fixed rate formula Mussels/Fried at €14.00. Plate Le Pescator (2 people): €57.60. The royal plate (2 people): €70.40. Terrace. The Pescator is the richness of the Sea brought to the city centre. With a menu to fade a lobster, the watchwords of the place are freshness and finesse. Deliveries are direct, and respect for the product are accepted here, it will taste the fine products of the méditérranéens sea. As for the lobster, it will be out of the pool and cooked in front of the customer. We can choose from several trays of seafood, or fish grilled or processed in tartar. One of the specialties of the house, the bouillabaisse is to try. How do you know it is authentic? It is that you will have to order it … 48 hours in advance! The service is very professional and simple and the decor is elegant, the wine list is taken care of and is for all budgets, appreciated in this type of establishment

■ PIRATES PARADISE
Odysseum
✆ + 33 (0) 4 67 68 06 80
www.pirates-paradise.fr
Open all year. Every day and public holidays for lunch and dinner. Booking advised. Menu from €16.90 to €25.90. Children's menu: €9.95. Lunch menu: €9.90. Wine by the glass. Salad-meal: €13.90.
Enter this dangerous looking den, a crew member of the pirates will lead you to your table, at the foot of the tower, in the den of the boat or the gaols of the ship. In addition to the imposing decorated surroundings of death's-heads, the storm and the cannons echo by surprise in the middle of the meal, and three times in an hour, the lights display. A long list of eclectic cocktails brings the highlight of to this festive atmosphere.
On the menu, there is something for everyone: salad-meal, pasta, pizzas, meat or fish. For dessert, the house opted for very classic: chocolate, crème brûlée or a scoop of frozen Bounty, composed of ice cream and chocolate, a sorbet and chips with coconut, and whipped cream. Children love this.

World Cuisine

African Cuisine

■ LE BOUZOU
753, avenue de la Pompignane
CASTELNAU-LE-LEZ ✆ + 33 (0) 4 67 72 33 08
www.lebouzou.net - contact@lebouzou.net
Open all year. Tuesday to Saturday for dinner. For lunch for groups only, by reservation. Booking advised. Set menu at €24.90. Children's menu: €8.50. Catering (on order, for lunch and dinner). Possible delivery. Evenings of groups, burials of life of boy or young girl, birthdays. Holiday voucher, Chèque Restaurant.

Between its curtains and its totemic masks, Le Bouzou welcomes you for a buffet of exotic specialities. The small islands of food, hot or chilled, are part of the decor. Among the hundred dishes offered, that come from Africa, the West Indies and Madagascar, you will find meat and fish in yassa, colombos, massalé, curry, or rougail, but also the original dishes such as chicken with vanilla, barracuda with coconut milk, cuttlefish with ginger, blue shark with red curry and giant mussels from New Zealand with basil. The caring team welcomes you with a colourful cocktail or achards (vegetable specialities) and accompanies you until the end of the meal where you will be served alcohol and aphrodisiac digestive seeds.

WORLD CUISINE - African Cuisine

■ **LE MOGADOR** ....**Moroccan**
3, rue Embouque-d'Or
✆ + 33 (0) 4 67 84 42 64
restaurantmogador.free.fr
Open Tuesday to Saturday for lunch; Wednesday to Saturday for dinner. À la carte: Around €12. Fixed rate formula: €10. Wine by the glass. Wine: from €12 to €25.

Tearoom in the day, Mogador is at nightfall a good place for amateurs of the Arab-Andalusian aimbiance. In beautiful medieval vaults, the kindness of Naser mingles with this warm and intimate place. Surrounded by antique objects from here and there, you settle around a table or on benches to enjoy the preparations of the chef. The carte is concise, but it has the merit never to disappoint. The most ferocious appetites are not left out: royal couscous, lamb tagine with dried fruits or chicken tagine with lemon confit already simmering on the stove. Each dish is served with a semolina and a small salad of a thousand and one spices.

Asian Cuisine

■ **FLAMME WOK**
6, rue Jules Ferry
✆ + 33 (0) 4 67 58 88 58
www.flammewok.com
Open Monday to Saturday for lunch and dinner. Fixed rate formula wok at €8.80. Fixed rate formula sushi €9.80 and all-you-can-eat buffet with 13,80€ (at lunchtime) and €15.80 (evening and weekends).

Opened in 2011, the property offers a modern decor and small terrace almost opposite the train station. There is a wide variation of dishes. The self service buffet menu for € 13.80 allows you to enjoy a whole range of Asian dishes ranging from caramel pork, sushi through sashimi, shrimp fritters, samosas, chicken skewers and spring rolls, of course! One can also choose beef, chicken, shrimp, fish or squid. The latter is accompanied by rice or noodles with vegetables and sauce of your choix. Nothing to say, especially in relation to the very low tariffs. The clientele is very eclectic and there is something for everyone, both the students (who, from wok menus, eat for € 8.80) than the rushing regulars who want to eat well and cheaply. The master of the place and his team are friendly and considerate. In the evening, the atmosphere is more convenient for two for the tasting of a real chinese fondue.

■ **PUJA**................................. **Indian & Pakistani**
3, rue Ferdinand Fabre
✆ + 33 (0) 4 30 10 83 57
Open all year. Daily for lunch and dinner. Booking advised. Menu from €16 to €20. À la carte: Around €20. Children's menu: €9. At lunchtime, about €10 approximately. Credit card not accepted. Chèque Restaurant. Take-away.

In India, Puja is the ritual prayer; in Montpellier, it is a restaurant not to be missed. In a typical oriental decor, you sample indian or... mauritian dishes! On the menu: fried squid or eggplant, samosas, Tikka Masala chicken, Pakora and *nans* with cheese or garlic. This is for the trip to India, and if you prefer a stopover on Mauritius island, taste the fish Cari (tomato and coriander) for example, or with semolina puddings called Sooji Meva. In Puja, the meal is copious, tasty and affordable, with the added bonus of a very welcoming staff.

■ **SUR LA PLACE**
Place François Jaumes ✆ + 33 (0) 06 12 57 16 84
Open all year. Monday to Saturday for lunch; Thursday to Saturday for dinner. Booking advised. À la carte: Around €20. Daily special: €9.50. Wine by the glass. Noodle'S Wok (Monday to Friday, for lunch): €9 to €13. Lunch box (take-away): €7. Breakfast from €4.80 to €9.80; from 8am. Chèque Restaurant. Terrace.

The table of Jean Van Thai is Well known in the neighborhood, and is a place that a good gourmet should know. «I would like my cuisine to have the taste of the wind because the wind always comes from elsewhere,» he says. And it can be said that he has succeeded, as its dishes have a taste for travel. Made with finesse and unknown flavors, this cuisine is that of a generous aesthete, a creator of flavors who knows how to be inspired by different traditions to take us towards a destination of his own. Tempura prawns and vegetables, wok of all kinds – and this time as they are made in Asia – Jean also works with French products that he makes his sauces with. You will find Aubrac beef to Sichuan pepper, lamb with green curry etc... The welcome, moreover, is of a rare kindness, and in short nothing is missing from this table, one of the most interesting in the city. The chef is not stingy with his secrets and the house also offers courses in Asian cuisine on reservation

■ **LES DEUX GRENOUILLES** ....**Japanese**
8, avenue Jean-Jaurès - CASTELNAU-LE-LEZ
✆ + 33 (0) 4 67 79 03 85
Open all year. Closed 3 weeks in August. Monday to Saturday for dinner; Tuesday to Saturday for lunch. Booking advised. À la carte: Around €20. Lunch menu: €12.

The Deux Grenouilles restaurant is a Japanese restaurant that is favored by Japanese of Montpellier, that offer sushis and other maki that are found everywhere. Mari and Jêrome offer a traditional cuisine. Why the frog? It is the symbol of the return. The menu is mouthwatering, iskaya

---

Bar Restaurant
SUR LA PLACE

Place François Jaumes - MONTPELLIER
Tél. 06 12 57 16 84

LES DEUX GRENOUILLES

Restaurant & Japanese bistro
8, avenue Jean-Jaurès - 34170 CASTELNAU-LE-LEZ
Tél. 04 67 79 03 85

cuisine, the names of the dishes are; yaki-oniguiri (grilled rice balls with soy), tofu hiyyayakko (organic). Pell-mell also on the carte, there is also a tonkatsu (bread-coated pork), zuke-maguro (tuna cooked a minute and marinated) or kara-aged (ginger chicken). For desert, the pineapple ginger crumble. Twelve sakés (rice wine) are available by the glass.

Mediterranean Cuisine

■ IL MERCATO .... **Italian & pizza**
Square de la Babote
✆ + 33 (0) 4 67 60 24 71
Open all year. Monday to Saturday from 10am to 11pm. Continuous service. Menu from €13 to €30. Day pass. Holiday voucher, Chèque Restaurant. Terrace. Kitchen 100% House, 100% Fresh products. Restaurant Italien. Cocktail bar.

Why Il Mercato?
Because it is summed up in one word: market cuisine. Here is a restaurant 100% fresh and 100% homemade products! a selection of vegetable and local products. We must admit that this place has some points to make. Starting with the terrace at the foot of the beautiful medieval Babote tower. Inside, you sit in a room, built on several levels. Behind his stoves Eric Torralba, a Chef from Montpellier who has been around, prepares fine traditional cuisine from Southern inspiration, judge for yourself: sautéed calamaretti and vongole zucchini flowers and ravioli Buratta, coastal anchovies put in salt and then marinated in white balsamic panisse of potimaron with saffron of Neffiès, you also treat yourself with tagliatelle «Aglio e Olio» on a spicy crushed green olives capers, bell peppers, basil, artichokes, the fish day, candied eggplant with bergamot lemon virgin vinaigrette of Combaillaux, to finish a cup of homemade mango sorbets, pineapple, delicious raspberry!

Market cuisine 100% fresh, 100% home made

Terrace on the square
Air-conditioned room

48, square de la Babote 34000 Montpellier
+33 (0)4 67 60 24 71 - www.ilmercato.fr
Hours 10 am to 11 pm
Near Comédie and train station
Near Observatoire station, lines 3

■ PIZZERIA DU PALAIS .... Italian & pizza
22, rue Palais-des-Guilhems
℡ + 33 (0) 4 67 60 67 97
www.pizzeriadupalais.fr
pizzeria.du.palais@sfr.fr
Open all year. Tuesday to Saturday for lunch and dinner. Menu from €13 to €16. À la carte: Around €16. Wine by the glass.
This pizzeria, open since 1965, became a montpellierian institution. In a typical vaulted room of the architecture of the Ecusson, the decoration is unpretentious with: green, red and white tablecloths, tables runner made of paper and some pretty lamps. The pasta is handmade and pizza cooked in a wood fire, of good quality. Gourmands can even choose the large pizza, and, even when hungry, it is not sure they will finish it! The menu offers a choice of thirty pizzas, and also pasta and antipastis dishes. The food and the reception is good, but we still regret that the prices are a little too high, considering the service offered.

■ TIBERIO .... Italian & pizza
121, rue d'Athènes
℡ + 33 (0) 4 99 51 67 40
Open all year. Closed in August. Tuesday to Saturday for lunch and dinner. Menu from €15 to €25 (Chef's suggestion between €13 and €18). Only Italian wine by the glass. Menu at €15 for lunch only. Terrace.
Tibèrio, Tibère, Roman soldier ending up a manic-depraved by casting the slaves in the sea in Sperlonga gave its name to this small restaurant serving Italian specialties in the Antigone district. Due fratelli, Antonio in the kitchen and Andrea - a former opera singer- in room are authentic Romans. You will be welcomed with open arms in a warm atmosphere. Elegant dining room, white tablecloths, red curtains, on the plate, Italian spaghetti all'vongolle, Sperlonga salad (tomatoes, ham, coppa, artichoke, Parmesan...), prawns, all'arrabbiata osso buco (veal shank tomato sauce), risotto with seafood or mushrooms. All washed down with an Italian light local wine of the famous wine merchant of the Jacques Cœur market.

■ LE VALENTINO........................ Italian & pizza
10, rue Alexandre Cabanel
℡ + 33 (0) 4 67 60 48 33
www.pizzavalentino.com
contact@pizzavalentino.com
Open Monday to Saturday from 12pm to 2pm and from 7pm to 11pm; Sunday for dinner. À la carte: Around €15. Wine by the glass. Lunch menus from €10 to €11.50. Pizzas: from €7 to €15. Desserts from €3 to €5.
In a setting decorated in red, gray and exposed stonewalls, Florian and his team offer a wide selection of pizzas, «red» (with tomato sauce) or «white» (with cream). The pizzas come in two sizes, for small and large appetites, and flavors range from classic to the original, as the Scallops, garnished with cream, mushrooms, with nuts of Scallops in white wine and raclette which creates the pizza version of the dish with cheese, also with the Grison meat and potatoes! We can also enjoy the homemade lasagna, Burrata (cheese from southern Italy) or the famous antipasti. The ovens are within sight of all the tables in the small room; the family atmosphere is very pleasant.

International & Fusion Cuisine

■ LA MANOLIA
8, place du Nombre d'Or
℡ + 33 (0) 9 82 32 68 03
lamanolia@gmail.com
Open on Tuesday and Wednesday from 8am to 6pm; Thursday to Saturday from 8am to 10pm. Wine by the glass. Starter and main course or main course and dessert: €14. Starter + main course + dessert: €17. Take-away.
At the foot of the imposing buildings of Antigone, in a small room in shades of ocher, red and chocolate, is a new little corner of Spain and Italy. The place also serves deli products with mainly Italian wines, De Cecco pasta, pesto and various condiments. Here, the cuisine is prepared with fresh ingredients. Also, we may, on a beautiful slate board or pretty plate, enjoy a plate of tapas or antipasti, a portion of pata negra ham, Italian salad (arugula, dried, cured ham, parmesan, basil tomatoes) or a velvety butternut, followed by tortellini with creamy mushrooms and artichoke. For dessert, we'll flambé seasonal fruits, or draw a portion of cheesecake or a jar of panna cotta. It is even possible to takeaway a dish! A perfect place for lunch.

Fast Food & Delivery

■ BAGEL STORE ....Sandwich
1-3, rue du Plan-d'Agde
℡ + 33 (0) 4 67 06 97 63
www.bagelstore.fr
Tram
Open Monday to Saturday from 8.30am to 11.30pm. Menu from €6.80 to €12.50. Terrace. Take-away. Shop.
Bagel Store now has a second shop in Montpellier! In the centre of the Ecusson, come and enjoy the thousand and one ways of this round sandwich. At the helm of this small restaurant, Cyril and Stéphanie who had been attracted by the product during a stay in the United States. The concept:

FAST FOOD & DELIVERY

an urban decoration and a menu inspired by the New York subway. Each bagel consists of fresh produce and is prepared before your eyes. On the menu: four menus and the salty and sweet bagels! Do not leave without tasting the desserts including the unavoidable cheesecake. We like the continuous service on the day, ideal for improvised lunches, and the American deli corner.

■ BURGER AND CO .... Fast food
4, rue Vanneau
✆ + 33 (0) 4 11 75 54 82
www.burgernco.fr
contact@burger-montpellier.fr
Open Monday to Saturday from 12pm to 2pm and from 7pm to 11pm. Burger with fried from €8.50, salads €8.50, burger vegetarian. Terrace. Take-away.

Burger and Co moved rue Vanneau but nothing has changed! Some claim that it is the best burger of Montpellier... After trying it, it is confirmed that they did not steal this reputation! The meat is soft and the fillings vary: the burgers are really to fall for. Accompanied by fries, they bear the names of symbolic songs of AC/DC, Dire Straits or Depeche mode... For an additional €3, you can have two steaks instead of one. Where to savour your burger? On site or as takeaways. Lovers of burgers and rock, rush to this place and you will not be disappointed!

■ FISH'N CHICK .... Fast food
1, rue En Gondeau
✆ + 33 (0) 4 67 63 57 04
Open Monday to Saturday for lunch and dinner. Menu from €12 to €15. Fixed rate formula: €11.20 (and €12). Terrace. Take-away. Heated terrace.

Li-Lan and her mother Anne Marie have recently opened a small restaurant where everything is eaten on the spot or taken away. The formulas are unique and offer breaded fish available in several variants or marinated and crumb-coated chicken : Chick 'Wrap (lettuce, cheddar, marinated and yellow crumb-coated chicken, curry sauce, coconut milk. The restaurant offers homemade sauces and its burger: Burger 'Chick (salad, marinated yellow breaded chicken and guacamole sauce.) And a possibility to create your own sandwich from chicken or fish between wraps, burgers or Viennese bread, along with ingredients and raw vegetables. vegetable salad or homemade fries. All made with fresh products. The owners also offer quiches, papillotte dishes and desserts (homemade clafoutis and fudge).

■ CHEZ FRIKOT
1 bis, rue Aristide Ollivier
✆ + 33 (0) 4 99 61 80 62
Open every day. Except Sunday in winter.

Marie called «Frikot» opened her small snack bar close to the Comedy, and gives Montpelliérains a little taste of Belgium. The more than twenty tables inside and outside will allow you to enjoy chips! They are excellent, crunchy and melting at the same time. It is a snack as there that offers the Mitraillette: a half baguette filled with meat, French fries and a choice of sauces, the famous balls, the hot dogs and sandwiches with rather original names. Judge for yourself: Van Damme, Amélie Nothomb, Brel, Capitaine Haddock... The dishes are delicious and the welcome is extraordinary! Faith in Petit Futé! In fact, it delivers at home too!

■ MADE IN FRANCE .... Sandwich & Salad
Place Saint-Côme
✆ + 33 (0) 4 99 58 10 74
www.le-made-in-france.fr
Open daily for lunch from 10am to 4pm and for dinner from 7pm to 11pm. A sandwich and a drink a dessert offered. Medium from €4.20. Large from €5.20.

After proving its worth to Nancy, this French style sandwich-bar landed in Montpellier facing Place Saint-Côme. Thanks to Audrey and Patricia, success is already waiting for you. The sandwich and salads are prepared infront of you now, you choose the (seasonal) ingredients and the type of artisan bread wanted from the baker (toasted or not, a nice medium size) along. The choice of composition is broad, and relected by the cheeses carte: Emmental, Edam, Camembert, bleu, goat, raclette and Reblochon! The meat is cured, prepared in marinade or grilled a la plancha. The star is the Big Boss, a sandwich with 2 meat choices (steak, chicken or pork), cheese and vegetables but Petit Futé has opted for the «duck» composed of duck breast, confit tomatoes and walnuts and other raw vegetables. Six homemade sauces, homemade fries, freshly squeezed fruit juice done infront of you, smoothies and snacks are also available to complete the range.

---

direct access to the beach	visually impaired disability	take away
bar	mental handicap	room service
laundry	motor disability	fitness room
air conditioning	garden or park	playroom / tv
nightclub	games	modern sanitary
cash machine	washing machine / laundry	water sports
drinking water	bicycle rental	tennis
horse riding	grocery store	archery
smoking area	airport shuttle	waterslide
non-smoking	fishing	fan
fitness	indoor swimming pool	toilet drain
miniature golf	outdoor heated pool	sailing
hard of hearing disability	outdoor pool	

Gourmet Escapes

■ **LE JARDIN AUX SOURCES**
30, avenue du Parc
BRISSAC
✆ **+ 33 (0) 4 67 73 31 16**
www.lejardinauxsources.com
contact@lejardinauxsources.com

Open on Tuesday and Thursday to Saturday for lunch and dinner; Sunday for lunch. Menu from €32 to €57. Children's menu: €12. Lunch menu: €23. Garden. Terrace. Shop.
A wonderful place where the pleasures of the table is combined with the beauty of the guesthouse. But it is above all a gourmet restaurant where Jérôme Billod-Morel takes an obvious pleasure to handle flavours and colours without distorting the product as in his sweetbreads with country crunchy tube and moss of fresh herbs, small aiguillette of supreme crust swindled Bresse chicken or a fillet of crust bar with chorizo, warm vinaigrette to olive and mashed potatoes with celery puree revisited and flavoured. The desserts are real artistic compositions, like this cheesecake revisited with citrus fruit on a success with cream of avocado and Grand marnier zest sorbet, or white chocolate and rhubarb, equatorial milk chocolate with mint tea and black chocolate guajana with passion. Regional wine list complements the meal; the vaulted dining room is generously flowered, the terrace overlooks the new balnéo pool, without forgetting the smile and the kindness of Isabelle that make the context all the more pleasant.

■ **L'OMBRINE**
Quai d'Honneur
LA GRANDE-MOTTE
✆ **+ 33 (0) 4 67 56 57 36**
www.restaurant-lombrine.com
restaurant-lombrine@hotmail.fr

Closed from December 26th to February 8th. Menu from €27 to €39.50. Children's menu: €9.50. Lunch menu: €19.90. Terrace. Take-away.
It is the number one address in la Grande-Motte, for shells! Monique and Jean-Louis Sans accommodate guests in their restaurant of the «Parisian chic brasserie» type. Moored in terrace (covered or closed), or in the warm and intimate room on the first floor, the view of the port and the sea is enhanced by the surrounding calm. The chef takes you on board to a cuisine of the «sea», products whose arrival is daily: royal or imperial seafood tray with their Breton lobsters and their lobster, fresh fish speciality, parillada, plancha, shellfish (oyster tartar speciality), seafood... As for the bouillabaisse, the fish are presented to the guests. And for those who do not have the marine legs, the chef offers a quality meat: beef fillet, chateaubriand, steak, duck breast. The desserts list will satisfy the most demanding, tiramisu with apple tart, via the terrine of fruit and red fruit gratin, without forgetting profiteroles.

■ **CÔTÉ MAS**
Route de Villeveyrac
MONTAGNAC
✆ **+ 33 (0) 4 67 24 36 10 / + 33 (0) 6 42 39 10 39**
www.cote-mas.fr

Open Tuesday to Sunday for lunch; Thursday to Saturday for dinner. Menu from €19 to €29. Daily special: €15.
Jean-Claude Mas made this restaurant in the «Rural Luxury» spirit. The place is elegant and the simple decoration is made with taste and refinement. Located in Montagnac, in the heart of 150 acres of vineyards, scrubland and olive trees, the gourmet stop will not disappoint. A menu very fusion, inspired by land and offering a completely new looks, with some detours on the land of the rising sun. Duck foie gras with the three flavours, «wakamé», honey and spicy red wine as starters; for the rest, grilled beef, seasonal vegetable casserole, red wine essence and Béarnaise sauce with wasabi. Finally, apples tatin, rice pudding cream and apple granite with Calvados. The wines chosen by lovers of the subject are of course excellent. A large room also allows the accommodation of groups, for seminars and private tastings.

Le Jardin aux Sources
Restaurant gastronomique — Chambres d'hôtes

Isabelle & Jérôme Billod - Morel

30 avenue du Parc – 34190 Brissac - **Tél. 04 67 73 31 16**

www.lejardinauxsources.com - contact@lejardinauxsources.com

GOURMET ESCAPES

Visit Millau

■ **HÔTEL DES CAUSSES**
2, rue Mathieu Prévot
✆ +33 (0)5 65 60 03 19
www.hoteldescausses.com
contact@hoteldescausses.com

Logis (2 cheminées). Open all year. Closed on Sunday in winter. Reception until 22: 15 rooms (new Eco categories or Comfort). Double room from €69 to €129. Half-board: €127 (at €153 as from two nights). Breakfast: €9.80. Extra bed: €15. Closed parking: €7. Stop-over with special rates with 75/90 €. Menu from €22 to €38. Restaurant open every evening and daily for lunch Tuesday to Friday – Express formula €16. Holiday voucher. Free Wifi.
Céline Dejay and Hervé Métayer took over this hotel in March 2011. Both knowing the trade, they completely renovated and refreshed the rooms and the Ardoise restaurant.
The result is there. At 3 minutes away from the historic centre, you can stay in one of the 15 rooms with contemporary tones, new bedding and TVs with flat-screen. The innovation of 2014 is the decoration of the hotel on the theme of the gloves and leather. In the restaurant with elegant and warm setting, we enjoy a gastro-bistro cuisine, including a snail fricassée with garlic cream, winemaker meat tart, homemade foie gras, mitonée of Aubrac beef, simply grilled chops of sheep, and finally its refined cheese board or a waffle with white and black chocolate. One of the best values for money in Millau.

■ **L'ARDOISE**
56, avenue Jean-Jaurès
✆ +33 (0)5 65 60 03 19
www.hoteldescausses.com

Logis (2 cocottes). Open all year. Low season: Monday to Friday for lunch and dinner; Saturday for dinner; Sunday for lunch. High season: Monday and public holidays for dinner; Tuesday to Sunday. Booking advised. Menu from €16 to €42. À la carte: Around €30. Children's menu: €12. Lunch menu: €16. Wine by the glass. Holiday voucher, Chèque Restaurant. Groups welcome. Terrace.
Hervé Metayer is the chef in the hotel des Causses. It is necessary to move the lines of the Millau catering. A restaurant with very elegant, cheerful and warm setting, in shades of brown and simple «» pink, red, it offers a very original cuisine with a bistro theme (themed menus; local, the river, around duck…), including its harlequin of spring vegetables with tuna, fillet of pike with crayfish and its crunchy vegetables, mutton chops simply grilled, and to finish your dish of refined cheese, a chocolate flavoured waffle or the forêt noire coupe. Homemade ice creams are served from 5 pm. An unmissable address in three years in homemade Millau produce.

MA MAISON
550, avenue du Salaison
SAINT-AUNÈS
✆ + 33 (0) 4 67 45 05 19
www.restaurantmamaison.com
restaumamaison@orange.fr
Open all year. Tuesday to Saturday for lunch and dinner; Sunday for lunch. Booking is essential. Menu from €36 to €59. À la carte: Around €40. Lunch menu: €20. Wine by the glass. Garden. Terrace. Entertainment.

Ma Maison, located at Saint-Aunés, a few kilometres from Montpellier, offers a rural setting and friendliness. This restaurant has become a reference in Montpellier in a few years. The recipe: a former bourgeois house, turned into a comfortable restaurant house, tables in mosaic, family furniture, the chandeliers and wrought iron chairs. The place has three rooms opening onto the pool and park. At mealtimes, Philippe delivers a cuisine from Nice with hints of cicadas and socca! Delicious is Philippe's pistou soup just like the sea bass fillet from the Mediterranean with lemon and its virgin olive oil fillet. Ma Maison organises tasting evenings from a program that you will also find on their website.

LA CHAPELLE
110, rue des Anémones
VILLENEUVE-LÈS-MAGUELONE
✆ + 33 (0) 4 67 07 95 80
Open all year. Sunday to Wednesday for lunch from 11.45am to 2pm; Thursday to Saturday for lunch from 11.45am to 2pm and for dinner from 7pm to 10pm. Menu from €12 to €25. Children's menu: €8. Lunch menu: €12. Wine by the glass. Chèque Restaurant. Garden. Terrace.

The place, undoubtedly, is original! A pretty chapel converted into a restaurant and a very secular enthusiasm to quickly make your mouth full with water. The outdoor setting is to be tried if the weather is nice, the small garden is very calming. Olivier the chef prepares Catalan specialities – suquet des peix (fish bouillabaisse and shellfish), chorizo cuttlefish à la plancha, guinea fowl with lobster... Several grills are offered (including bull), pata negra fillet with espelette pepper is also a safe bet. For dessert, chocolate cake and rum babas will delight the most unrepentant gourmets.

Accommodation

Hotels → 32
Hostel → 37
Camping → 37
Guesthouses → 38
Cottages → 38
Other Accommodation → 40

Hotels

High Budget

■ **HOTEL LE GUILHEM**
18, rue Jean-Jacques-Rousseau
✆ + 33 (0) 4 67 52 90 90
www.leguilhem.com
contact@leguilhem.com

Open all year. 35 rooms (exemption from payment for the accommodation of the children accompanying their parents). From €99 to €189. Breakfast: €12. Extra bed: €20. Pets allowed. Internet access. Wifi. Cleaning service. Special rate with the parking of Peyrou Pitot. Breakfast of terrace depending on weather. Satellite TV, Canal+.
At a few steps from the beautiful jardin des plantes, the hotel offers the harmonious comfort of a 16th century residence that is tastefully renovated. Each room has an atmosphere and a decor that is unique with a level of comfort and amenities of high – quality. Some rooms open onto a garden offering a little freshness for the summer season. The address is one of the safe values of the Ecusson for a charming stay.

■ **LE JARDIN DES SENS** .... 1 Star
11, avenue Saint-Lazare
✆ + 33 (0) 4 99 58 38 38
www.jardindessens.com

Open all year. 15 rooms (2 suites). High season: single room from €175 to €215. Breakfast: €22. Closed parking. Suite from €415. Pets allowed. Wifi. Cleaning service. Catering facilities (gourmet restaurant « Le Jardin de Sens «). Satellite TV, Canal+. Whirlpool. Adjacent club of fitness.
Hotel Jardin des Sens is a design hotel where everything invites luxury, calm and voluptuousness. Located close to the city center, in a quiet environment, it has 13 rooms and 2 suites, one with a private pool. The place is striking beautifull and the pure and simple lines give, as if by magic, a warm and cozy atmosphere. In the rooms, the mahogany wood floor, the small room lamps and cozy armchairs contribute to the charm. This refined and elegant atmosphere blending with the comfortable room offers a true charming holiday .

■ **KYRIAD PRESTIGE** .... 4 Stars
135, rue de Jugurtha
✆ + 33 (0) 4 67 64 56 45
www.hotel-prestige.fr

Open all year. Reception 24/24. 100 rooms. Double room from €100 to €140. Half-board. American Express, Diners Club, Holiday voucher. Seminars. Receptions and weddings. Internet corner. Free Wifi. Cleaning service. Catering facilities. Canal+. Hammam, whirlpool, sauna.
Close to the business district and just 5 minutes from downtown, at 10 minutes from the beaches and the airport, the hotel Kyriad Prestige enjoys a privileged location. It has a hundred rooms and offers upscale features, is equipped with meeting rooms, an outdoor and indoor pool, a relaxing spa and massages, as well as a piano bar. The rooms are spacious and have a central office and all the computer connectors you might need. A restaurant, «Rest'Ô « will even allow you to eat a market cuisine on spot .

■ **LA MAISON BLANCHE**
1796, avenue de la Pompignane
✆ + 33 (0) 4 99 58 20 70
www.hotel-maison-blanche.com

Open all year. Reception 24/24. 34 rooms (2 suites). Double room from €83 to €136. Buffet breakfast: €10. Extra bed: €16. Parking included. Pets allowed (€9). Internet access. Wifi. Cleaning service. Catering facilities.
Anne-Marie and Jean-Pierre Casalta have transformed this old abandoned (for twenty-five years) farm of the nineteenth century, into a beautiful colonial-style mansion inspired by the great houses of white Louisiana woods. The hotel also has a park, filled with cedar, chestnuts and lindens ... and an aviary of exotic birds! with a refined line, the rooms receive essentially a high-end clientele. The Maison Blanche has already received its share of celebrities: Rostropovich, Noiret, Beckenbauer, Delon, Johnny Hallyday etc... Not forgetting to mention the pool, which overlooks the park and the restaurant which serves a traditional cuisine.

■ **OCEANIA MONTPELLIER LE METROPOLE** .... 4 Stars
3, rue du Clos-René
✆ + 33 (0) 4 67 12 32 32
www.oceaniahotels.com

Open all year. Reception 24/24. 84 rooms. Double room from €110 to €185. Breakfast: €17. Garage: €14. American Express, Diners Club, Holiday voucher. Pets allowed. Free Wifi. Cleaning service. Catering facilities (menu from €18 to €35). Satellite TV, Canal+.
A few steps from the train station, the hotel is nestled in a beautiful nineteenth century building, built on the model of the great palaces of the Côte d'Azur. It has eighty four spacious air-conditioned rooms, some with views over the garden. The hotel has its charm of yesteryears: the immense hall welcomes warmly guests, while the wooden classified elevator, takes you upstairs. In summer, the garden is the perfect place for breakfast to the sound of

cicadas. A bar, a library area with club chairs, lounges and restaurant perfectly complement the offer of this hotel. A solarium in the park will offer you the opportunity to quietly enjoy your tea and cake by the pool after a few races at the Polygon or in Ecusson.

■ **PULLMAN** .... **4 Stars**
1, rue des Pertuisanes
✆ + 33 (0) 4 67 99 72 72
www.pullmanhotels.com
H1294@accor.com

Open all year. Reception 24/24. 88 rooms (2 suites). Single room €140. Buffet breakfast or in room: €26. Closed parking: €14. American Express, Diners Club, Holiday voucher. Pets allowed (€8/night). Seminars. Internet corner. Free Internet access. Free Wifi. Catering facilities. Satellite TV, Canal+. Whirlpool.

Completely renovated in July 2011, the Pullman is located in the heart of the city centre, attached to the The Polygon mall. Its location and services seduce both men and business couples and families on holiday. Discreet luxury and quality are the hallmarks of this hotel decoration inspired by the awakening of the senses. With 86 spacious rooms (connecting rooms for families) and 2 suites combining tranquility and new technologies, the hotel ranks among the finest in Montpellier. We appreciate the free wifi, heated pool, Mediterranean restaurant and bar located on the top floor.

■ **ROYAL HÔTEL** .... **3 Stars**
8, rue Maguelone
✆ + 33 (0) 4 67 92 13 36
www.royalhotelmontpellier.com
resa@royalhotelmontpellier.com

Open all year. Reception 24/24. 46 rooms. Single room from €70 to €110; double room from €75 to €125. Buffet breakfast: €8. Parking (special rate parking of the Comedy: 18 €/midnight then €8/day extra). Pets allowed (€4.60). Free Wifi. Cleaning service. Satellite TV, Canal+.

This hotel, ideally located in the city centre in a quiet environment, between the station and place de la Comédie, offers 46 comfortable rooms in contemporary surroundings. The reception of Evelyne and her team is friendly, professional, and the value for money is excellent. An address to remember for those looking to make their way to Montpellier most practical and as comfortable as possible.

■ **L'HÔTEL DE MASSANE** .... **3 Stars**
Domaine de Massane
BAILLARGUES
✆ + 33 (0) 4 67 87 87 87
www.massane.com
reception@massane.com

Open all year. Reception 24/24. 32 rooms (more 52 apartments). Double room from €128 to €148. Half-board: €36. Breakfast: €11.50. Parking included. Tourism label & Disability. Pets allowed (with supplement). Free Wifi. Cleaning service. Catering facilities (menu from €25 to €75). Satellite TV. Sauna.

At a few kilometers from Montpellier, between the Camargue and the Mediterranean, Hotel Massana is a true luxury resort nestled in the heart of golf. It is ideal for a holiday combining sport and recreation. The hotel has tennis courts, volleyball court, an outdoor pool and a golf course. After exercising go to the Aromassane spa where many treatments and massages are offered. The rooms are tastefully decorated in the colors of the region. They are warm, calm and spacious, and are an invitation to relax. As for catering, the restaurant le 360 is available.

■ **DOMAINE DE VERCHANT** .... **5 Stars**
1, boulevard Philippe-Lamour
CASTELNAU-LE-LEZ
✆ + 33 (0) 4 67 07 26 00
www.verchant.com
reservation@verchant.com

Open all year. 26 rooms. High season: double room from €230 to €450. Pets allowed (animal supplement from €20 per day). Seminars. Receptions and weddings. Internet access. Wifi. Cleaning service. Catering facilities. Sale (wines of the estate of Verchant). Satellite TV, Canal+. Hammam, whirlpool, sauna.

Inspired by the «Montpellier follies» of the seventeenth century, this castle has a high-class clientele in large rooms (from 30 to 90 m² for the apartments) tastefully decorated, combining the old and the modern (open bathroom with spa bath, exposed beams, stone walls). The authenticity of the setting, the estate surrounded by vineyards, and contemporary decoration, make this hotel a place with unique charm, just a few away minutes from Montpellier. This luxurious estate offers absolute comfort and omnipresent calm, in the rooms, around the pool or in the restaurant where a light and tasty cuisine accompanied by wines from the estate. Note: rooms are available to rent for banquets, weddings and seminars.

Medium Budget

■ **HÔTEL D'ARAGON** .... **3 Stars**
10, rue Baudin
✆ + 33 (0) 4 67 10 70 00
www.hotel-aragon.fr
info@hotel-aragon.fr

Open all year. 12 rooms (room Luxury: Netbook, Netpresso, Tea. European Ecolabel). High season: double room from €92 to €139. Breakfast: €14. Internet corner. Internet access. Wifi. Satellite TV, Canal+.

In the city center, close to the Place de la Comédie, the Hotel Aragon welcomes its guests with charm and elegance. In a harmonious space, the harmony of colors and quality materials offers a place between imagination and functionality, nobility of ancient times and high-tech technology. The fully equipped rooms are spacious and soundproofed.

HOTELS - Medium Budget

LES JASSES DE CAMARGUE
Route d'Aimargues
30660 Gallargues-le-Montueux
+33 (0)4 66 806 400

reservation@jasses-de-camargue.com
www.jasses-de-camargue.com

Outside, the porch is nestled among green plants and is a perfect place to sit for breakfast! A service that is intended to satisfy perfect man and woman business or discerning tourist. The hotel also offers services such as car rental, boat, concierge service ... The establishment is very involved in eco-tourism and has implemented a green tariff: a discount on price of your stay in exchange for light housekeeping every 3 days.

■ **LES JASSES DE CAMARGUE**.................. **3 Stars**
Route des Plages
GALLARGUES-LE-MONTUEUX
✆ + 33 (0) 4 66 80 64 00
www.jasses-de-camargue.com

Open all year. Single room from €69 to €89. Breakfast: €9.80. Pets allowed (€5 extra). Internet access available for a fee. Wifi. Cleaning service. Catering facilities. Satellite TV, Canal+. Hammam, whirlpool, sauna. Excursions.
Les Jasses De Camargue, is more than a simple hotel, it is a real hotel and residential area. Its location makes it an ideal place to stay overnight, one week, or even a month or more! You will immediately be seduced by the charm of this estate located in the heart of a huge 8 acres park between the Camargue, the Cévennes and Provence. Comfort, modernity, is what will immediately draw your attention in the rooms, very spacious and beautifully designed. All the elements are gathered for an immediate relaxation: spa, indoor swimming pool and massages. At Patio des Jasses, you will have the opportunity of enjoying a cuisine with Provence flavours. Les Jasses de Camargue also have a spacious dining room of 200 m² that can host weddings, seminars and any other event.

■ **HOTEL DU PARC**................................... **2 Stars**
8, rue Achille-Bégé
✆ + 33 (0) 4 67 41 16 49
www.hotelduparc-montpellier.com
hotelduparcmtp@wanadoo.fr

19 rooms. Double room from €59 to €107. Breakfast: €10. Parking. Internet access. Wifi. Canal+.
Here's a great address. For the record: the Hôtel du Parc is located in an old XVIIIth building century where the family of Count Vivier de Chatelard lived... Claire and Frances lived, the owners of the place were beautifully landscaped hotel in classic style to preserve the authentic character of the building. The rooms are all now personalised, and well equipped (the owners have not forgotten the mini-bar). You will enjoy your breakfast on the terrace of the hotel, giving onto an attractive shaded garden.

■ **HÔTEL EUROCIEL** .... **3 Stars**
1, avenue du Pont-Juvénal
✆ + 33 (0) 4 67 07 51 61
www.hoteleurociel.fr
Double room from €118 to €135. Breakfast: €10.50. Extra bed: €20.

An invitation to travel, relaxation and peace for this new 3 star hotel that opened in March 2012. Immersed in a contemporary and warm atmosphere, the journey can start. Spain, Italy, Germany, the Benelux, England and Greece: 6 floors/ 6 stopovers, it is left for you to choose. A decoration subtly combining journeys and the charm of Montpellier. A set of services and amenities worthy of a 4 star at the cost of a 3 star. An independent and family-run hotel where service and the help of the guest are the motto of the house.

■ **HOTEL LES ALIZES**
14, rue Jules-Ferry
✆ + 33 (0) 4 67 12 85 35 / + 33 (0) 4 67 12 85 30
www.hotellesalizes.com
info@hotellesalizes.com

Open all year. 12 rooms. High season: double room from €80 to €90. Breakfast: €9. Holiday voucher. Internet access. Wifi. Satellite TV, Canal+.
This small hotel is just across the Saint-Roch station. The area is a bit noisy, but the twelve rooms have the advantage of being bright, soundproofed, acceptable comfort and all equipped with shower, satellite TV and telephone. You can choose between a single, standard and comfort (double and single bed). Breakfast (fast or continental) is served in your room from 6 am. An address has a very interresting value for money.

■ **HÔTEL KYRIAD MONTPELLIER AÉROPORT.....3 Stars**
273, rue Roland Garros
MAUGUIO
✆ + 33 (0) 4 67 99 20 00
www.kyriad-montpellier-aeroport.fr
kyriad.montpellier@free.fr

Open all year. Reception 24/24. 51 rooms. Double room from €59 to €120. Half-board: €90. Breakfast: €9.50. Closed parking included. American Express, Diners Club, Holiday voucher. Free Wifi. Catering facilities (menu starting from 13,50€). Canal+.
Le Kyriad located 2.5 km from the airport, in the commercial area, was revamped in 2011. The carpet has been changed, the beds the duvets and the walls have been painted. Family rooms for three and for four people with a mezzanine. The setting is good, a restaurant with a large floral fresco and pool completes the offer. Pastaboxes allow you to eat if you arrive after 21: 30.

■ **LE MAS DE GRILLE ....3 Stars**
93, rue Théophraste-Renaudot
Mas de Grille
SAINT-JEAN-DE-VÉDAS
✆ + 33 (0) 4 67 47 07 45
www.hotelmontpelliermasdegrille.com

Open all year. Reception 24/24. 53 rooms. Double room from €92. Breakfast: €12. Closed parking included. Pets allowed (€10 extra by animal). Seminars. Free Wifi. Catering facilities (menu from €10.90 to €28.90). Satellite TV, Canal+.

Located near the highway and the tram, Mas de Grille is ideally located. The welcome is warm and attentive. The rooms are calm, tastefully decorated, simple and comfortable. They offer views of the park and the swimming pool. The bar is the place for cocktails and viewings. In summer, the terrace overlooking the pool and the petanque are perfect places to relax or arrange a seminary.

Small Budget

■ **HOTEL NOVA .... 2 Stars**
8, rue Richelieu
✆ + 33 (0) 4 67 60 79 85
www.hotelnova.fr
hotelnova@free.fr
Open all year. Closed period of Christmas. Reception until 23: 00 (access by badge the night). 16 rooms (3 rooms 4 people). Double room from €50 to €65; triple room €77. Breakfast: €8. American Express, Holiday voucher. Internet corner. Free Wifi. Satellite TV, Canal+.
Some parts of the building in which the hotel Nova settled dates from the thirteenth century; it is to say that's how history hangs over this place. In the centre of the Ecusson, the total immersion, walls in old stones, vault for the breakfast room, again, you are just a few steps from the Comedie. The welcome is warm and the rooms are limited in number, which provides a good cosy character. The rooms, with pastel tones, are pleasant and are equipped with a telephone, Internet access and double glazing for most of them.

■ **À LA VOILE BLANCHE .... 3 Stars**
1, avenue Louis-Tudesq
BOUZIGUES
✆ + 33 (0) 4 67 78 35 77
www.alavoileblanche.fr
alavoileblanche@wanadoo.fr

Open all year. Low season: double room €65; suite €110. High season: double room from €85; suite from €190. Half-board: €125 (the room in low season at €145 the room in high season and from €170 for a suite in low season at €250 the suite in high season). Breakfast: €9. American Express, Holiday voucher. Pets allowed. Free Wifi. Catering facilities. Canal+.
Easily identifiable thanks to its orange façade, it is the last hotel on the quay of the port of Bouzigues. Opposite the Lake Thau, it has eight rooms with different atmospheres, including a suite and four with terraces. All rooms overlook the port, which is pleasant. The decor is refined and the metal and design furniture, are reduced to the essential. All these offer a modern and relaxing atmosphere, with an interesting touch of originality, witnesses the room with the leopard walls and the full of chrome metal bed. A bar-restaurant with a lounge atmosphere with terrace will offer to taste the shells of the nearby pond as well as fish grilled à la plancha and other seafood platters. In high season, from 3.pm to 6.pm, you can also go for the tea room with tasting of coffees, teas, pancakes and waffles!

HOTELS - Small Budget

■ **HÔTEL LE NEPTUNE** .... 3 Stars
Port de Plaisance
1, rue de L'Etang-de-l'Or
CARNON
✆ + 33 (0) 4 67 50 88 00
www.hotel-neptune.fr
hotel-neptune@wanadoo.fr

Closed from December 18 th to January 11 th. Reception 24/24. 53 rooms. Single room from €85 to €140; double room from €75 to €130; triple room from €70 to €95. Breakfast: €12. Closed parking. Seminars. Internet access. wi-fi. Satellite TV, Canal+.
A marine atmosphere for this hotel bathed by the air of the Mediterranean and opening onto the ponds and Camargue, just a little further. The complete renovation of the hotel is underway. The peaceful atmosphere that reign there is perfect for a relaxing stay and the location, 300 metres from the beach and within walking distance of the port, is ideal. Holidaymakers will stop here with pleasure, but the place can satisfy businessmen wishing a little more peace than in the city. Three conference rooms are available and the hotel used to receive business trips and seminars. The offer is completed by a swimming pool, solarium and a restaurant in the regional touches, Le Trident.

■ **LE BRASILIA** .... 3 Stars
9, boulevard Maréchal-Joffre
PALAVAS-LES-FLOTS
✆ + 33 (0) 4 67 68 00 68
www.brasilia-palavas.com
hotel@brasilia-palavas.com

Closed from December 15th to January 15th. 22 rooms. Double room from €56 to €119; triple room from €98 to €133. Garage. Holiday voucher. Free Wifi. Canal+.
Brasilia is ideally situated as it is close to the port, right in front of the Phare de la Méditerranée. The beach is at its feet and Montpellier is just a few kilometres away. The sea can be appreciated from the balconies of a good part of the rooms, perfect for a breakfast facing the Sea. The service is efficient and smiling and the the price/quality ration is very interesting.

■ **HÔTEL DE LA PLAGE**
99, avenue Saint-Maurice
PALAVAS-LES-FLOTS
✆ + 33 (0) 4 67 68 95 43
www.hotel-palavas-plage.fr
contact@hotel-palavas-plage.fr

Open all year. Reception until 10.30pm. Double room from €69 to €110. Breakfast: €7.50. Extra bed: €10. Closed parking: €10. Holiday voucher. Seminars. Internet corner. Free Wifi. Cleaning service. Satellite TV, Canal+. Lent bicycles.
Recently renovated, the Hotel de la Plage today offers a different face. The façade was renovated and he 34 rooms were redesigned, the result is a modern décor and a new layout which adds to the comfort of the place. For the view, you will have the choice between sea and ponds, and a private parking allows you to leave your car safely. The beaches are just 50 metres away and the sporting stays, in partnership with local partners, are organised.

■ **AUBERGE DU BERANGE**
N110
SAINT-GENIÈS-DES-MOURGUES
✆ + 33 (0) 4 67 87 75 00
www.hotel-auberge-berange.com
contact@hotel-auberge-berange.com

Open all year. Reception until 11pm. Single room from €40; double room from €45. Breakfast: €6. Closed parking. Pets allowed. Free Wifi. Catering facilities (menu from €17 to €30). Surrounded by nature in an environment of olive trees and geraniums, this hotel and restaurant, run by Emmanuelle and her mother, offer camargue cuisine in the pure family tradition. The room in south colours is extended by a beautiful terrace in a pleasant setting for a good meal. Wide range of starters with, among others,

Port de Plaisance - 34280 CARNON
Tél. 04 67 50 88 00 - Fax 04 67 50 96 72 - www.hotel-neptune.fr

well-stocked buffets of vegetables and meats (more than fifty different choices). Homemade salads – aubergines, pepper, grilled chickpeas, mussels with escabeche, fresh anchovies, sardines with escabeche, cold cuts of the Cévennes – can be complemented by a bull sausage or serrano ham. For the main course: bull or gardiane rib but also duck or olives according to the season, all liven up with fresh vegetables. For desserts, with the choice between rum baba, prunes with wine and tart grapes. The bar and its patrons make the entertainment. You can visit the herd next to the inn. Many hotel rooms in the garrigue await you for a quiet nap.

Hostel

■ **AUBERGE DE JEUNESSE**
Impasse Petite Corraterie
Rue des Ecoles-Laïques
✆ + 33 (0) 4 67 60 32 22
www.fuaj.org
fuaj@hifrance.org
Open all year. Annual closing of semi December to January 3rd. Reception uninterrupted from 8am to midnight. from €20.20. Breakfast included.

The auberge de jeunesse has a good idea to be installed in the student area of the city center. To get there, the best mean is to take the tram and get off on the Boulevard Louis Blanc. There, go up the street this until you reach this old building that has been beautifully renovated ... from the inside. Through a contribution, you will be housed in rooms of 3 or 4 or in larger dormitories. It is usually quite friendly, but always crowded in summer. Once spring arrives, it is recommended to book several days in advance.

Camping

■ **CAMPING-CLUB LE PLEIN AIR DES CHENES ...4 Stars**
Avenue Georges Frêche
CLAPIERS
✆ + 33 (0) 4 67 02 02 53
www.sandaya.fr
contact@pleinairdeschenes.net

Open all year. Campsite from €20 to €57 per night for 2 people. Mobile homes 6 to 8 people from €85 to €165 per night. Area for camper van. Internet access. Activities.

Camping-Club Plein Air des Chênes is known for its water park that delight children and teenagers during the summer months. But it is also the only alternative for campers on the area in the north of the city. In the shade of oaks, tourists can plant their tent or rent mobile home - from two to eight people - or chalets - three rooms maximum - and enjoy the many activities that offer the complex. This establishment is a good alternative for those wishing to discover the inland montpellier.

⚓ direct access to the beach	♿ visually impaired disability	☕ take away
🍸 bar	🧠 mental handicap	△ room service
🧺 laundry	♿ motor disability	🏋 fitness room
✳ air conditioning	🌳 garden or park	📺 playroom / tv
🎵 nightclub	🎲 games	🚿 modern sanitary
€ cash machine	🧺 washing machine / laundry	🏄 water sports
🚰 drinking water	🚲 bicycle rental	🎾 tennis
🐎 horse riding	🛒 grocery store	

Guesthouses

■ **MAS DE FOURNEL**
Saint-Clément-de-Rivière
✆ + 33 (0) 4 67 67 00 85 /
+ 33 (0) 6 40 32 36 20
www.masdefournel.com
amb137@yahoo.ca

Open all year. Reception up to 20. Double room from €115. The week from €400 in low season. As from three nights €105. Parking. Cottage from €600 to €780. Pets allowed. Free Wifi. Whirlpool. Park of 14 ha.

Anne-Marie Boullais Bernabé welcomes its guests in a superb location overlooking the scrubland and the village of Montferrier, seven kilometres north of Montpellier. For short stays, four charming suites await their guests. For longer stays, the Farmhouse has five apartments and a studio open onto the garden and pine forests. All apartments, particularly bright, are equipped with a kitchen (dishwasher, stove, fridge, oven...). A common lingerie is also available. The setting is well maintained and comfortable, not forgetting the exceptional setting that makes Fournel one of the most popular cottages of the Montpellier area. Pool (on site), golf, horseback riding and tennis (nearby).

■ **CASTLE COTTAGE**
289, chemin de la Rocheuse
CASTELNAU-LE-LEZ
✆ + 33 (0) 4 67 72 63 08 / + 33 (0) 6 75 50 41 50
http: //castlecottage.free.fr
castlecottage@free.fr
tram line 2, just 500m, station « clairval »

Open all year. 4 rooms. Single room from €82 to €116; double room from €92 to €126; studio/apartment the week. Breakfast included. Extra bed: €22. Rates rental studio for a week on request. Pets allowed (on request). Wifi.

In this village adjoining Montpellier,, Mrs Carabin-Cailleau is fortunate to live in a mansion protected from the bustle by a park. In her house, there are two guest bedrooms sharing a bathroom. And in an independent house, it is a full apartment that opens directly onto the greenery. The cottage is accompanied by a large living room with kitchenette to an end, and armchairs to the other. The setting is charming, you will quickly feel at home.

Cottages

■ **MAS DE FOURNEL**
Saint-Clément-de-Rivière
✆ + 33 (0) 4 67 67 00 85 /
+ 33 (0) 6 40 32 36 20
www.masdefournel.com
amb137@yahoo.ca

Open all year. Double room: €115 per night (between €450 and €1100 for a week); Small cottage (show, kitchen, room, mezzanine) with €780/week. Internet access.

Just 7 km from Montpellier, wide open spaces are available in Mas de Fournel. Pine forests nearby, an 18th century farmhouse, everything invites you to escape. It is in this privileged setting that Olga Bernabé welcomes you with the choice in one of the four suites, for short breaks, or one of the five apartments, for longer stays. Particularly right, from their windows overlooking the gardens and pine forests, all the apartments have a kitchenette – stove, fridge, dishwasher and wireless system. On-site, guests will enjoy the pool and hot tub, if not, you have tennis courts and a green nearby.

■ **CHÂTEAU DE LA BANQUIÈRE**
Vauguières-le-Haut - MAUGUIO
✆ + 33 (0) 4 67 65 79 95 / + 33 (0) 6 74 19 49 44
www.chateau-la-banquiere.com
chateaulabanquiere@wanadoo.fr

The château de la Banquière is in Marie Varenne de Bordas' family since six generations. Today set up to receive guests, the place still exudes the daily life of the time. The layout of the farm evokes the traditional small square of languedoc village, which adds to the place a sure charm. Four cottages are offered, two in a historic building and two more modern houses, all well-equipped. If the activities around are many, a meal in the shade of nettle trees where you can stroll among the trees in the park will already offer a certain delight. You can also visit the family wine warehouses, with the castle enjoying its own wine production! Information and rates on request.

The digital version of this guide is available!

Only available from the online shop of Petit Futé.

1. Go to the online shop of Petit Futé: http://boutique.petitfute.com
2. Click on the **« Cherchez votre destination »** tab and type the title of your guide, then click on **OK**.
3. Click on the **« Guides numériques »** link of **« Type Guide »** in the left column and scroll covers using left or right arrows, then click on **the cover** of your guide.
4. On the presentation form of your digital guide, click on the **« Ajouter au panier »** button below and then on the **« Valider »** button on the right.
5. Type the **« Code de remise »** below and click on **« Utiliser un bon de réduction »**.

99GHBL9E5UQP

The code can only be used once. It is necessary to respect the characters in capital letter of the code

6. Click on the **« Passer la commande »** button with a global amount of 0€.
7. Log into your account by clicking on the **« Se connecter »** button or create your account by clicking on the **« S'enregistrer »** link (after creating an account, click once more on the **« Valider mon panier »** button on the right and repeat stage 6).
8. Select your billing address and click the **« Poursuivre »** button, or fill in the **« Informations de facturation »** fields before clicking the **« Poursuivre »** button.
9. Select the **« Valider ma commande offerte »** payment method and click the **« Poursuivre »** button, then the **« Valider la commande »** button.
10. Simply click on the **« Mes guides téléchargeables »** link, or click on the **« Mon compte »** link at the top and then below on the **« Mes guides téléchargeables »** link in the **« Mon compte »**, left column and on the right, select the digital version using the **« Télécharger »** link.

*ffer is valid until 31/12/2014 subject to a stop the marketing of certain titles in France and around the world and provided that the number of downloads is less than or equal to the number of printed paper guides. so available for smartphones, tablets, e-readers and PC or Mac computers.

Other Accommodation

■ **APPART HOTEL SMART LIVING**
12, rue Hippolyte
✆ + 33 (0) 6 76 20 84 70
www.smartliving.fr
contact@smartliving.fr
Tram: lines 1, 2 and 3 according to apartments.

Open all year. Charming apartments, from studios to T2 in the Arches, Antigone and Comedie neighbourhoods. Reception up till 11 p.m. 9 rooms. Studio / Apartment from 85 € to 140 € per night, from 70 € to 120 € per week, from 60 € to 96 € per month. Extra bed: 15 €. Open car park. Pets allowed. Free wifi. Housekeeping. Satellite TV.

With innovative accomodation offers, the «ready to live» apartments of Smart Living will charm many. Individual apartments located at various strategic locations of the city, all-inclusive and all modern amenities of a real home. Decorated in a contemporary and rather trendy manner, the apartments are well located and can meet the needs of a diverse clientele. Be it for a few days, weeks or months, it is probably a home that meets your expectations, and which successfully replace the traditional hotel offer.

■ **LAGRANGE CITY MONTPELLIER**
1684, avenue Albert Einstein
✆ + 33 (0) 4 99 64 29 40
www.lagrange-city-montpellier.com

Breakfast: €9. Parking: €10 (€60 per week). From €75 to €116 per night for an apartment 2 people. From €113 to €148 for 4 people From €122 to €170 for 6 people Pets allowed (€7/night).

In the center of business district of Montpellier, the hotel takes you in the heart of the new centres of Montpellier activities, while enjoying a quick access to the city via the nearby tram. The same goes for leisure, since the Odysseum center is within walking distance, and access to the beaches is direct by road, towards the sea without trapping into the town! The architecture of the residence is decidedly avant-garde, the furniture is stylish and the works of contemporary art adorn the rooms; you will still enjoy the heated pool on the roof of the residence! The hotel offers a certain standard yet relatively affordable, you can certainly provide some hammam or additional sauna sessions.

■ **VILLAGE CENTER – RÉSIDENCE LE DOMAINE DU GOLF**
Chemin de l'Aire
Launac-le-Vieux
FABRÈGUES
✆ 0 825 00 20 30
residences.village-center.fr

218 accommodations. F1 from €378 to €945 per week; F3 from €490 to €1,141; F4 from €672 to €1,477. Weekly rental. Children's club. Games for children. Pets allowed (€2.50 or €5.50 depending on the duration of the stay). Internet access available for a fee. Cleaning service. Catering facilities. Outdoor lounge. Satellite TV. Hammam, sauna. Entertainment.

Halfway between the languedoc vineyards and the Hérault beaches, the Village Center residence Domaine du Golf is a resort with exceptional services, dedicated to sports and relaxation. The 218 houses of the southern type are spread over a landscaped grounds planted with Mediterranean trees and bordered by a fitness trail and a compact golf. Pedestrian trails allow you to reach houses and services in peace. On-site, guests will enjoy a bar restaurant with a terrace overlooking a small heated pool, a spa and beauty salon. What more could we ask?

Having Fun – Going Out

Bars – Coffeehouses → 42
Clubs – Nightclubs → 46
Shows → 46

Bars – Coffeehouses

■ **BARBEROUSSE** ....**Rum bar**
6, rue Boussairolles
✆ + 33 (0) 4 67 58 03 66
www.barberousse.com
montpellier@barberousse.com
Open all year. Tuesday to Saturday from 6pm to 1am. Happy hours. Bottle of grower: €16; bottle to shoot: €24; €2.50 drink to shoot; cocktails from €7; beer from €3 to €4; tapas. Activities.
The façade does not look like much: a simple gate, rather narrow and guarded by two doormen, opens onto rue Boussairolles. But behind, a diving staircase takes you in the belly of a pirate ship. In a setting made of wood, Montpellier Barbarousse (it is a national chain) displays its huge bar where you consume the homemade specialities made with rum, Shooters and planter's punch: apricot, lychee, mandarin, chartreuse or pear. The hotel offers more than sixty different tastes! You can also be tempted by the old rums. The decoration is very nice, but the place is quickly stormed by partygoers! It is possible to drink in the calm until 09: 30 pm… After, in a crazy atmosphere, part of the room is waddle. For those who do not like rum, the half is 3.50 €.

■ **LE CAFE DE LA MER**
5, place du Marché-aux-Fleurs
✆ + 33 (0) 4 67 60 79 65
Open Monday to Friday from 8am to 1am; Saturday from 10am to 1am; Sunday from 3pm to 1am.
Café de la Mer, is the most famous gay bar of Montpellier. Ideally located in a popular district, it also attracts a mixed clientele. In addition there is crowd throughout the day, the place is ideal for meetings! The welcome is very warm, waiters are very attentive and charming. The decor, very beautiful counter in mosaics in the red shades and remarkable contemporary chandeliers. The drinks and their prices are the same as everywhere else, but the terrace, with the tranquillity of the place of Marché-aux-Fleurs, is very popular at the first rays of the sun.

■ **CAFE DES ARTS**
3, rue Saint Guilhem
✆ + 33 (0) 4 67 60 81 87
stelaupo1950@hotmail.fr
Open all year. Every day from 7am to 1am. Catering facilities. Concerts.
On the Castellane square, café brasserie des Arts displays its tables on a large terrace. It has become a reference in Montpellier in a few years. Its location at the top of the rue St Guilhem is an asset. Two rooms, one on the ground floor with the bar and the other, air-conditioned, is upstairs with a musical atmosphere and some high bar tables, linen-laid tables and exposed stone walls. A pleasant decoration, and the choice between cocktails, ice cream, soft drinks throughout the year.

■ **CAFE JOSEPH**
3, place Jean-Jaurès
✆ + 33 (0) 4 67 66 31 95
www.cafejoseph.com
Open all year. Low season: every day from 9am to 1am. High season: every day from 9am to 2am. Free Wifi. Catering facilities.
Probably the trendiest café of Montpellier since 21 years now! The non aficionados will find this place a little too «brags». The Café Joseph, enjoys the large terrace that extends over half of place Jean-Jaures. An impressive concentration of young people is permanently installed! If you do not dance outside, a DJ is there to light up the evening regularly, and other events enliven the bar throughout the year. As for catering: the charcuterie boards to share or the hamburger Joseph is the house speciality. The floor of the café, with magnificent decor, can be reserved for birthdays and other events.

■ **LE CIRCUS** ....**Pub**
3, rue Collot
✆ + 33 (0) 4 67 60 42 05
www.circus-mtp.com
jean@circus-mtp.com
Open all year. Every day from 6pm to 1am.
This pub within walking distance of place Jean-Jaures fits in the setting. A long zinc, small lounge lounges cut off from the bar, leather sofas: Annie and her brothers wanted to give it a New York soul. Red billiards and decorative elements showing the theme of the circus complete the picture. The sound atmosphere is very pleasant, with a trendy playlist of current music while remaining original. The 250 m² bar, very lively from Thursday to Saturday evening, attracts a lot of Erasmus students and Montpellier partygoers. You will need to find way way through the crowd to touch the bar and don't expect to find a place on a sofa. During the week, the atmosphere is different, cosy, and the music is not too loud, which makes it possible to hold discussions without screaming (quite pleasant because it is less and less common!) On The other hand, whether in group or alone, the service is always desperately slow. The draught beer goes from €3 to €3.50, the mojito at €8. Possibility to book lounges.

■ **COULEURS DE BIERES** ....**Beer**
48, rue du Faubourg-Saint-Jaumes
✆ + 33 (0) 4 67 03 31 54
hopsandgrapes34@gmail.com
Open all year. Monday from 5pm to 11pm; Tuesday to Saturday from 5pm to 1am.

BARS – COFFEEHOUSES

It is at the square of one of the oldest bars that Couleurs de Bières settled. The latter offers a new concept in Montpellier: here, you can eat on the spot with an upstairs room or take home, after choosing one of the eight hundred mousses stored in the shop part, on the ground floor. On the other side of the bar, Francis invites you to taste or retaste these fermented drinks. Real liquid gold passionate, he gets busy putting together in his shop of excellent beers from Belgium, Ireland, Germany and England and France. The atmosphere there is friendly and the beers are delicious! The football and Rugby evenings are particularly busy.

■ DELECTO .... Fruit juice bar
3, rue des Ecoles-Laïques
✆ + 33 (0) 4 67 02 08 96
contact@delecto.fr

Open all year. Tuesday to Saturday from 9am to 3pm; Sunday from 11am to 4pm. Fixed rate formulas lunches: €8.90 and €10.90; hot soup: €4; wraps: €5.50. Wifi. Terrace. Juice from €3.50. Brunch (cakes, salads, cakes and soups house: €15.90. Saturday and Sunday. Booking advised). Shop.

Very fashionable for a few years now, the concept of bar offering fruit juice has been widely imitated. In a corner of the place de la Chapelle-Neuve, the team of Delecto offers fruit lovers a myriad of juices and smoothies to refuel with vitamins. We recommend the diabolico: strawberry, raspberry, apple and banana. The hotel also offers a package of breakfast: perfect tea or coffee, bread and jam (fruit salad, muesli and cottage cheese) and fresh juices. The prices are reasonable and the welcome is very friendly. At noon, in the summer a menu of salads and wraps (set menu with with juice of the day €8.90) and the winter, you will enjoy the soup menu.

■ LA FABRIK ....Live music
12, rue Boussairolles
✆ + 33 (0) 4 67 58 62 11

Open all year. Tuesday to Saturday from 6pm to 1am. Happy hours (from 6pm to 8.30pm). Concerts (aperitifs live once per week).

Opposite the cinema le Royal, La Fabrik properly bears its name. In an industrial surroundings modernised and designed by its owner (the same as Barbarousse), we sit on a comfortable sofa or bar. All, with soft lighting, gives the place a rather pleasant trendy appearance. A variety of beers specially come from Belgium, such as Estaminet and the famous and renowned Palm. Quality and local oblige, you will also find wines of the region, whisky, cocktails and Sweets (sausage boards, tapas) at affordable prices. With its friendly atmosphere and its menus (of all styles, but always the best), la Fabrik will delight the active young people from central Montpellier for a drink after work. Note that the place has a smoking room worthy of this name!

■ FITZPATRICK'S ....Pub
5, place Saint-Côme
✆ + 33 (0) 4 67 60 58 30

Low season: open Monday to Saturday from 12pm to 1am. High season: Monday to Saturday from 12pm to 2am.

Undoubtedly montpellieran pub par excellence. We even wonder if the establishment did not become a real Irish embassy in Hérault... Guiness and Kilkenny is served on tap (6 euros), the clover decorating the beer. This pub is the favourite haunt of the english who has managed to create and share a warm atmosphere. People flock to the bar where the beer flows nonstop, and people gather around the screen in the evenings to watch Rugby games. Fitz is victim of its success, so do not expect to spend a night sitting on the weekend. The Irish beer, here, is a precious cultural asset: it comes directly from Dublin, and it is stored and served as a «wine». In summer, the pub offer a selection of board games to better enjoy the terrace.

■ GRAND CAFÉ RICHE
8, place de la Comédie
✆ + 33 (0) 4 67 54 71 44
www.cafe-riche.com
contact@cafe-riche.com

Open every day from 7am to midnight. Free Wifi. Terrace. Catering facilities. Brunch.

Opened at the end of the nineteenth century, this café is one of the oldest in the city. Its best asset is its southern terrace on the place de la Comédie, where guests – especially tourists – massively come for the sun. Despite its standard and its strategic location, the service is fast and efficient.

■ INGLORIOUS BAR
6, rue Cope-Cambes
✆ + 33 (0) 4 99 63 54 10
www.ingloriousbar.com
news@ingloriousbar.com

Open all year. Low season: Monday to Saturday from 6pm to 1am. High season: Monday to Saturday from 6pm to 2am. Happy hours. Beer half: €2.50 in the evening. Checks are not accepted. Free Wifi. Terrace.

Salva and Steph, two boys with impeccable figure, but also with strong breadth and a kind of ZZ top look, of course welcome you in Inglorious Bar with rock. Do not think to annoy them! To start up the evening carefully, from 6 pm to 8 pm, happy hours in a friendly atmosphere: a good plan. From 9 pm, the rock minimalist regained its rights for the delight of our ears: Led Zep, Elvis, Johnny Cash, Blues Rock, Rock Sudiste with no holds barred... and the good beer run there in litres. The atmosphere is very nice, the clientele too. One of the popular places of the city! «Quiz nights» are held regularly, and are presented by regulars bar.

■ LATITUDE CAFE
1, rue Sainte-Croix
Place de la Canourgue
✆ + 33 (0) 4 67 57 72 47

Low season: open Tuesday to Saturday from 8am to 8pm. High season: Tuesday to Saturday from 8am to 10pm. Coffee: €1.90; Teas: €3.20; wines: €3.20; pressure: €3; Belgian beers: €4.

Latitude Café extends its terrace in the shade of nettle trees of the most beautiful square in the Ecusson: the place de la Canourgue. The brand is a lawyer den, a quiet place to sip a soft drink, even an espresso at any time of the day while going through the news of the day, provided freely to guests. Inside, the atmosphere is cosy with parquet flooring, wooden ceilings, leather club chairs... and decoration inspired by Afro-chic style, and it can be privatized! A trendy place where people come for the setting, although the prices are a bit high.

HAVING FUN – GOING OUT

BARS – COFFEEHOUSES

■ **MILK SHAKE COFFEE**
7, rue de l'Aiguillerie
www.milkshake-coffee.com
Open Monday to Saturday from 11am to 1am; Sunday from 3pm to 7pm.
Here is an address still brand new and unprecedented in Montpellier. The Milkshake coffee invites you to discover more than 200 flavours of milkshakes, hot chocolate, American coffee, fresh juices and smoothies, all for the pleasure of your taste buds, summer and winter. There will be something for everyone and you won't be able to exhaust the range of sweets available!

■ **O' CAROLANS** ....**Whisky bar**
5, rue du Petit-Scel
℃ + 33 (0) 4 67 60 98 18
www.go-montpellier.fr/ocarolans/
contact@ocarolans.fr
Open Monday to Friday from 3pm to 1am; the weekend from 1pm to 1am.
This is undoubtedly the most famous place for all Irish who who passed through Montpellier. Probably because of the accent of the owner who then comes to fill a small moment of nostalgia? Anyway, here, Ireland is honoured, from the decor to the menu and daily specials allowing to eat without going bankrupt. Its main attraction: its terrace on the place Sainte-Anne!

■ **PAPA DOBLE** ....**Cocktail bar**
6, rue du Petit-Scel
℃ + 33 (0) 4 67 55 66 66
www.papadoble.com
Open all year. Monday to Saturday from 6pm to 1am. Cocktails from €9; glass of wine: €4.80 (bottle: from €19 to €35). Wifi. Catering facilities. Concerts (theme parties and DJ evenings).
Classified in 2011 among the 50 best bars in the world, this both authentic and glamorous property is the creation of Sète native Julien Escot, elected in 2004 Barman «of the year» in London. Then, while we are at it, the «best cocktail barman of the world», more recently! Needless to tell you that his creations are real jewels both in terms of flavours and presentation. In a very sophisticated setting, both simple and stylish, Papa Doble stands as an important After Work meeting point of Montpellier. The advantage of the place: menu of original cocktails created by the owner, therefore making the bet to erect «mixocology» in a culinary art in Montpellier. In fact, the establishment is one of the only downtown do not target the student public (tighter budgets, go your way!). An ideal meeting place for those who wish, according to the principle of After Work, to start their evenings after working hours and have fun without having to sleep at dawn. The standard evening starts in an intimate atmosphere, then quirky music delights revellers. The hotel also offers a quality snacks service.

■ **THE BEEHIVE** ....**Pub**
15, rue du Plan d'Agde
℃ + 33 (0) 9 66 94 53 71
Tram
Open every day from 12pm to 1am. Happy hours (every day from 6pm to 8pm). Terrace.
This pub with 100% British influence is open in the Saint-Roch neighbourhood of Montpellier. On draft or bottled, the English beer flows profusely; a quiz evening takes place every tuesday at 9 pm and, of course, «Live Sports» evening are held during football and Rugby games broadcast mainly on TV. The food too is so *british*: mushrooms soup, salads, Fish & The Beehive fries, burgers, cheesecake, without forgetting the unmissable English breakfast!

■ **THE BLACK SHEEP** ....**Beer**
21, boulevard Louis-Blanc
℃ + 33 (0) 4 67 58 08 65
Low season: open every day from 6pm to 1am. The summer, until 2: 00 Variety of draught beers, between €2.50 and €3.80 the half. Wide range of beers in bottles. Concerts.
Le Black Sheep, it is a friendly beer bar on boulevard Louis Blanc. The beer list is displayed on the large black board: on tap or bottled, the choice is wide: Cuvée des Trolls, Guinness, Kwak, various Abbey beers... If you don't know what to choose, do not panic: the bartenders will provide you with some advice. During crowded evenings, it is difficult to find a seat – on the other hand, the bar is lively! Evening concerts, rather rock or metal, are regularly held in the basement, a second large vaulted room a little rock'n'roll with a second bar, toilets and a smoking lounge. The entrance to the latter is sometimes free, or at least very cheap (rarely more from €5). In case of peckish, order a sausage board at €5. The hotel is very easily accessible with the hirrondelles tram (1).

Wine Bars

■ **BISTROT CHEZ FÉLIX**
1, rue Vanneau
℃ + 33 (0) 4 67 92 66 83
Open all year. Every day from 9am to 1am. Happy hours (6pm/8pm). Chèque Restaurant. Catering facilities.
This is one of the most beautiful in the city. Heterogeneous style décor: staue of the Virgin, wooden canoe, comfortable armchairs of the 1970s... On the tables, various delicacies of the house are available: meats, cheeses, tapenade... Nice selection of wines by the glass, champagnes, rums, brandies and full of liqueurs. Concerts every Sunday evening.

■ **A L'HEURE DU VIN**
7, rue du Puit-du-Temple
℃ + 33 (0) 6 27 51 39 11
alheureduvin34@gmail.com
Open all year. Monday to Saturday from 9am to 1am; Sunday from 6pm to 1am. Fixed rate formula bruschetta €9.90. Free Wifi.
Aznavour on the screen in the morning, jazz and rock in the evening. Joris and Florent, Inhabitants Of Avignon, receive in their wine bar canteen in the middle of the coat of arms. High tables, wooden counter, small terrace. A menu of salads (Italian, salad, ham, basil, tomatoes, parmezan) and bruschetta and especially a glass of wine at €1 of the month in cubi very popular with students in the neighbourhood... All day from coffee accompanied by small deserts.

Tea Houses - **BARS – COFFEEHOUSES**

Internet Cafés

■ **CYBERCAFÉ WWW**
1, rue de la Victoire-de-la-Marne
✆ + 33 (0) 4 67 56 84 16
www.sobra.com
cybercafewww@hotmail.fr
1am: €1.80. 2am: €3.60. From 9am to 1am. 7 days a week.
At a time when Internet entered almost all the houses, there is still a little space for Internet cafés. This one, which has – we can say – a well-established reputation, is divided into three locations and offers quality services: powerful computers, individual offices, peace. The clientele is mainly composed of students who spend much time on the screen. We liked the advice and the equipment offered including the webcam, scanner and the burner... without forgetting the beverage vending machine (alcoholic or not, €1 a coke tin, a bottle of water at €1.50, a coffee at €0.60.

Tea Houses

■ **CAFÉ BUN**
5, rue des Etuves
✆ + 33 (0) 6 70 86 43 24
luc.beaur@gmail.com
Tram
Open Tuesday to Friday from 8.30am to 7pm; Saturday from 9.30am to 7pm. Chèque Restaurant. Wifi. Terrace. Shop.
The Café Bun is a convenient place! It is a bit the temple of the café. After studying physics, Luc was strained by Antoine Netien, who won the Meilleur Torréfacteur de France title in 2011. The café is its passion as well as roasting. Luc decided to create his café in Montpellier he named «Bun», «coffee» in ethiopians. Craftmanship is given pride of place here! On the menu, carefully selected products like the Rishi teas. He favours homemade pastries. Brownie tested and approved. We liked the teacups, made by Lise Meillan, which wonderfully matches with the colour of glass. A nice touch. For the decor: metal, wood and stone. Simple and attractive.

■ **COFFEE CLUB**
12, rue Saint-Guilhem
✆ 07 86 17 81 56
www.coffeeclub.fr
bonjour@coffeeclub.fr
Tram
Open Tuesday to Friday from 8.30am to 7pm; Saturday from 11am to 6.30pm; Sunday from 11am to 5pm. Checks are not accepted. Free Wifi. Terrace.
Nicholas and Sarah mounted this small area «like in London», inside, a dozen people, (not more) who enjoy good cappuccino, mocha coffee, tea or excellent espresso. The place is cosy and open to the young couple who come to prepare excellent sandwiches that are extra ordinary (Ham, goat cheese and crushed tomatoes) salads nicely presented such as salmon, shrimp, cherry tomatoes, avocado and lamb's lettuce calm down the hungriest. Soups, brownies, cookies, cheese cake of very good quality but also, organic juices and smoothies. The small lunch menu changes with the seasons and is made with fresh ingredients. Takeaway or on site, this coffee club is truly a place where everyone speaks often in English to each other! At any time of day, friendliness, exhibition of photos, some books here and there and a small terrace on the rue St Guilhem. And what about the kindness and smile of this charming couple. An address that lacked this side of Clapas. There is everything there

■ **FAIRVIEW COFFEE**
6, rue Loys
✆ + 33 (0) 9 80 56 39 39
http: //fairview-coffee.tumblr.com
contact.fairviewcoffee@gmail.com
Open all year. Tuesday to Saturday from 9.30am to 7pm; Sunday from 11am to 5pm. Brunch Sunday. Chèque Restaurant. Free Wifi. Terrace.
A coffee shop in the british tradition but not only... Pastel colours, jazzy atmosphere, relaxation, warm and armchairs as at home. On the spot or takeaway, a list of tea (Tea & Company, varied menu, control of the infusion time) like the Mango Mambo and the espresso coffees. For pastries: whoopies, muffins, cookies, scones or pancakes, not only homemade, but prepared before your eyes. Cinthya and Didier offer for lunch, sweet pancakes, savoury cake, small soup and hot drink (€8).

■ **LE KALYSTHE**
14, rue du Collège
✆ + 33 (0) 4 99 62 97 28
Open all year. Closed in August. Monday to Saturday from 8.30am to 7pm. Daily special €8.50. Chèque Restaurant. Terrace.
It is one of the rare tea rooms in Montpellier which makes pastries, cakes and chocolates. Emilie, Marie-Thérèse, and Jean-Louis Cabezos come from rue de Verdun, where they already run, Le Palais Romain, a famous tea room. Upstairs, the manufacturing workshop, two rooms including one vaulted. At noon we have salads, ravioli with casserole, veal stew, for a cuisine, all in all, family. In the afternoon, the summer on the terrace, the Dammann tea is served (ginger lemon green Tea, Darjeeling...) as well as the hot chocolate à l'ancienne and delicious homemade pastries, pies à l'ancienne (lemon, crumble) or royal chocolate- praline feuillantine and chocolate mousse. Without forgetting the café croissant at 2 € every morning. The best value for money of the city.

Find all our best deals and good addresses on our website www.petitfute.uk.com

Clubs Nightclubs

■ **LE FIZZ**
4, rue Cauzit
✆ + 33 (0) 4 67 66 12 89
www.lefizz-discotheque-montpellier.fr
Open Tuesday to Saturday from midnight to 5am. Free admission for girls on weekdays.
Located in the city centre, near the Saint-Ravy square, this small nightclub on two levels has become over the years the meeting point of students in the late evening, including the young people of Erasmus. On a music in general, the latter have a field day, especially the girls, for whom the entrance is free on weekdays. Although the atmosphere is often with the more or less alcoholic euphoria «boys will be boys» all remain folksy as students openly come to party and hit on, but not to pick a quarrel. Of course, after 25 years old, it might not seem that exciting, but to every age its pleasures.

■ **MILK**
Complexe Le Palladium
1348, avenue de la Mer
www.lemilk-club.fr
Open Wednesday to Saturday from 11pm to 5am. Rate depending on the evenings. Free admission for girls Friday. Checks are not accepted.
It is the meeting point of a good number of high school students and young students of the city. This nightclub offers a general musique *dance* but also themed parties. Every Wednesday evening it is «Gossip Girl», a rather hip-hop and r'n'b, party with, for girls, champagne bar open from midnight to 1: 30 am and every month a gift to be won (generally a bag of great brand). Friday, it is «Ladies Night», with free entry and glass of champagne, always available for girls of course. However, for girls and boys, the owners make a point of maintaining a festive atmosphere but relaxed: a decent dress and a proper behaviour are therefore essential.

Shows

Cinemas

■ **DIAGONAL CAPITOLE**
5, rue de Verdun
✆ + 33 (0) 4 67 58 58 10
www.cinediagonal.com
Admission: €7. Subscription card 5 places, €25; 10 tickets, €47; 15 tickets, €63. Sessions of 12pm at €4.20. Child rate at €4.20. Cinema of the children at €3.70.
In this cinema, a room is devoted to exhibitions, digital creations combining photographic stereotyped and software applied to the image processing. For the film fans, the cinema also offers short films followed by sessions debates, in the presence of actors and directors. Another device allows children and teachers of the elementary schools to benefit from a sensitization programme to the cinema. This program features projections in room, an educational work accompanying, artistic workshops practices, and training courses. For the colleges, «College in the movie» from 1719 serving tasty the foundations of a film culture. And «High School Students in the movie» sessions and conferences of films. The smart idea: Movies for children: films chosen to form the taste of the future movie fans.

Concert Halls – Opera – Dance

■ **OPERA BERLIOZ**
Esplanade Charles-De-Gaulle
Le Corum
✆ + 33 (0) 4 67 60 19 99
www.opera-montpellier.com
location@opera-montpellier.com
Billetery open Monday to Friday from 12pm to 6pm. Various subscription options exist. Rates depending on the shows. Possibility of online booking.
Set in the Corum, Berlioz opera is a beautiful room, with optimal acoustics. Two thousand people can attend the opera performances and concerts of the National Orchestra

Pop & Rock Concert Halls - SHOWS

Opéra-comédie of Montpellier.

of Montpellier, seated in its very pleasant grey armchairs. Its manager, Jean-Paul Scarpitta, present a 2013 season of classics and discoveries, with contemporary creations. A panel is devoted to young people, to get acquainted with classical repertoire through educational concerts. The ticket prices vary tremendously according to the show and camping. But no need to break the moneybox to enjoy an opera, some performances are accessible from €10 in normal rate, whereas others cost €60. It is up to you to go through the programme.

For access, underground parking allows you to reach the interior of Corum directly, Palais des Congrès, and the hirondelles tram drops you at the foot of the complex.

■ **OPERA COMEDIE**
11, boulevard Victor-Hugo
✆ **+ 33 (0) 4 67 60 19 99**
www.opera-montpellier.com
location@opera-montpellier.com
Schedule ticket office Monday to Friday from 12pm to 6pm. Rates depending on the shows.

Arena

Inaugurated by Indochina in September 2010, the large room adjoining the Exhibition park has wide paths and compete the multiplicity with three possible configurations: 14,000 spectators – including 7,500 seats – configuration show, 9000 fans in sports version and 13,500 m² gross area for exhibitions. Everything has been designed to allow updates in the most creative scene (a fully removable scene and adjustable surface, height, etc..). The structure hosts shows, concerts and events throughout the year!

Montpellier is very proud to have two operas, like the big cities. L'Opéra Comédie is the oldest in Montpellier. In a sumptuous setting with gilding and draperies, which reminds the Opera Garnier de Paris, the programming gives pride of place to famous opera titles, soloists, and chefs whose talent is no longer to prove, but also creations and discoveries. In June 2012, the beautiful room of the 18th century reopened after 20 months of work. Its baroque atmosphere is enchanting, with great comfort henceforth!

Pop & Rock Concert Halls

■ **LE JAM**
100, rue Ferdinand-de-Lesseps
✆ **+ 33 (0) 4 67 58 30 30**
www.lejam.com
Concerts (jazz, world music, blues) in the evening. Closed in August.

Le Jam, pretty dining area in concert with 350 seats, belongs to the school of jazz of the same name – which is known and recognised in all France. In addition to the music of the courses, you can discover artists in various styles such as jazz, funk, the French music... Its strong points is: the quality of the musicians and human scale of the place. Some music lovers prefer to walk down the velour and red armchairs in the centre of the room to enjoy a concert – the others remain standing on the platform on the stage, which allows you to admire the skills of the musicians! The decor of Jam is pleasant, with its leather seats in the bar and the piano. Practical: Montpelliérains go there now by street-car. Several concerts take place every week, mainly from Thursday to Saturday. The details of the programming is on the website.

SHOWS - Pop & Rock Concert Halls

■ **LE ROCKSTORE**
20, rue de Verdun
✆ + 33 (0) 4 67 06 80 00
www.rockstore.fr
webmaster@rockstore.fr
Nightclub rock and concert hall and electronic music. Open Tuesday to Saturday. From 11pm (except concert).
Opening of the bar rock: 18: 00
Former church turned into a rock temple in the 1980s, Rockstore is a monument of Montpellier nightlife, with its characteristic red Cadillac embedded in the façade. In 2013, it closed for 9 months of renovation – to the dismay of night owls. On the programme: insulation work and compliance. Over the years, French and international stars have trod its stage – in all musical genres: M, NTM, Les Sheriffs, Brigitte Fontaine, Franck Black, Lenny Kravitz, Poppa Chubby… More than a concert hall, the place is also a nightclub – often free entrance – and the meeting point of revelers at the closure of bars. You will have to wait for the duration of the work – from January to September 2013 - to remake the festival within its premises. A blessing in disguise: you will find a dapper Rockstore in compliance with standards!

■ **SECRET PLACE**
ZI de la Lauze
25, rue Saint-Exupéry
SAINT-JEAN-DE-VÉDAS
✆ + 33 (0) 9 64 00 87 11
www.toutafond.com
tafeur@gmail.com
Variable price depending on the concerts.
Concert hall dedicated to rock, Secret Place offers throughout the year programming generally varying between – roll, punk and metal, in sharp styles. Some evenings are free, but the entrance fee for concerts varies between 5 € and 20 €, often with several groups to shout their electric guitars on stage. The rock singers closely follow up its programming thanks to Tafeur, the diary of concerts that hold in the region. It is housed in bars by Tout à fond, the association that holds Secret Place. Also, there are rehearsal rooms and a recording studio for local groups.

■ **LA PLEINE LUNE**
28, faubourg Figuerolles
✆ + 33 (0) 6 72 79 03 03
www.lapleinelune.fr
la.pleine.lune@laposte.net
Open Monday to Friday from 8am to 1am; the weekend from 10am to 1am.
This small hotel bar – well-known by night owls of the city - has built its reputation on its concerts and its artistic and popular atmosphere. From rock to Brazilian music via funk, many musical styles rub shoulders during concerts. Regularly, you can see exhibitions of artists. An authentic cultural emulation.

Community Centres – Youth Centres

■ **CENTRE CHOREGRAPHIQUE NATIONAL DE MONTPELLIER**
Couvent des Ursuline
2, boulevard Louis-Blanc
✆ + 33 (0) 4 67 60 06 70
Open Monday to Thursday from 10am to 6pm; Friday from 10am to 5pm. Schedule of the shows on the site of Montpellier dances.
The national choreographic centre until the end of 2013 is run by Mathilde Monnier. It is a beautiful equipment. Housed in a former convent, the Ursulines convent. It is dedicated to contemporary dance. It is a place of mixings, meetings and residences for artists. The invited choreographers succeeded it, and the buildings also open with other arts that are always interesting for events and often very surprising too.

Sports & Leisure

Air Sports	→ 50
Individual Sports	→ 50
Water Sports	→ 52

Who says Montpellier was a city where idleness was the only way of life? To see the list of popular disciplines, there is no doubt that the city is sportive. Of course beach sports have their place with kite surfing, diving or beach volleyball but not only that … Everyone at Montpellier is runninf, all Montpellier is swimming, Montpellier is on wheels, on horseback, on the mat, on the green, bicycle, at the net, with a stick, a ball … The Montpellierians maintain their shape. In the morning at dawn, on the banks of the Lez, throughout the day on the bike paths, on Friday evening on rollers … Come on, motivate yourself and choose a sport that you will practice this year!

Air Sports

- **HELISUD LR**
Mas Garrigou
Le Village
LAGAMAS
✆ + 33 (0) 6 01 72 18 01
www.helisud.fr
helisud@club-internet.fr
Open all year.

If you have always dreamed of flying and seeing the world from above, it's time! Of great diversity, the area lends itself perfectly. You can fly environments as diverse as the coast or the Camargue, the vineyards of the hinterland, the Salagou or peak-saint-loup. The tours are made in consultation with the client, according to his expectations. And Regis will certainly help you over 15,000 flight hours. He crisscrosses the sky for many years and will take you on the most imposing sites. He and his helicopter move over a large area, from the Bassin de Thau to Millau viaduct through the valley of the Buege. The hardest thing for you will be to choose which landscapes to fly! (Watch the video on the site).

Individual Sports

- **GOLF MONTPELLIER MASSANE**
Domaine de Montpellier Massane
BAILLARGUES
✆ + 33 (0) 4 67 87 87 87
www.massane.com
contact@massane.com
Open all year. Catering facilities. Shop. Hotel. Spa.

This international golf course is composed of a 18-holes course and a compact of 9 holes located in a very quiet environment.
It is surrounded by amenities that make the approval of major hotels, namely tennis courts, swimming pool, spa (sauna, jacuzzi, hammam).
The restaurant is one of the best restaurants around. An outdoor terrace overlooking the golf course, and a restaurant lounge offers a menu based on méditerra-néenne cuisine.

10 minutes from Montpellier, in the village of Baillargues, on the Montpellier Massane Resort, fly you to relaxing break SPA Aromassane. In an enchanting sleek, our team will make you discover our menu of treatments and rituals for body and face: massage world, care with essential oils...

The spa includes a sauna, hammam, jacuzzi, relaxation room and indoor pool.

We welcome you from Monday to Saturday from 9am to 7pm, Thursday until 9pm and Sunday from 10am to 6pm.

Informations & bookings
04 67 87 87 81 • spa@massane.com
www.massane.com

Before or after a golfcourse, a relaxing spa break or just for pleasure, come to discover the exceptional setting of the **restaurant Le 360.**

On the restaurant, our chef offers tasty cuisine, gourmet and evolving with the seasons.

Side bar, enjoy a cocktail and tapas assortments on our panoramic terrace.

Open 7d/7d for lunch and diner .

04 67 87 87 87
Domaine de Massane
34670 BAILLARGUES

MONTPELLIER
MASSANE
GOLF · HÔTEL · SPA

INDIVIDUAL SPORTS

■ **ACCRO ROC**
Les Infruts
CORNUS
✆ + 33 (0) 6 83 19 22 39
www.acrorocdesinfruts.com
info@acrorocdesinfruts.com
Open all year by reservation.
In the heart of the Larzac, not far from the Regional Park of Grands Causses, is friendly and sports opportunity to discover the place in another way.
Through a dozen courses, making speleology or simply hiking, the Addicted Rock welcomes you to discover the historic wonders of the area. Whether you are beginners and experienced, they can accommodate your level and helps you, why not, take speleological discoveries that will delight children and adults.

Water Sports

■ **AXEL'AIR**
Rue du Mont Saint-Clair
CARNON
✆ + 33 (0) 4 67 50 62 60
www.axelair.com
contact@axelair.com
Monday to Saturday from 10am to 12.30pm and from 2.30pm to 7pm.

The kitesurfing international school run by Stéphane Breton offers packages of kitesurfing classes, from the complete beginner to the expert via the intermediate practicing. The Axel'air school is one of the first schools of kitesurfing in France. The courses that take place from March to November welcome a good number of foreigners, making the courses often bilingual (anglo-french). And also supports intercultural meetings that are very interesting for the trainees.

Shopping – Fashion – Gifts

Jewellery – Clocks ➜ 54
Good Tips ➜ 54
Gifts ➜ 55
Shopping Centres ➜ 57
Naughty – Sex ➜ 58
Art Galleries ➜ 59
Games & Toys ➜ 60
Bookshops ➜ 61
Fashion – Clothes ➜ 62
Multimedia – Picture – Sound ➜ 62
Music ➜ 63

Jewellery – Clocks

■ **FRANCK DESEUSTE**
16, rue du Palais-des-Guilhem
✆ + 33 (0) 4 67 66 37 19 / + 33 (0) 6 43 33 03 08
franck.deseuste@orange.fr
Open on Monday, Tuesday and Thursday to Saturday from 10am to 12.30pm and from 2pm to 7pm. Closed on Wednesday.
For twenty years, Franck Deseuste has worked precious metals, but, silver, platinum and classic stones like emerald, the ruby, sapphire. But it does not neglect any so the less known stones such as tourmaline. His shop resembles a setting where each room is unique. Even if Franck Deseuste makes a little transformation or repair, it is primarily a design of a talented jeweller. It for his job as a trade of excellence and attempts to look after the detail. Enter into his shop and you will be amazed by the beauty of the rooms. Real jewels!

■ **KIARA CREATION**
9, rue du Plan-d'Agde
✆ + 33 (0) 6 25 02 38 29
www.kiaracreation.com
contact@kiaracreation.com
Open Tuesday to Saturday from 10.30am to 7pm.
Kiara left the Vers Anis shop to to do othe things. Its broches, earrings, rings, necklaces are tempting and the choice is as delicate as jewels of Kiara are original. There is something for all budgets. What we love, is its pépettes, nice dolls with the expressive faces suspended from necklaces. All rooms are unique and Kiara devotes a shelf to Kimado, an artist who specialises in jewellery for children. So that, there are no room for jealousy. When moms, choose their young girls do as much.

■ **SIDNEY CARRON**
6, rue de l'Ancien-Courrier
✆ + 33 (0) 4 67 63 99 75
Open Tuesday to Thursday from 10am to 1pm and from 2pm to 7pm; Friday and Saturday from 10am to 7pm.
Located in the city centre, this shop is full of marvels. Here, the owner of the place has been exhibiting for 10 years, jewellery of contemporary style in silver or gold metal and in brushed silver. The creations showcased in their windows, are for some, inspired by sculptors. It is easy to fall for, whether it is for this Angel necklace, this pendant in the form of Montre Molle de Dali or this bracelet with pure and original lines. In this shop, with a beautiful setting, you will probably find your happiness or «the rare gem» for someone of special. As its name suggests, the place is the reseller of Sidney Carron, but not only it! Marina de la Roche added some ropes to its arch by offering other designers such as Scatolarossa or Plata Pa'Ti. Marina also offers nice and affordable Italian leather bags and totes (from 120 € to 170 €). Above all: these accessories are single (unique), you will never see another person wearing the same! New Collection: Mexican cuff bracelets with coloured woven cotton and silver hand-embroidered patterns, symbols of Mexico.

Good Tips

■ **LES DIMANCHES DU PEYROU**
Jardins du Peyrou
www.ot-montpellier.fr
contact@ot-montpellier.fr
Sunday from 7.30am to 2.30pm.
Created at the initiative of the Municipality of Montpellier and managed by a passionate antique vintage girl, this flea market has become the place of rendezvous for lovers of beautiful antiques. In the majestic setting of Peyrou Gardens, in the heart of the town, about fifty antiques come every Sunday to offer rare art deco coins of the 1970s or older. Each week, a specialist ensures the upstream texture and verifies that the proposed objects and furniture are genuine and that prices are in line with their value. Here you can come and hunt but also have coffee or eat, since a tavern is installed.
Approximately six times per year, the flea market continues exceptionally until late afternoon (the dates are announced on the upstream site of the town hall and tourist office).

Gadgets – Unusual Objects - **GIFTS**

■ **LE GRAND BAZAR**
www.montpellier.fr
Mid-May and mid-October.
Twice a year (usually mid-May to mid-October), the historic center is inspired by the Grande Braderie de Lille (Great Fair of Lille). For two days (Friday and Saturday), traders bringout tables and racks in the street to settle for their leftovers, sold at bargain prices. In parallel, especially on Saturdays, individuals empty their cellars and attics and settled in the streets and place de Ecusson and the city turns into a giant flea market.
It is friendly, sympathetic and often the opportunity to do good business. It is one of the major popular events downtown.

Gifts

Carteries

■ **IMAGES DE DEMAIN**
10, rue de la Vieille
✆ + 33 (0) 4 67 66 23 45
Open Monday to Saturday from 9.30am to 7.30pm.
In this very small street set between rue Saint-Guilhem and rue de la Loge, here is a shop that takes us out of the world Or almost. On both sides of passage, on the walls of the alley, are spread colourful or black and white images. You will find funny or more serious quotations, the humorous cards, photos of famous. Also, on entering the shop, large postcards are leave room for the posters of art and cinema, with a multitude of decorative objects. There is something for all prices and especially for all tastes. Search for the image that suits you, it is a real little pleasure! Even better: you can frame it in the workshop hidden at the back of the shop, which realises a pretty job and gives expert tips. The most loyal guests, owners of a loyalty card, will be even entitled to discounted rates.

Gadgets – Unusual Objects

■ **L'ESPRIT DES LIEUX**
21, rue du Palais-des-Guilhem
✆ + 33 (0) 4 67 57 36 27 - www.lespritdeslieux.net
Open on Monday from 12pm to 6pm; Tuesday to Saturday from 10am to 7pm. L'Esprit des Lieux, is the most kitsch store in l'Ecusson. The garden dwarfs welcome you on the doorstep, and you cross the shelves from one discovery to the other especially that there are from floor to ceiling. Fawns, birds and colorful patterns are available on decorative accessories. Beautiful thermos with Asian design, shifted fridge magnets, a suitcase, a set of pastel colored porcelain: you will find wonders and kitsch galore! What to redecorate your entire house or prepare very original gifts to your loved ones. The nostalgic can get vintage schoolboy glue with the smell of almonds and enjoy gourmet olive oils in perfume bottles.

IMAGES DE DEMAIN

CARTERIE
DECORATION
FRAMING

10 RUE DE LA VIEILLE
34000 MONTPELLIER

+33 (0)4 67 66 23 45

Elegant savings or solidarity purchase: the Koala solution

In September 2011, Alexander Martin-Rosset and Jean-Yves Bernard launch a new concept, Koala Capital, to help families finance future projects and higher education for their children. The principle: for every purchase made on the Internet in one of their 1400 traders partners, Capital Koala reimburses an average of 5 % (and up to 20 %) of total purchases, such repayments are then transferred to a savings account opened in the name of the children. Capital Koala offers a savings account paying through its banking partnerships with Monabanq and Crédit Lyonnais. Registration on the site is free and without obligation. This savings solution is inspired by loyalty programs, allows you to place accumulated money during shopping on saving children booklet automatically. All family members and friends can participate and save together for one or more children. Members also have the opportunity to donate their refund to UNICEF. A new way to shop.

■ **ETAT D'AME**
12, rue En-Gondeau
✆ + 33 (0) 4 67 60 79 20
Open Monday to Saturday from 10am to 7pm.
Etat d'âme is a shop in kitsch decor is an unavoidable retro in Montpellier! On its shelves, there is an abundance of unlikely objects, gadgets, accessories, crockery, preferably in pastel colour, with floral or fawns. To add some vitamin (taste) to your habitat by a little crazy touch of decor, this is the place you need! On condition that you do fear nor the neither the many kitsch styles, nor the pink. If that is the case, have a look at it, it is worth the detour.

■ **LE PRINCE DE SAINT-GILLES**
11, rue des Soeurs Noires
✆ + 33 (0) 9 51 56 23 12 /
+ 33 (0) 6 72 73 84
www.leprincedesaintgilles.com
contact@leprincedesaintgilles.com
Open Tuesday to Saturday from 11.30am to 7pm.
Hear, hear enthusiasts of the Middle Ages, this is the place for you! Jean Barbier welcomes you in his shop, open since autumn 2011, for a trip back in time. His passion for objects of medieval inspiration is communicative – he offers for example jewellery, clothes, soaps, weapons, everything to create an atmosphere the time in his humble castle. In addition to the facilities, the Prince De Saint-Gilles also makes us discover medieval drinks like the Hypocras, the Hydromel or the Clos des Sentinelles of the Saint-Loup peak, a red wine with fruits. Lovers of life-size role-playing games can equip themselves from head to toe whether they prefer to fight with the sword or arm yourself with an arch! On the programme: chain mail, wraps, leather flask or a horn as a cup, and a variety of accessories. The shop gives favour to the achievements of local craftsmen and offers books on the Middle Ages. This is an original place for a break out of time!

Souvenirs

■ **LE BOUTIK'R**
41, boulevard Bonne-Nouvelle
✆ + 33 (0) 4 67 66 35 93
www.leboutikr.fr
contact@leboutikr.fr
Low season: open Tuesday to Saturday from 10am to 7pm; Sunday from 1pm to 6pm. High season: Monday to Friday from 10am to 8pm; from 1pm to 7pm.
Souvenir shops do not roam the streets in Montpellier. From where comes our crush for this shop located opposite the Esplanade, near the Corum, Fabre Museum and Comedy. A strategic point for which Thierry fell in love with. it must be said that the place has character. Installed and thoroughly renovated in the former stables of a mansion, Boutik R (R as air de Montpellier) deploys media treasures that benefit both tourists and Montpellier: local crafts with Old Montpellier earthenwares that are recognized by their yellowish background decorated with a blue flower, mosaics bulls, key-holder: the choice is vast. It is just as this gourmet area with these pots of jam raisiné de Montpellier and also pineapple or banana flambe, meats and wines from the south. Thierry loves unique tastes and does not hesitate to open the doors of his shop to bee-keepers that produce – among others – lemon tree honey or rhododendron or a local cannery that provides organic mixtures as artichoke with white pepper or dark chocolate with red peppers. A real mine of gift ideas.

Pen – Tobacco

■ **LA MAISON DU STYLO**
1 bis, rue de Verdun
✆ + 33 (0) 4 67 58 35 34
www.syll.fr
Open Monday to Saturday from 9.30am to 7pm.
This home based in Montpellier since 1936 and is the benchmark for pens. Whether as gift or for yourself, you will find your happiness from the simplest to the most luxurious pen pen. Major brands are referenced here: MontBlanc, Dupont, Cartier, Parker, Faber-Castell, Waterman, Caran d'Ache etc... In addition to the pen boxes, the house is specialized in wooden boxes for precious watches, jewelery and cigars. We must not forget to mention the Œuf de Montpellier an original souvenir of the city, its name originally given to the Place de la Comédie, in close proximity to the store. Created a little more than ten years ago, this egg contains the Trois Grâces. It will delight lovers or collectors. La Maison du Stylo is also specialist in Dupont and Cartier lighter and diaries, especially of the Filofax brand.

Shopping Centres

■ **ODYSSEUM**
2, place de Lisbonne
☏ + 33 (0) 4 67 13 50 50
www.centre-commercial-odysseum.com
Open Monday to Saturday from 10am to 8pm. The Géant Casino hypermarket is open from 9am to 9pm Monday to Friday. Until 9.30pm Saturday. Possible delivery (giant Casino).
The recent Odysseum open-air shopping mall became the headquarters of the new trends of the world of fashion, of the house and leisure with its hundred shops. Designed in the 1990's, packed full, controversial, this complex was made of cinemas, ice rink, aquarium, planetarium, bowling or laser game and channels of catering half an hour away by tram from the centre. Car parks are also many to accommodate the drivers who come for shopping. As for shopping, there are above all, brands of clothes: H&M, Desigual, Zara, Le Temps des Cerises, Pull& Bears, Celio, Bérénice, Tally Weijl, etc. The Sauramps bookseller on two floors offers a paper shop, books and some cds. Added to that, shop's for; toys (La Grande Récré), jewelleries, gifts (Nature&Découverte), cosmetics (Sephora), utensils for the house and the kitchen and an Apple Store for technophiles. A Géant Casino is integrated into the mall, and the direct neighbours are Ikea and Decathlon.

■ **POLYGONE**
1, rue des Pertuisanes
☏ + 33 (0) 4 67 99 41 60
www.polygone.com
Open Monday to Friday from 10am to 8pm; Saturday from 9.30am to 8pm. Parking the least expensive in downtown.
One of the largest shopping centers in the area! If not all youthful, it intends to maintain its status and compete with the latest and its open-air shopping: Odysseum. Le Polygon offers the advantage of being located in the heart of town, next to the Place de la Comédie. There is no need for a car to get there – even if it has a large car park for Motorists (free after a certain amount of purchase). On the menu of a shopping trip are: more than a hundred shops on three floors, starting with a range of services like: banking, kiosk, cafe, catering, bakery, dry cleaning, shoe repair pharmacies and Para pharmacies. Two large ensigns on several floors are signs to visitors: Galeries Lafayette and Inno (food and cosmetics). Fashion shops for men and women have the spotlight (Naf Naf, Zara, C & A, Celio, etc.), as well as shoes, leather goods, accessories etc... You can find everything in Polygon: cosmetics (Sephora, Body Shop, Yves Rocher), house (Habitat), gifts (Nature & Discovery), toys (La Grande Recre) Culture (FNAC), a small music store, watches or pens ... If you put a foot you can stroll for hours.

Place des Grands Hommes at the matt Odysseum.

Rue Foch, Heart of the luxury

Whether in the decor, clothing or accessories, Montpellier has no shortage of high-end boutiques. Do not also hesitate to walk to the street of the l'Ancien-Courrier or l'Argenterie, where are more chic and trendy multibrandes are found. A large majority of luxury brands, however, are clustered along the rue Foch, which by its width and chic, has nothing to envy the Parisian avenue of the same name. It has also become the inevitable shopping appointment of the Montpelliéraine select. Along its palm trees and its little green spaces, with the arc of triumph Peyrou end point of view, those who like to dress with taste (and have a large budget, admittedly) will easily find their happiness here. Brands such as Agnes b, Eden Park, Hugo Boss, Gérard Darel or Zapa are well established there on the street for years. Less classic brands such as Zadig & Voltaire, have joined more recently. There is even a hair salon Jacques Dessange. A touch of the great Parisian boulevard, the midday heat and the palm trees.

Naughty – Sex

■ **REX CLUB CINEMA**
12, rue Boyer
✆ + 33 (0)7 60 07 34 48
Open Monday to Saturday, from 1pm to 11.30pm and Sunday, from 2pm to 8pm.
Traditional shop with sex toys, gadgets, magazines, lingerie and DVD you can watch in personal cabins and two projection rooms.

Art Galleries

In Montpellier, city of art and culture, the places of exhibitions and galleries abound: traditional art galleries displaying paintings and sculptures, photo galleries, video, installations, performances, collectives of artists who are places of creation and exhibition, and others.

■ **CARRE SAINT-ANNE**
2, rue Philippy
✆ + 33 (0) 4 67 60 82 11 /
+ 33 (0) 4 67 60 82 42
www.montpellier.fr
carre.sainteanne@ville-montpellier.fr
Open Tuesday to Sunday from 10am to 1pm and from 2pm to 6pm. Free admission.
The Saint-Anne Square is an not a common exhibition centre for ordinary exhibitions. Housed in a deconsecrated church, it offers its picture rails to the frequent exhibitions of contemporary art, and follows closely the work of young local artists. Since 1991, its 600 square metres served for in situ, video installations, plastic facilities... Many artists of regional, national and international fame even displayed here. Moreover, the entrance is free!

■ **EN TRAITS LIBRES**
2, rue du Bayle
✆ + 33 (0) 4 34 11 38 43
entraitslibres.blogspot.com
entraitslibres@gmail.com
Free and variable schedule depending on the presence of the artists.
Both a workshop, exhibition venue and retail space, En Traits Libres is a new kind of art gallery: evolving and multidisciplinary. The place is shared by artists from different and diverse worlds: drawing, painting, illustration, cartoon, animation, writing, mail-art, sculpture and photography. The exhibition space will allow you to discover all in turn. As for the shop corner, it will delight fans of comics and fanzines, but also offers single-copy postcards, posters, badges, CDs and original t-shirts. The added advantage of the house: it gives you the opportunity to place a customized order for portraits, landscapes, posters and other illustrations.

■ **FRAC LANGUEDOC-ROUSSILLON**
4-6, rue Rambaud
✆ + 33 (0) 4 99 74 20 36
www.fraclr.org

ART GALLERIES

Open Tuesday to Saturday from 2pm to 6pm.
Like all FRAC, the Montpellier's main purpose is the creation of a collection of contemporary art, representative of the actual contemporary creation. The Regional Contemporary Art Fund has as a mission, through exhibitions and publications, to creat public awareness of contemporary art and participate in the development, dissemination and knowledge of all forms of contemporary creation. In this beautiful scenic area, each artist chooses according to its uniqueness and occupies its own way and the public was able to discover: Pierre Giner, Ghazal Radpay, Dora Garcia, Closky etc...

■ GALERIE 13
13, boulevard du Jeu-de-Paume
✆ + 33 (0) 4 67 02 87 92 / + 33 (0) 6 08 84 81 45
www.artgalerie13.com
artgalerie13@gmail.com
Open Tuesday to Saturday from 10.30am to 12.30pm and from 2.30pm to 7pm.
This gallery chose to settle in Montpellier after exercising activities for many years on the Tuscan coast, Italy and Spanish Catalonia. The gallery offers in a beautiful area of 130 m² of already recognized or emergent talented artists, in the different aspects of the current contemporary art: painting, sculpture, photography, graphic, young Art. the place is surrounded by the artists of the region, the Italian painters, the Spanish sculptors, graphic designers and photographers from all horizons.

■ GALERIE ALMA
14, rue Aristide Olivier
✆ + 33 (0) 9 51 30 27 01 / + 33 (0) 6 63 27 15 63
www.galeriealma.com
Open Tuesday to Saturday from 3pm to 7pm. Possibility of visit the morning. Between two exhibitions, the gallery is closed; it is more advisable to telephone before you to return there.
Founded in 2002 by four friends willing to share their enthusiasm for contemporary art, gallery Alma left the outskirts of Sainte-Anne for those in the Place de la Comédie. Max Charloven was the first artist hung on the new picture rails, on two levels. The gallery has succeeded in the challenge of a significantly different programming trends in contemporary art. At each exhibition, the public discovers new talents. Mostly paintings and volumes are exposed, and more rarely videos and photos are exhibited. On the mezzanine an important place is reserved for artists' books and of Méridianes editions.

■ GALERIE DE L'ANCIEN COURRIER
3, rue de l'Ancien-Courrier
✆ + 33 (0) 4 67 60 71 88
www.galerieanciencourrier.com
contact@galerieanciencourrier.com
Open Tuesday to Saturday from 10.30am to 1pm and from 3pm to 7pm.
Danielle Benzimra and Mongin Martine opened their gallery twenty years ago, in the heart of the Ecusson, in the mansion of the Marquis de Montcalm. One and the other being very attached to artists that reflect the subtleties of light, they have recently passed the baton to Claire Bornerand, which ensures continuity with the same taste and the same passion. The latter still has art lovers of contemporary works by artists with very different sensibilities and diverse pallets

■ GALERIE DE L'ECUSSON
11, rue de l'Ancien Courrier
✆ + 33 (0) 4 67 52 80 14
www.galerie-ecusson.com
Open Tuesday to Saturday from 11am to 7pm.
For over fifteen years, the gallery promotes eclecticism in its choice, a path that works well. Contemporary and figurative art, original prints and bronzes. Here nationally recognized artists and even international exhibit themselves... And the official painters of the Navy, like Bourrier. The gallery is often open all day, but sometimes happens to be closed, at lunch time. Do not thus hesitate to phone before going there, you will moreover be well received.

■ GALERIE HELENE TRINTIGNAN
21, rue Saint-Guilhem
✆ + 33 (0) 4 67 60 57 18
www.galerietrintignan.com
contact@galerietrintignan.com
Open Tuesday to Saturday from 10.30am to 12.30pm and from 2.30pm to 7pm.
When, in 1974, Hélène Trintignan opened a contemporary art gallery and exhibited abstract and contemporary artists of the 1950s, it disturbed and surprised people. With the same passion and an impressive knowledge of art, she has always followed her tastes and defended artists she had chosen. There are those that she followed since from the beginning and who have remained faithful, among whom are Boumeester C., O. Debré, H. Goetz and Pelayo, and others very young, met through the «Movement Support-surface et de la nouveau figuration libre»... Its walls welcome different generations of artists, among them are G. Bartholomew, V. Bioules, P. Buraglio, L. Cane, R. Combas, C. Lopes-Curval, P. Loste J.-P. Pincemin, S. Plagnol, A. Slacik and C. Viallat, A. Clement, etc..

■ GALERIE LE MAT
3, rue Voltaire
place Saint-Roch
✆ + 33 (0) 6 19 60 37 71 / + 33 (0) 6 20 84 59 07
www.lematgalerie.com
nilssplasher@hotmail.fr
Open Tuesday to Saturday from 3pm to 7pm. Free admission for the exhibitions.
Gallery Le Mat is a young underground gallery located in the heart of Ecusson. It is multitasking in: exposure, projection, concert, residency, research, dissemination and encounter. It is founded by Nils Bertho and Marjorie Accarier, two artists who are graduates of the Ecole des Beaux-Arts de Nîmes. The gallery offers a parallel circuit, a platform of independent distribution to artists. Fans of fanzines and independent magazines run the gallery. It includes an important background of editing, creations of artists and collectives, screen prints, albums, books and art objects. A real trade hub of the fanzine in Montpellier. More than an art gallery or center, it is a platform for the creation and distribution where artists go to expose, meet and make themselves visible.

ART GALLERIES

■ GALERIE PLACE DES ARTS
8, rue de l'Argenterie
✆ + 33 (0) 4 67 66 05 08
www.place-des-arts.fr
place-des-arts@wanadoo.fr
Open Tuesday to Saturday from 10am to 12pm and from 3pm to 7pm. Calendar of the exhibitions available on the site.
It is in 1981 that Françoise Polack is an art gallery dedicated to creations of the master glassworkers: Navaro, Zoritchak or Zuber. In his shop set under a beautiful medieval vaults, she displays vases, sculptures and pieces of collections. These contemporary works are carved into the an optical crystal or shaped in the molten glass.

■ GALERIE RENO
10, rue Saint-Firmin
✆ + 33 (0) 4 67 66 37 30
www.galerie-reno.com
galeriedart.reno@wanadoo.fr
Open Tuesday to Saturday from 10am to 12pm and from 2.30pm to 6.30pm.
A little away from the main traders of Ecusson, is this gallery created in 1984 that features contemporary artists, colorists and figurative, often of national and international reputation. Painters and sculptors will exhibit regularly, like Jean-Pierre Baldini, Roger Bonafé Gerard Calvet, Maria Penraat, Eric Bapttista Antoine Lombardo, Gabriel Couderc, René Pialot Alain Gaudry … Jean-Claude Reno is also responsible for the expertise, restoration and sale of antique paintings.

■ GALERIE TALBOT
16, rue Saint-Firmin
✆ + 33 (0) 6 16 19 09 87
www.galerietalbot.com
contact@galerietalbot.com
Open Tuesday to Saturday from 2pm to 7pm.
Created in 2007 in Saint-Germain-des-Prés, the Talbot gallery settles in the historic center of Montpellier. The artistic line is completely contemporary and showcases the painters and sculptors. The gallery owner is also present in Saint-Martin-de-Londres, where he continues to share his discoveries. Works are displayed in an ancient vaulted room of the xii^e and xv^e centuries, an association that is worth a look.

■ LIVING ROOM
550, avenue de la Justice-de-Castelnau
✆ + 33 (0) 6 62 52 61 59
www.livingroomart.wordpress.com
livingroomart@hotmail.fr
It is a combination of contemporary creation open only during the exhibits that it organises. This place of experimentation was created by Valérie Séverac, trained at the school of applied arts and the visual arts. The idea is to cross the fields and paths of art. To come across the creations of a photographer and a dancer for example. A voluntary and courageous company follows…

■ PAVILLON POPULAIRE
Esplanade Charles de Gaulle
✆ + 33 (0) 4 67 66 13 46
www.montpellier.fr
Low season: open Tuesday to Sunday from 10am to 1pm and from 2pm to 6pm. High season: Tuesday to Sunday from 11am to 1pm and from 2pm to 7pm. Weekly guided tours Saturday 11am, 2.30pm and 4pm Guided tours in group. Bookings required by e-mail: visites@ville-montpellier.fr or by tel: + 33 (0) 4 67 66 88 91.
The Photo gallery of the city of Montpellier welcomes all year round exhibitions of photographic works on different themes. Its artistic headquaters was entrusted to Gilles Mora until 2014, on the principle of invitation of commissioners around new projects. It presents modern and contemporary photographers of international reputation.

Games & Toys

■ LA CLINIQUE DES POUPEES
5, rue d'Alger
✆ + 33 (0) 4 67 58 76 66
www.poupees-reparateur.com
Open on Monday from 3pm to 7pm; Tuesday to Friday from 9.30am to 12pm and from 3pm to 7pm; Saturday from 9.30am to 12pm.
Guy Geraud does not show off. Its window never changes and heads, limbs and trunks of dolls are accumulated there. Elsewhere, white sandals and clothes are waiting to dress brand new body. We are not in a spare parts store, but at a repairer of antique dolls. These small masterpieces of porcelain or celluloid find a second life here. Guy Geraud may also occasionally sell spare parts and if he has the right model. A leg, an arm then come to replace the missing part. Ah, if Lady Réant had known Guy, Sophie (that of «Misfortunes») could have preserved her wax doll!

■ POMME DE REINETTE – POMME D'API
35, rue de l'Aiguillerie
✆ + 33 (0) 4 67 60 52 78
www.tradition-jouet.com
Open on Monday from 2pm to 7pm; Tuesday to Saturday from 10.30am to 12.30pm and from 2pm to 7pm.
Pomme de Reinette and Pomme d'Api, are two fantastic stores dedicated to toys of all ages. Adults and children

go to Apple Pippin with expectation; adults will find their inner child by going through the different themed rooms overloaded with wonders. For the décor, you will find yourself in the jungle or in a spaceship! The adorable pastel shop window showcases doll houses accessories and other toys. A true museum, that mixes toys of all generations.

There is everything! Card, company, construction games, music boxes, stuffed animals, etc... Difficult to go back empty – kids want to take everything ... and adults are even worse! Beside it, the little sister Pomme d'Api is for the youngest children, with wooden toys, games and developmental games and for baths, puppets and incredible go-carts in front of the shop.

Bookshops

General Books

■ **GIBERT JOSEPH**
3, place des Martyrs-de-la-Résistance
✆ + 33 (0) 4 67 66 16 60
www.gibertjoseph.com

Open Monday to Saturday from 9.30am to 7pm. Membership card (it is used to resell with one on estimate).
The good plan for novels, specialised works, Cartoons and nice books at low prices, is Joseph Gibert! The concept of the house is to offer at low prices, new works by second-hand goods on shelf. It is left to the reader to make his choice! The brand known in France since 1956 in the centre of Montpellier is spread over 5 floors. A beautiful area is dedicated to schoolbooks, novels, practical works, cookbooks, travel guides, youth books... Not all of them can be listed, for the themes covered are numerous – and there is even a section for novels in English. A place not to miss if you are a bookworm. Note that the shop has as bonus, a paper shop, CD and DVD player shelf.

■ **SAURAMPS**
Le Triangle - Allée Jules-Milhau
✆ + 33 (0) 4 67 06 78 78 - www.sauramps.com
Open Monday to Friday from 10am to 7pm; Saturday from 10am to 7.30pm. American Express.
Sauramps is a brilliant maze of books that takes shape on six levels and offers novels, practical books, beautiful books, comic strips, «mooks» (those thick magazines distributed in bookstores), etc. the independent bookseller is a must for lovers of reading. Sauramps is an institution in Montpellier, with this shop located in front of the Polygone, next to the Comédie square, another one at the Oddysseum shopping mall, and the third, dedicated to children, at the end of the Triangle gallery. When you step foot in Sauramps, you do not know when you will come out of it, or with how many books in your arms!

Specialist Books

■ **LE BOOKSHOP** ....
Languages
8, rue du Bras-de-Fer ✆ + 33 (0) 4 67 66 22 90
www.lebookshop.com
Open on Monday from 1pm to 7pm; Tuesday to Saturday from 10am to 7pm. The concept of Bookshop is very simple: the bar is also an English bookstore, even including a bookshelf of Spanish and German literature. Language activities are offered regularly in two small rooms at the bar: initiation to foreign languages, literary circles and lectures. Basically, it is a café ... and a bookshop! A bar where you can stop for a drink and read a British magazine. For English and others, VOs are a treat. Certainly there is a choice, but obviously a good one! Note that Booskhop is a partner of Fairview Coffee (rue Loys), where cupcakes are worth dying for ...

■ **LES CINQ CONTINENTS** ....
Travel
20, rue Jacques-Cœur ✆ + 33 (0) 4 67 66 46 70
www.lescinqcontinents.com
Open on Monday from 1pm to 7pm and from 10am to 7pm Tuesday to Saturday. This shop's globe-trotters booksellers will help you make a good choice among the numerous works on the five continents. Trip accounts, touristic guides, art books, maps, cuisine and musical books will enable you to better understand the different countries of the world and regions of France. Regularly, the bookshop organises encounters and entertainments (quarterly programme available on the spot).

Find all our best deals and good addresses on our website www.petitfute.uk.com

Fashion – Clothes

Shoes

■ **CHAUSSURES LAFFITE**
14, rue de la Loge
✆ + 33 (0) 4 67 66 10 99
Open on Monday from 2pm to 7pm; Tuesday to Saturday from 9.30am to 7pm.
The must shop in montpellier, established for generations now, the same family manages Mephisto, another reference in town. At this great shoemaker's, only one rule: «to fit well, fit comfortable». The Laffite house offers a wide choice of renowned brands for their quality and their solidity, such as Kickers, Arche Dr. Martens, Fly London, Geox, Pikolinos, Karston, Paraboot, Think, etc. Shoes to walk without neglecting elegance. The collections are constantly renewed.

■ **ESCASSUT**
25, rue des Etuves
✆ + 33 (0) 4 67 66 00 00
www.escassut.fr
contact@escassut.com
Open Monday to Friday from 9.30am to 7pm; Saturday from 10am to 7pm. Custom-tailored shirts and costumes.
Shop of reference in Montpellier, Escassut offers a range of shoes, as elegant as comfortable. According to its style, you will go for Geox, Timberland, Paraboot, Sebago, Cat, Mephisto, Rockport, Campers, Dr. Martens, Lloyd... But you can dress from head to toes, from socks to the hats and the sweaters to the coats, modern or classic, city dweller or country, according to your taste. It is still in this venerable house found on the second floor that you will find professional garments. As the Escassut slogan says, «Nothing above»!

Lingerie

■ **DAUDE**
25, grand-rue Jean-Moulin
✆ + 33 (0) 4 67 60 76 51 /
+ 33 (0) 4 67 60 43 15
Open on Monday from 10am to 7.30pm; Tuesday to Saturday from 10am to 7.30pm.
There are shops of lingerie and there is Daudé. For forty years now, the family has been specialising in the fine lingerie signed by great names of fashion: Armani, Hugo Boss, Dolce and Gabbana, Versace, Gautier. The collections are renewed twice a year. With black and white in winter, complemented by a line of swimsuits of the same designers during the summer. An elegant and intimate setting where briefs, pants, and bras are carefully locked in white drawers. Over the years, the shop developed a sexier corner, let's say a bit cheeky to satisfy some crazy fantasies...

Multimedia – Picture – Sound

Computers – Internet

■ **ITRIBU**
36, rue Saint-Guilhem
✆ + 33 (0) 4 67 55 51 11 - www.itribustore.fr
Open on Monday from 2pm to 7pm; Tuesday to Saturday from 10am to 1pm and from 2pm to 7pm.
In this little shop, Itribu is for lovers of Mac, became within a few years, an unmissable in Montpellier. You will find all the Apple range in the following demonstration; iMac, iPod, iPad, AppleTV but also software and peripheral devices. The professional advices are popular because, Mac, it is primarily a passion. Itribu: Apple Premium Reseller, is fifteen years of experience, and also a showroom in Mauguio with a certified training centre and free introductions three times a week. New: a fast and without prior appointment after-sales service in Montpellier.

■ **PLANET SI**
14, rue Bernard Délicieux
✆ + 33 (0) 4 67 70 85 11
www.planetsi.fr
contact@planetformation.fr

Open Monday to Friday from 9am to 12pm and from 2pm to 6.30pm.
At Planet Système Informatique, you can follow formations combining convenient exercises and theory to learn how to handle classic office suite or take over other specialty tools. You will then learn the secrets of Word, Excel, Access, or graphic creation programs including Illustrator or Photoshop. The classes are of different levels and suit your occupation. They are given individually, for two or as a small team. Planet SI sells computer equipment, peripheral devices and consumable, and has assistance and repairing service at home for users of PC and Mac.

■ **MACTRIBU**
39, rue René-Fonck
Fréjorgues Ouest
MAUGUIO
✆ + 33 (0) 4 67 65 65 26
www.mactribu.fr
mactribu@mac.com

MacTribu was established 10 years ago with the main aim to develop the Apple brand in Languedoc-Roussillon. His reputation is now well established.
Companies and individuals rely on this company. Besides the sale of computers, software and peripherals, MacTribu organizes training sessions for an introduction to the world of Mac.

Music

Record Dealers

■ **GIBERT JOSEPH**
3, place des Martyrs-de-la-Résistance
✆ + 33 (0) 4 67 66 16 60
www.gibertjoseph.com
Open Monday to Saturday from 9.30am to 7pm.
First independent bookseller in France (there are thousands of second-hand books), Gibert Joseph however is also open to music! On the top and fourth floor of the shop, second hand CDs are sold or bought at low prices.
You can find here various artists at 2 or 10 € or in the few shelves available. Several styles are represented: French songs, pop, rock, rap, etc. By the side, a large room has an impressive choice of films, DVD boxes of series or mangas, and second hand video games.
Cinema enthusiasts seeking second hand DVD: do not miss this place. You will also find everything that can be related to the paper shop: ream of papers, notebooks, envelopes of all sizes, pens, files, etc.

Instruments – Equipment

■ **MUSIC LEADER INTERNATIONAL**
9, avenue de Nîmes
✆ **+ 33 (0) 4 99 63 28 82**
www.music-leader-montpellier.com
Open Tuesday to Saturday from 10am to 12.30pm and from 2.30pm to 7pm.
At the foot of Corum, this store has a wide selection of musical instruments and accessories. Neighbor to pianos Hamm and is managed by the same team. Within its walls, we discover acoustic, electric or bass guitars, batteries, keyboards, saxophones and accordions. As for accessories, there is – of course – the partitions, and also amplifiers for violin, effects, pedals and all the necessary electronics (micro, DJ equipment or recording).
The striking force of Music Leader International (as the name suggests), is to offer products from many brands, unbeatable prices, similar to those found on the Internet. Grégory welcomes you in his shop, behind which lies a workshop, and will lavish you with precious and wise advice on repair and maintenance of your gems.

Gourmet Products – Wines

Coffee – Tea – Herbal Tea	→ 66
Delicatessen	→ 66
Cheese Shops – Dairies	→ 68
Markets – Covered Markets	→ 69
Breads – Cakes Chocolates – Ice Creams	→ 70
Fish – Seafood	→ 72
Local Products	→ 72
Products Of The World	→ 73
Caterers	→ 74
Wines & Spirits	→ 74

Coffee –Tea – Herbal Tea

■ **BETJEMAN AND BARTON**
1, rue de Pertuisanes
Centre commercial Le Polygone
✆ + 33 (0) 4 67 15 07 28
www.betjemanandbarton.com
contact@betjemanandbarton.com
Open Monday to Saturday from 9.30am to 8pm. The tea room closes at 6.30pm.
In this English-style boutique, located on the third level of the shopping Centre of Polygon, Pascal kindly welcomes you for a purchase, lunch or for tea tasting. Wooden shelves of the store contain quantities of teas and a variety of teapots, cups and bowls, as well as chocolates and gourmet products. The carte contains more than 250 kinds of teas from India, China and Ceylon. The Darjeeling from the foothills of the Himalayas is round in the mouth and offers a woody and nutty taste, others like Chinese Lapsang Souchong, slightly smoky and smell like spruce can perfectly accompany a salty meal. The second floor is especially dedicated for tasting all the sweets and lunch menu is also offered.

■ **COFFEA**
Centre commercial Le Polygone
✆ + 33 (0) 4 67 64 35 61
www.coffea.fr
siege@coffea.fr
Open Monday to Saturday from 9.15am to 8pm. Package of coffee or tea from €5 approximately.
Located in the heart of the most important commercial center of the city centre, Coffea is a quiet boutique in a beautifully cozy decor where a smile is required. The ensign offers more than a hundred different coffees and teas, from the most classic to the finest and most unexpected flavors. One can also buy homemade and fine chocolates, as well as cookies, caramels, honey, jams or cookies, developed from exclusive recipes or specially selected by the brand .. The coffees to purchase are also ground in front of you and at your convenience for more freshness and friendliness.

■ **FRENCH COFFEE SHOP**
40, rue Saint-Guilhem
✆ + 33 (0) 9 84 09 26 59
www.frenchcoffeeshop.com
contact@frenchcoffeeshop.com
Open Monday to Saturday from 8.30am to 7pm.
This is the latest addition to the rue Saint-Guilhem, well known by Montpellierians for its fine and quality shops (coffee, cheese, grocery shop …). In a cozy space with mahogany shades and coffee shop (obviously), the establishment offers a relaxing and tasting moment in the heart of the often excited central-town. You can take a coffee or hot chocolate there and also gourmet beverages such this delicious Chocotella, made with hot chocolate and a famous spreadable pâte. You also crunch cookies or muffins, or treat yourself to a creamy cheesecake.

■ **LA QUINTESSENCE**
26, rue de l'Aiguillerie
✆ + 33 (0) 4 67 60 58 22
www.laquintessence.net
contact@laquintessence.net
Open Tuesday to Saturday from 9.45am to 12.30pm and from 1.30pm to 7pm.
This address is unique to Montpellier and is one of the last herbal-medicine shop of France. For herbal teas, Jean Rey and her daughter Geraldine proportion clever combinations for cough mixtures – eucalyptus, fir, marshmallow root, capillary of Montpellier … For over-eating, herbal tea for liver, artichoke, Boldo, combretum (Senegal), rosemary, fumeterre. Teas, ancient sweets, essential oils, health food, natural cosmetics and essential oil diffusers are also available.

Delicatessen

■ **LE COMPTOIR GOURMAND**
Halles Castellane
✆ + 33 (0) 6 75 07 12 64
lory.caselli@orange.fr
Open Monday to Saturday from 9am to 1pm and from 3.30pm to 7.30pm; Sunday from 10am to 1.30pm.

Present in the Castellanes halles for a few years now, Lory Caselli is a beautiful offers delicacies and products of delicatessen. It starts with the productions of the country, olives and olive oils, tapenades, craft tarama, anchoïades, fresh truffles in season (and variations)… to extend to the whole country, and even in the world!

DELICATESSEN

The products presented translate the pleasure of sharing and the discoveries. Classic lentils from lauragais with penja pepper, from Cameroon, there is something to satisfy the tastes and curiosities. You will also find rare dried fruits, sweets, rare spices (such as the salt from the Himalayas)... There will be surprises and you will discover unexpected needs. The best is to go to the site and let yourself to delicacy, you will not be disappointed!

■ ÉCRIN ET SAVEURS
47, rue Saint-Guilhem
✆ + 33 (0) 4 67 60 87 95
www.ecrinetsaveur.com
Open on Monday from 2pm to 7pm; Tuesday to Saturday from 10am to 7pm.
Fine, subtle, but balanced, this is the motto of this lovely little neat and tidy grocery store which opened in fall 2013 at the corner of Saint-Guilhem and the Boulevard du Jeu-de-Paume. The young hostess, assisted by her mother to the sale and advising clients, has indeed been trained as a dietician and makes it a point of honor to provide you some relevant and needed advice. In this cozy shop, there are mainly French products: tapenade, oils Nîmes, foie gras from Gers, surprising alcohols currant and cassis, and even caviar 100% French. The few foreign products will probably surprise the most demanding taste buds, as this amazing Japanese whiskey. And it does not hurt and the smile and kindness are always waiting for you.

■ ÉPICERIE FINE – AU PÈRE SIMPER
35, boulevard du Jeu-de-Paume
✆ + 33 (0) 4 99 66 78 32
www.auperesimper.fr
street-car tracks
Open on Monday from 2pm to 7.30pm; Tuesday to Saturday from 10am to 7pm.
This recently installed Epicerie fine is a very nice discovery on the Boulevard du Jeu-de-Paume. Eric Bernard Simper shares his passion of the best craftsmen and producers in France that he gleaned from many years in the course of his previous journeys. These products are his passion and the grocery, his dream... And it is felt by what he does. Anser Foie gras, caviar Petrosian, Ibérico Bellota ham or San Daniel of 18 months, fresh Alba truffle, olive oil of Camille mill, Olivier Roellinger spices, fish rillettes from l'Atelier du Poissonnier (Fishmonger Workshop), cooked food, smoked salmon, caramels, jams, chocolates Castelane, Monin syrup, crystallized petals of flowers, wines from winemakers, champagnes and Japanese, Irish moult whiskey... An Epicurean choice, the best of the best in all these delicacies. And what can be said about the eloquence of the father Simper on all these beautiful discoveries selected here and there. Expert advice and discoveries guaranteed! All these exceptional products will be found at your table for parties or to regain your meal with friends. A resolutely epicurean address! Everything is there.

■ L'EPICERIE ITALIENNE ALBERT
4, rue de la Vieille ✆ + 33 (0) 4 67 66 00 75
www.epicerie-italienne-albert.fr
Open Tuesday to Friday from 9am to 1pm and from 4.30pm to 7.15pm; Saturday from 9am to 1pm and from 2.30pm to 7.15pm. Open on Sunday afternoon for the festivals.
The shop created by Albert exists since 1961, a real institution in Montpellier! It is now Enza who continues the adventure and continues to treat us with Italian delicacies. It offers sicilian pasta, pasta of the pouilles, calabrèses pasta, each with different colours and taste. To enter this delicatessen, is to find yourself in the sun on the peninsula. You go from the ham shelf, San Daniele to the cut – a delight – with ravioli with truffles and fresh ravioli, fresh tomatoes with balsamic vinegars. You will be surprised by the varieties of sauces that match so well with the pasta: cream with truffles and mushrooms, cream with five cheese, artichokes cream. Without mentioning the spices that jump to the nose through their translucent paper. At this point in time the eye is set on the small rum babas or the limoncello, Gianduja chocolates, craft panettone of Sicilia and flavoured amaretti. Also, a renewed wine carte of Barolo and Brunello di Montaccino. A bit of boot in the tastebuds...

■ LE PANIER D'AIMÉ
6, rue du Plan-du-Palais ✆ +33 (0)9 83 29 98 62
www.lepanierdaime.fr
Open Monday to Saturday from 9.30am to 7pm.
It is strolling in the streets of the Patch that one falls on attractive showcase. Baskets richly filled with preserved preparations and other fine, fine bottles, sweets... The shop offers a selection of products from five departments in the region, plus the Aveyron: brandade, rouille sétoise, grisettes of Montpellier, chestnut jam and lozérien clover, pâtés artisanaux and candied Aveyron duck... You will also find a selection of wines and oils. A great opportunity to discover products from local know-how, as well as a bookshop that offers regional art books and literature on the subject.

■ AU PÈRE SIMPER
35, boulevard du Jeu-de-Paume
✆ + 33 (0) 4 99 66 78 32
auperesimper.fr
tram, bus
Open Monday to Saturday from 10am to 7.30pm. Open from 2pm to 7.30pm only Monday.
Five minutes' walk from the Ecusson and close to several parks and tram stations, this shop offers a wide variety of quality and upscale ingredients made according to traditional methods. You will find sweet, salty, caviar, foie gras or the meats or a wide choice of jams and spices. Foie gras Anser, Pétrossian caviar, ibérico Bellota ham or 18 months San Daniel, fresh Alba truffles, Camille mill olive oil, spices from Olivier Roellinger, fish rillettes from Atelier du Poissonnier... Also note a shelf of quality cheese and a varied and substantial selection of wines, whiskeys and rums.

GOURMET PRODUCTS – WINES

Find all our best deals and good addresses on our website www.petitfute.uk.com

DELICATESSEN

■ PINTO
14, rue de l'Argenterie
✆ + 33 (0) 4 67 60 57 65
www.pinto.fr
contact@pinto.fr

Open on Monday from 2.30pm to 7pm; Tuesday to Saturday from 9am to 12.30pm and from 2.30pm to 7pm.

Pinto is according to the words of Jean-Pierre Coffe: It is without call, «The most brilliant deli that any amateur can dream of». And the most interesting part is that it is now more than twenty years that it lasts! The store is a real institution in Montpellier, and its reputation has never been tarnished. Who by chance went through the streets of l'Argenterie, and was not intrigued by the scents that emerged from the shop, which on fine puts its stalls in the open air. The motto of the house is quality above all. Also, you will need to spend for some delicacies, but you will not regret it, for the choice of supply made by the grocer is demanding and lit. You will find specialties of the Montpellier region, sometimes unknown: the inevitable Saint-Roch steak (almond cake in a fine paste of comfit orange peel enlarged with pure cocoa powder and a mixture of soft spices), oreillette... then all Pinto's wonderful discoveries, humble tielles sétoises with truffles and other caviar vintage and foreign spices, which you have never heard about. And this is better because then, greed will mingle with the pleasure of discovery.

■ PLAZA DE ESPANA
Halles Jacques Coeur
Boulevard d'Antigone
✆ + 33 (0) 4 34 11 37 16

Open Thursday to Saturday from 11am to 8pm; Sunday from 11am to 4pm. Open 7 days a week by reservation for the special privatizations and orders. Possible delivery. Fixed rate formula entrée+plat+tapas sweetened and coffee for €10. Variety of tapas as of approximately 2.50.

Within the Jacques Coeur halls, at Antigone, Natalie offers a part of Spain in the grocery-bistro. You can taste the Spanish tapas, especially with its personal touch. At noon or evening, we will gladly stop to chew a piece. Natalie knows Spanish chacuterie on the fingertips, and the tasting session of lomo or chorizo turns out to be both exciting and delicious! Products are imported from the Iberian breeders: do not miss the famous pata negra bellota, the French equivalent of foie gras from our expert! The grocery section delights lovers of Spanish products or wines. Note that Natalie offers a catering service, and can arrange private aperitifs on site. Two nice little summer terraces welcome visitors in a relaxing atmosphere. And here, even the coffee is served in the Iberian way. Natalie, origining from the Peninsula, is happy to share her passion for gastronomy!

Cheese Shops – Dairies

■ LA CLOCHE À FROMAGES
23, rue Saint-Guilhem ✆ + 33 (0) 4 67 66 17 32
www.fromagerie-tourrette.com

Open on Monday from 10am to 1pm and from 4pm to 7pm; Tuesday to Thursday from 8.30am to 1pm and from 4pm to 7pm; Friday and Saturday from 8.30am to 7pm. Because nothing is too good for the cheese service, the Puig family is fully committed in it. After having occupied only one stand in the Castellane market place for long, in 2000, they took up residence in the lively rue Saint-Guilhem. The name of the shop has changed not long ago, but the spirit remains intact. The Tout-Montpellier goes there and prepares a plate of cheese or offer a sweet treat at the stroke of noon for himself. We take the time to taste and discover what cheese makers are pleased to advise us on the tone of a gourmet confidence. They naturally love praising the virtues of country cheese like pélardon or Pérail.

Markets – Covered Markets

■ HALLES CASTELLANE
Open Monday to Saturday from 7.30am to 7.30pm; Sunday and public holidays from 7.30am to 2pm.
Set under a modern structure made of confined of wood, the Castellane Markets are located in the city centre. Thirty boutiques provide for the residents in the district. Greengrocers, butchers, fishmongers, cheese and caterers have succeeded in recreating the friendly atmosphere of yesteryear, where everyone – or almost – knows each other. It is more smart than before, but a little expensive. Oh yes, everything is bought here in Montpellier!

■ HALLES DES QUATRE SAISONS
Avenue de Heidelberg
℃ + 33 (0) 4 67 75 76 81
Open every day from 7am to 1pm.
In this popular Paillade district, the market existed before the markets and continues to do with them. They group on their part the merchants of food supply, although the mint and coriander are sold on the run, outside, while around and along the avenue, the stalls offer in all types: clothes, fabrics, shoes, hardware store, haberdashery, sound recordings etc... But what was there on one day will disappear the following day, it is the rule. Then we dawdle, we search and we rummage about …

■ HALLES JACQUES-CŒUR
Boulevard d'Antigone
Open Monday to Saturday from 8am to 9pm; Sunday and public holidays from 8am to 3.30pm.
The market places precided over by the statues of Jacques Cœur, the most famous merchant that mattered in the city, have made a nice place in this neighborhood. Opposite the Central Library, served by the streetcar, are characterized by modern architecture. Thirty traders have settled here, they are divided between the two spaces, the actual market place, closed but very perforated with open stands, sheltered by a wings-shaped canopy. The offer is complete. The food supply makes the beautiful part, with fruits and vegetables, meats, fishes, bakery, prepared dishes and sandwiches, cheeses, wines, etc.., without forgetting florist, press and shoemaker. An undeniable advantage is that these market places are open all day long.

■ MARCHE DE L'ESPLANADE
Open Tuesday to Thursday from 7am to 1.30pm; Friday from 7am to 7pm.
We have a particular tenderness for this market of the city center which has lost a lot in passing from the place Jean-Jaurès at the edge of la Comedy. The proof is, the number of traders there is very variable, and also depend on time and open-air market is obliged. We dream to see it becoming established proudly on the egg next to Trois Graces. We like strolling among the displays of shoes, jewels, clothes for adults and children – Petit Bateau marked-down! And just opposite, there is a flower market, in new flambants boxes!

■ MARCHÉ DES ARCEAUX
Boulevard des Arceaux
Tuesday and Saturday from 7am to 1pm.
Marché des Arceaux is an unmissable appointment for enthusiasts of organic and fresh products «directly from producer to consumer.» It is located in the famous Arches, in beyond the Peyrou gardens, a few steps from the center. Meats, cheese, honey, olive oil, fruits, vegetables: here everything is fresh and organic, and comes from the region. There are also, especially in summer, handcrafted jewelry, scarves and more. Of course, all this is quite «bobo», and the prices may be slightly higher than elsewhere, but we have the assurance of eating healthy foods. Moreover, when fine weather comes, the place can be a very pleasant walk.

■ MARCHE PAYSAN
Avenue Samuel-Champlain
Open on Sunday from 8am to 1pm.
The country market does not in any way seem to suffer from the presence of the halles Jacques Cœur a few metres away! Every Sunday morning, for ten years, it has made a real culinary festival. The merchants, all producers proudly display on their stall what their best goods. Everything is beautiful, good and fresh and in season: radishes in spring, melons in summer, grapes in autumn, squash in winter. Poultry, game, cheeses and flowers are a feast!

⚓ direct access to the beach	👁 visually impaired disability	♨ take away
🍸 bar	🛡 mental handicap	△ room service
🧺 laundry	♿ motor disability	🏋 fitness room
✳ air conditioning	🌳 garden or park	📺 playroom / tv
🎵 nightclub	🎲 games	🚿 modern sanitary
€ cash machine	🧺 washing machine / laundry	🏄 water sports
🚰 drinking water	🚴 bicycle rental	🎾 tennis
🐴 horse riding	🛒 grocery store	

Breads – Cakes – Chocolates – Ice Creams

■ **ATELIER DU CHOCOLAT DE BAYONNE**
17, rue des Etuves
✆ + 33 (0) 4 67 66 48 17
www.atelierduchocolat.fr
contact@atelierduchocolat.fr
Open Monday to Saturday from 10am to 7pm.
For several years, chocolates Bayonne has enhanced the Montpellierian palace with its assortment of subtle and captivating fragrances. Flavors delight the senses by the richness of the cocoa beans. Chocolate nirvana for foodies. In cones, in plates, in bouquet, in a basket, in bulk, as you please. Petit Futét loves chocolate cake all sold box in a camembert way. To be consumed warm with homemade crème anglaise, on condition that you know how to do it...

■ **BOULANGERIE TEISSIER**
8, rue Saint-Guilhem
✆ + 33 (0) 4 67 60 77 07
patisserieteissier.free.fr
sarl.teissier@wanadoo.fr
Open Tuesday to Sunday and public holidays from 6.30am to 8pm. Possible delivery (on Montpellier only). Chèque Restaurant.
In four generations, the bakery of the Castellane place had time to make a name, it is an inevitable in the city center. Adrien is the fourth generation to handle the business. Tradition and expertise are combined to offer you the best (bread) baguettes (sarmentine, grand siècle …) and cakes. The house is developed with a snack area for selling sandwiches. In addition to the manufacture of its classics such as chocolate eclair and cabbage, the Teissier house has now developed a catering line to meet new needs. The window case also hosts macarons on weekend to enrich its flavors and get the tastes of its customers. For communions, birthdays, baptisms, weddings, puddings and showpieces will surprise more than one!

■ **CABIRON**
Odysseum
✆ + 33 (0) 4 99 64 58 54
www.cabiron.com
traiteur@cabiron.com
Tram line 1
Open Monday to Saturday from 10am to 8pm.
The famous Montpellier caterer settled in Odysseum, to the delight of gourmets. The shop has Gérard Cabiron's creations, voted best confectioner in France in 2007 in the ice-cream category. Flutes of chocolate with multiple flavours, classic and revisited macaroons, homemade ice cream… The creativity of the maître pâtissier is much unbridled staying lit. The offer is very large, blackberry-violet macaroons, pistachio-chocolate, mint leaf, more original with lemon – yusu (Asian variety of citrus fruit) and the vanilla- tonka. The 70% chocolates are available in mixtures with chocolate praline, coconut, cinnamon, pecan caramelised or candied orange. The most difficult in this shop… Will be to leave without falling for it!

■ **CHOCOLATS THIERRY PAPEREUX**
8, rue Saint-Paul
✆ + 33 (0) 4 67 63 90 64
www.chocolats-thierry-papereux.com
contact@chocolats-thierry-papereux.com
Open on Monday from 2pm to 7pm; Tuesday to Saturday from 9.30am to 7pm.

Baker and pastry chef
Confectioner – Ice-cream maker
Caterer

3 adresses
à MONTPELLIER :

6, et 8 rue Saint Guilhem
23, rue de la Saunerie
5, rue de Barralerie

Tél. +33 (0)4 67 60 77 07
Fax. +33 (0)4 67 60 70 95
Email : sarl.teissier@wanadoo.fr

A tradition of quality… since 5 generations

BREADS – CAKES – CHOCOLATES – ICE CREAMS

From the doorstep, our nostrils are tickling by the sweet aroma of chocolate. Inside, in a warm atmosphere where wood and ocher dominate, the chocolate comes in a thousand ways: in bites, tablets, olive etc... Nadine and Thierry love surprising mixtures such as chocolates with bell pepper and essential flavour of peppermint, with salted butter. Latest news: chocolates with red berries and praline and chocolate with jasmine and tangerines will make you melt with pleasure. Amidst the mouthfuls called Jamaica, Tahiti, are macarons, homemade spreads, candied chestnuts and other marzipan. Do not miss the pure original ganaches, its a real treat. Notice to gourmets who want to train for making macarons. Three hours of preparation for €65, this is a very nice gift that you can do for yourself.

■ CREMERIA VIENNA
1, rue En-Rouan
✆ + 33 (0) 4 67 54 16 24
Low season: open Tuesday to Saturday from 8am to 8pm. High season: Monday to Saturday from 8am to 11pm.
What a pleasure to enjoy a delicious Italian ice cream! Eric has just moved near the Place Saint-Cosmas and offers nineteen perfumes that are all more attractive as each other. As her icecreams are homemade, you will find a beautiful range of sorbets that change with the seasons. In this small shop, it is Thibault, who prepares the ice creams of the day in the early hours of the morning. Eric welcomes you with a smile and serves you with generous ice creams. The house also offers milkshakes and zuccotto, a bombe glacée, a specialty of Florence. And as there has to be something for all tastes and all seasons, needless to deprive you from an Italian crepe, that is soft inside and crispy on the outside.

■ LO MONACO
8, rue Jean-Jacques Rousseau
✆ + 33 (0) 4 67 60 76 07
Open Monday to Saturday from 7am to 1.30pm and from 4pm to 8pm. Closed on Sunday.
The address was known as one of the best bakeries in Montpellier. It is today Lucien Goudar who took over, and he does it beautifully. Somewhat hidden, between Place de la Canourgue and plants garden, this address is worth seeing. Payse bread, flax baguette, spelt pie, wheat pie and Cevennes, the choice is vast and of quality products. Some chocolate muffins, cakes with lemon and orange are also present. A taste of priority: autumn steak and the festive, both awarded by the 2013 Gourmand Hrault contest.

■ MARQUISE DE SEVIGNE
4, rue de la Barralerie
✆ + 33 (0) 4 67 66 36 90
www.marquise-de-sevigne.com
Open Tuesday to Saturday from 10.30am to 12.30pm and from 2pm to 7pm.
Created in 1898 in Auvergne, this chocolate factory has since open several shops in Paris, in the province, and even a museum in Alsace! In his montpellier shop, Marquise de Sévigné exhibits all creations that contributed to its success such as: Mazarin, Taragona or Montespan. These delicious delicacies are taken away in pouches or in sets. A good address for lovers of real chocolate.

■ VALGALIER CATHERINE
18, rue du Faubourg Saint-Jaumes
✆ + 33 (0) 4 67 63 30 61
Open Tuesday to Saturday from 6: 30 am to 12: 45 pm and from 2: 30 pm to 7: 45 pm; Sunday and public holidays from 6: 30 am to 7: 30 pm. Possible delivery.
Catherine Valgalier was introduced in the chocolate business while she was still a kid ... Inheriting a tradition which runs over three generations, she continues today with gusto, having learned to put thereon her own creativity. Holder of the Master Artisan title, she defends constantly renewed inventiveness, in accordance with tradition and open to modern culinary intuitions. From saint-honoré classic and rum babas with checkered crisp chocolates to pistachio or coffee, happiness is as much aesthetic as gustative. It's beautiful, it's good, the products are top quality ... Simply irresistible!

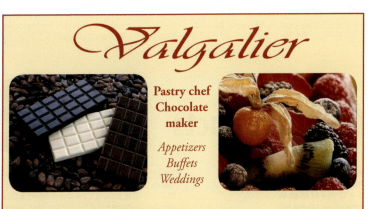

Valgalier
Pastry chef Chocolate maker
Appetizers Buffets Weddings

18, rue du Faubourg Saint-Jaumes • MONTPELLIER • Tel. +33(0)4 67 63 30 61

BREADS – CAKES – CHOCOLATES – ICE CREAMS

■ **MY CUPCAKE BY LILA**
2, rue du Bayle
✆ + 33 (0) 4 67 63 05 01
Open on Tuesday and Sunday from 11am to 7pm; Wednesday to Saturday from 10am to 7pm. Take-away or to eat on the premises. Cupcake from €2.80.
This little tea room specialized in cupcakes is located in an alley behind the Foch Street. In an all white world, these colorful cupcakes are a delight for the eyes... and the taste buds. You taste one of these typically Anglo-Saxon pastries not knowing what to expect, and you discover a fishing grout under the glaze decorated with sugar stars! Miam. Anis and Faty, the couple who opened this place in late 2012, will welcome you with a smile and advise you on the tea to drink in agreement with your choice of cupcake. Every day, varieties change according to their inspiration. Sweet mouths will be delighted, and the others will try the savory cupcakes! If that exist: for example salmon, avocado, fig- foie gras, olives and roasted chicken. A small original address!

■ **GONZALEZ CHOCOLATIER**
La Plaine
Espace Bocaud
JACOU
✆ + 33 (0) 4 99 77 10 82
www.chocolateriegonzalez.fr
chocolateriegonzalez@neuf.fr
Open Tuesday to Saturday from 9am to 1pm and from 2pm to 7pm; Sunday and public holidays from 9am to 12.30pm.
Patrice Gonzalez a renowned artisan confectioner officiates in the region for over 13 years now. First at Castelnau, he is now settled in Jacou, at Bocaud area. Commander to the brotherhood of chocolate makers of France since 2006, this passionate man continues to draw on inspiration and renew his art. This results to a variety of homemade designs, about ten of pure origins, Madagacar, Venezuela and the Caribbean. You will appreciate better the tremendous creative work when you know one of the cakes is present in the year (the famous Royal: dark chocolate mousse, almond cookie and crunchy praline) or macaroons (praline speculos, almond pasta, passion fruit). An expertise acquired through experience and real intensive finesse in gourmand associations for this peerless chocolate. Regular news, for individuals with a dark chocolate mousse cake, raspberry coulis, bell pepper, and for businesses: the 'boîte croquez le sud': is a thinning-out of the leaves of the Languedoc cross. Chocolates of a local flavor, apricot flowing caramel, rosemary thyme ganache, almond paste with olive oil...

Fish – Seafood

■ **LA PECHERIE**
30, rue du Faubourg-Figuerolles
✆ + 33 (0) 4 67 92 54 18
Open Tuesday to Friday from 8am to 1pm and from 4pm to 8pm; Saturday from 8am to 2pm and from 4pm to 8pm; Sunday from 8am to 2pm.
Fish lovers certainly know the fish shop at the rue du Faubourg-Figuerolles. The choice of fish and shellfish from the Mediterranean is huge. The goods are of exceptional freshness, it comes from the Sète wet market every morning.
On the caterer shelf, rouille squid, stuffed squid, brandade, bouillabaisse makes the passers-by salivate. A good address for fish gourmets, they are so rare in this category that it should be mentioned. Who would think that Montpellier is located in the Mediterranean suburb?

Local Products

■ **OLIVIERS & CO**
30, rue des Etuves
✆ + 33 (0) 4 67 66 63 46
www.oliviersandco.net
oco.montpellier@free.fr
Open on Monday from 2pm to 7pm; Tuesday to Friday from 10am to 1.30pm and from 2.30pm to 7pm; Saturday from 10am to 7pm. Closed on Monday in January and February.
Olive oil in all its forms: it is the offer of Oliviers & Co, a shop dedicated to the men of the olive tree. And it is pretty olive trees that welcome you at the entrance of this original shop. After, room is given for all olive oils from the cradle

of the Mediterranean: Spain, Italy, Greece, Lebanon, etc. then perfumed oils with bergamot, basil, the mandarin, without mentioning fig or poppy vinegars. Here, the olive oil is endlessly available in tapenades, pesto and multitudes of preparations. But the Dominique Guillon's shop also opens onto cosmetics, the plates made of clay, the oil-cans, in short on a world that exudes Mediterranean flavours.

■ **AU COMPTOIR PAYSANS D'OC**
Tournezy 2
2, rue Montels-l'Eglise - LATTES
✆ + 33 (0) 4 67 55 75 79
comptoirpaysan.doc@orange.fr
Open Monday to Saturday from 9.30am to 1pm and from 2.30pm to 7pm.
This is an address to relax! A multitude of producers, breeders, market gardeners, poulterers, cheese makers, wine growers and so many others from the vintage offer live, through this beautiful country bar, the best of their production. Alternately, the farmers take this stall and boast their products. Fruits, vegetables, meat, poultry and cooked meats, honey, wine... As weeks and seasons go by, the stalls change, develop and regularly the open houses are organised and allow you to discover all these producers. The choice is large in these 300 m² and the quality is obviously there. Finally, an address that was lacking in Montpellier. Producers live, friendliness, choice, everything is of extremely high quality. Make your shopping differently!

■ **L'HUILERIE BLANC**
Mas de la Laune
Chemin de la Laune
SAINT-GENIÈS-DES-MOURGUES
✆ + 33 (0) 4 67 86 21 94
lhuilerieblanc.fr/
Open Tuesday to Sunday from 9am to 7pm.
It is on 18 acres that Robert Blanc planted his olive trees, 3 500 trees grouped by variety on adjacent plots. Olivière, aglandau, négrette and picholine therefore share the ground, exclusively maintained by shearing and turnaround of land. Here, everything is managed by the White: from manual harvest to the grinding made in a small latest generation compact mill. Oils are a mono variety, in green fruity for aglandau and the picholine, and in ripe fruity the négrette and the olivière.

Products Of The World

■ **AGOSTINO RAVESE** .... *Mediterranean*
Halles Laissac
Place Alexandre-Laissac
✆ + 33 (0) 4 67 58 53 75
Open Tuesday to Saturday from 7am to 1pm. Possible delivery (for disabled people). Chèque Restaurant.

Agostino Ravese manufactures its own fresh pasta, to which it offers to add Italian cheeses and cold meats. For twenty years that he has worked in the Laissac halles. But he has not lost the original vision he had the art, «Everything is made on site and in hand. I have no need for bulky equipment but time, «he says. That finally convinced us, if it was not already done by the appetising stall. Always busy, you will certainly see him immersed with two guests, making one of his quality ingredients. The kind of passionate attention of which are born the good things.

LES ESTIVALES

■ **LES ESTIVALES**
Esplanade Charles-de-Gaulle
✆ +33 (0)4 67 34 73 25
From end of June to beginning of September, every Friday evenings from 6pm to 11.30pm.
The city of Montpellier has this demonstration organised around wine now for almost 10 years, with the growing success. From the end of June to the beginning of September, each Friday evening is devoted to the now traditional wine tastings and to the night market of local handicraft. Both support the wine industry and the possibility of meeting with the winegrowers of the vintage. The event became popular, as the prices are reasonable (3 drinks for €5). The nearby Bosc kiosk will serve as stage for free concerts.

■ **SUR LA ROUTE DU SAFRAN**
6, rue Clos-René
✆ + 33 (0) 4 67 29 62 24
www.surlaroutedusafran.com
surlaroutedusafran@gmail.com
Open Tuesday to Friday from 10am to 1pm and from 3.30pm to 7pm; Saturday from 10am to 7.30pm.
Between the station and Comedie, Kazem Karimi opened at the end of 2013, a cave of the Iranian gastronomic culture. The colours and products are legions, equally known and recognised as these famous pistachios of Iran, saffron obviously and many other prepared spices, pastries, dishes, honey, jams, sweets, teas, rice, cherry fruit juice or with granada (among others) but also syrup, olive oil, Turkish and Armenian wine, Rakis, Turkish delight, Baklava, dried fruits, rose water or pistachio Ice Cream (delicious!) and caviars, of course!

The choice is too large to name it all. Iran is honoured, obviously but not only, the best of Greece, Armenia, Lebanon, Turkey delights gourmets that we are and the prices, given the quality of products offered, seem the most competitive. Note that Karem advises on the preparation and the tasting of its products and also organises discovery workshops of Iranian cuisine every fortnight. Non-standard reception! A moment of escape, you will go back!

■ **WEI SIN** .... **Asia**
45, avenue Georges-Clemenceau
ⓒ + 33 (0) 4 67 06 92 43 / + 33 (0) 4 67 34 01 86
Open Monday to Saturday from 9am to 1pm and from 3pm to 7pm; Sunday from 9.30am to 12pm.

Wei sin, it is the unavoidable shop on Clémenceau for whoever wants to enjoy Asian cuisine. You might ask yourself why your dishes do not have this special and unique flavour that foreign. It is for sure that you lack some of the basic products of this cuisine, obvious products for all «cooks» from these traditions which you do not even know the existence! Fortunately you will find it here, and more importantly, you will be thought on how to discover it and use it. It is the time to get some advice and tricks essential to the authenticity of your dish.
The shop also offers products of the other continents and you can stroll through the African, Indian Ocean and South American shelves, in search of new flavours to impress your guests.

Caterers

■ **CABIRON TRAITEUR**
350, avenue du Maréchal-Leclerc
ⓒ + 33 (0) 4 67 65 48 02 - www.cabiron.com
No corkage charge. Possible rental of chairs.
Cabiron Traiteur, it is an experience which runs on three generations of professionals of the trades mouth. Reference on Montpellier and the region, the company is popular both for the quality of the gastronomy as it develops than for efficiency and originality of its logistics services. The catering is a member of the prestigious club of the Caterers in France, has had the label Qualitraiteur and Gérard Cabiron, who watches over the operations, was voted meilleur ouvrier de France in 2007.
In short, call Cabiron, it is the guarantee of a successful reception, in the purest tradition of French culinary expertise.

Wines & Spirits

Cellars – Wine Shops

■ **LA CAVE DES ARCEAUX**
7, rue Marioge ⓒ + 33 (0) 4 67 92 44 84
http://www.cave-arceaux.com
Open Monday to Thursday from 9am to 1pm and from 4 pm to 7: 30 pm; Friday from 9 am to 1 pm and from 4 pm to 8 pm; Saturday from 9 am to 8 pm. Vineyard meeting every Saturday. What could the definition of «merchant of pleasure» be for you? we can see you coming. Well it's not what you think; Frédéric Jeanjean does not deal in the illegal but in wine. Since 2001, this wine merchant, neighbourhood in size, delivers precious advice to its many guests. Partners of winemakers of Languedoc, they select at home the best including vegetables. Its wines: mas Bruguière, domaine de Cazeneuve, domaine Clavel- Pierre. This wine waiter by profession does not neglect the wines of Burgundy and Bordeaux, the Loire wines or champagnes. A little place is reserved for gourmet gifts such as tapenade or olive oils. And the little plus of this wine lover, the layout of cellars where guests can store and make age in serenity their precious bottles. Is this not pleasure!

■ **AUX GRANDS VINS DE FRANCE**
1 & 3, rue de l'Argenterie
ⓒ + 33 (0) 4 67 60 75 48
www.auxgrandsvinsdefrance.com
Open on Monday from 3pm to 7.30pm; Tuesday to Saturday from 9am to 1pm and from 2.30pm to 7.30pm. Possible delivery. American Express. The house founded in 1944, is undoubtedly one of the oldest wine cellars in the region. Son of a winemaker from Lavérune, Jean Guizard instigated

the address. In these four cellars (whose latest; Megavin, opened its doors in Fréjorgues, exit of the airport, near Jean Truffaut) Jean and his team continue the tradition of wine merchant at the origin of this place. Its armagnacs vintages of over 60 years old are worth visiting as well as the whiskies. But these passionates of good drinks make a point of honour to present what the French vineyards have as the best. From the Languedoc with Château de la Salade fermented in 1803 in Pic-Saint-Loup or Mas des Armes on the fabulous village of Aniane and its delicious perspective vintage, but also Val de Loire, Alsace, Provence, Côtes-du-Rhône... and Champagne. The choice in this cellar is impressive, all kinds of prices are available and the council is highly recommended here.

■ **MAISON REGIONALE DES VINS ET DES PRODUITS DU TERROIR**
34, rue Saint-Guilhem
✆ + 33 (0) 4 67 60 40 41
maisonregionaledesvins@orange.fr
Open on Monday from 10am to 8pm; Tuesday to Saturday from 9.30am to 8pm. Possible delivery.
The region did not deserve less than these large vaults and this atmosphere to show what it has as best. It is in a former mansion of the sixteenth century renovated in the nineteenth century, enhanced by its slabs of Castries, its walls and ceilings with exposed stone, that Jean-Marc, big expert of local delights shares his passion with not less than 1600 wines and 600 local produce. On saturdays, tastings are enlivened by the producers. A beautiful champagne shelf of 80 references. The favourites; Château de Gaure, Mas de Chimère, a superb shelf of yellow wines of the Jura. Also, the Gangloff national references (condrieux), Pierre Auvernoy (Jura) and Romanée Conti.

Wine Merchants

■ **CAVE CELLIER ET MOREL LA MAISON DE LA LOZERE**
27, rue de l'Aguillerie
✆ + 33 (0) 4 67 66 46 36
Open Monday to Saturday from 10am to 9pm.
Adjacent to the reception of famous restaurant city of the same name, a wine cellar representing the jewel of the Languedoc wines and elsewhere, judge in: Bruguiere, Aupilhac, Peyre Rose, Petite Sibérie, Roucaillat... These names that make you dream. There are nearly a thousand references in region and except region. Wines from star: Gérard Depardieu collects 2011. Also a list of champagne, Dagueneau, Beaucastel, Guigal, Château Simone... Of whiskies, range of the house Roofer. Convenient for your evenings the biberon' art of High Puech. At the end of the day (in times of a normal shop) think of your bottle of bench or rosé, it will be kept in the shade. A wine selection for all budgets.

■ **CAVES D'OCCITANIE**
259, rue Jean-Baptiste Calvignac
BAILLARGUES ✆ + 33 (0) 4 67 69 02 55
cave.doccitanie@wanadoo.fr
Open Tuesday to Saturday. Smoking-room for the amateurs

of Havana, initiation to tasting, evenings tasting.
The Stéphane Lebesgue's cellar is one of the most famous in the region. Rightly so, as it is one of those where you can find the largest number of bottles of exception. Rare crus of Burgundy (Boillot, Dauvissat, Coche Dury...) or Bordeaux (Mouton, Figeac...), champagnes of exception (Clos du Mesnil, Selosse...). But also all the vintages of Mas Julien or Grange des Pères, jewels of the region. It is not for nothing that it occupies the tables of the greatest restaurants of the town. There are also bottles at less than 4 €. With excellent advice, you can follow it with your eyes closed. Tasting on Saturdays with winemakers generally from the region. Also, storage of wines for individuals. Upstairs, there is a reception area to organise banquets and meals. Also unique in Montpellier is a smoking room for cigars.

Cooperatives

■ **MAISON DES VINS DES COTEAUX DU LANGEDOC**
Mas de Saporta - LATTES
✆ + 33 (0) 4 67 06 04 44
www.coteaux-languedoc.com
Open on Monday from 2pm to 7pm; Tuesday to Friday from 10am to 7pm; Saturday from 10am to 1pm and from 3pm to 7pm.
Mas de Saporta is an old winemaker farmhouse of the seventeenth century, revalue by the winemakers in order to promote their wine. It houses the headquarters of the vast name; coteaux-du-Languedoc. You will find the cru trade union of winemakers, but especially the wine counter that offers a wide choice of wines and regional produce, and the Les Cuisiniers Vignerons restaurant, open every lunch and dinner upon reservation only. In a friendly setting, you will discover a beautiful menu of regional specialties and a solid selection of coteaux-du-languedoc. Documentation on the wines and the soils, tasting courses, and large reception room for festive evenings and cocktails.

WINES & SPIRITS - Cooperatives

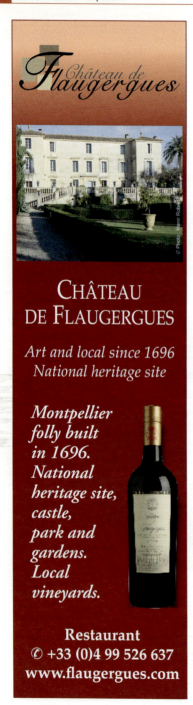

Château de Flaugergues

Art and local since 1696
National heritage site

Montpellier folly built in 1696. National heritage site, castle, park and gardens. Local vineyards.

Restaurant
© +33 (0)4 99 526 637
www.flaugergues.com

■ LES COSTIÈRES DE POMEROLS
68, avenue de Florensac - POMÉROLS
© + 33 (0) 4 67 77 01 59
www.cave-pomerols.com

Open Monday to Saturday from 8.30am to 12.30pm and from 2pm to 6pm. Founded in 1932, the cellar of Pomerols continued growing, thriving and being modernised. In 2003, the cellar merged with the cellar of Castelnau de Guers and in 2007, with the cellar of Mèze in order to produce quality wines. Its wines with culinary qualities confirm the specificity of their origins. The specialty is white wines. 400 ha are classified in AOC area. If the reputation of the wines of picpoul-de-pinet largely exceeds the region, it serves as ambassador to the other whites made with chardonnay, viognier and sauvignon, as well as red and rosé wines made with syrah, merlot and cabernet. The Beauvignac label signs the most noticeable vintages. Range from 4 € to 14.90 €. In 2014, three newcomers, the slopes of Languedoc white, red and a soft rosé. Equally discover Caveau de Mèze, open for sale, wine tasting and also friendly entertainment around wine.

■ LES VINS DE SAINT-SATURNIN
Avenue Noël-Calmel
SAINT-SATURNIN-DE-LUCIAN
© + 33 (0) 4 67 96 61 52 / + 33 (0) 4 67 96 49 08
www.vins-saint-saturnin.com

Open Monday to Saturday from 8.30am to 12pm and from 2pm to 6pm. Closed at 19: 00 in summer. Open on Sunday from mid-June to mid-September, from 10am to noon and from 3pm to 7pm. Visit of the farm and entertainment on appointment. Located at the gates of the village, on the road to Arboras, the cellar called La Cathédrale produces of coteaux-du-Languedoc Saint-Saturnin. This name had its heyday in the region in the 1960s, because its winemakers were the first to market in a dynamic way their production. Today they produce excellent wines, like; la cuvée du Seigneur des deux Vierges, la Cuvée Cinquantenaire, le Vin d'une Nuit... Very different from each other, they have in common balance and quality.

Vineyards

■ CHÂTEAU DE FLAUGERGUES
1744, avenue Albert-Einstein
© + 33 (0) 4 99 52 66 37 - www.flaugergues.com

Open Monday to Saturday from 9: 30 am to 12: 30 pm and from 2: 30 pm to 7 pm. High season: Sunday from 2: 30 pm to 7 pm. Visits Tuesday to Saturday. No visits in August.
Close to the city, towards the sea, the property of Brigitte and Henri de Colbert can be visited in more than one way. The castle, «madness» of the eighteenth century, was built by the same family that manages the estate since 1696; the souvenirs that tell Mr and Mrs. de Colbert, to illustrate antique furniture, monumental tapestries... The gardens with French floors and «gardens of the senses» request the view, hearing, the smell... And beyond, the view embraces a vineyard planted on pebbles, these «sandstones» left by the Rhone at the Quaternary era; on the 33 acres are planted mainly syrah, grenache and mourvèdre for the reds, marsanne, roussanne and

role for the whites. You will no doubt appreciate the Colbert vintage (raised 12 months in oak barrels), the Foliæ vintage for the white, and the Délix vintage, red rosé white wine of local d'Oc.

■ DOMAINE DU RIEUCOULON
2420, avenue de Toulouse
✆ + 33 (0) 4 67 47 32 76
contact@rieucoulon.com

Low season: open Monday to Thursday from 9am to 12pm; Friday and Saturday from 3pm to 6pm. High season: Monday to Saturday from 9am to 12pm and from 3pm to 6pm. Anne and Benoît Lacombe perpetuate an already known long family tradition in the nineteenth century with the Family of Lunaret. On a small special land, the vineyard extends from a single unit between Montpellier and Saint-Jean-de-Védas over about twenty hectares where combines – sauvignon, merlot, cabernet-sauvignon, carignan and grenache. Small outputs, the sun and wind combine to create the perfect conditions for the production of Mediterranean fine wines. Vintages «Las Pillas» local wines from the hills of Moure, great bottles signed «Cuvée du Pont de Vassal», a reference with «Merlot L'Enchanteur» and the vintage «Lucentum» a 100 % Alicante from footbridges of grapes, the result is amazingly beautiful. The site is visited with delight.

■ MAS DE DAUMAS GASSAC
Haute Vallée du Gassac - ANIANE
✆ + 33 (0) 4 67 57 88 45
www.daumas-gassac.com

Low season: open Monday to Saturday from 10 am to 12 pm and from 2 pm to 6 pm. High season: Monday to Saturday from 9:30 am to 6:30 pm. Visit and tasting all day. Groups (starting from 10 people) visits by appointment.
Nestled in a wild valley for more than twelve centuries now, near the romanesque Saint-Guilhem desert abbey, this estate offers the opportunity to discover a Gallo-Roman winery in full scrubland 3 km from Aniane. From the eyes to the tongue, with tasting, you can enjoy: Mas de Daumas Gassac red 2008 or 2010 (drawn from the barrel), Mas de Daumas Gassac Blanc 2010, as well as the wine of Laurence, the wines of Gassac Mills, Guilhem, Elise, Albaran and the new wine Fauna.

■ DOMAINE DE MUJOLAN
RD613 - Mas de Mante - FABRÈGUES
✆ + 33 (0) 4 67 85 11 06
www.mujolan.com

Open Monday to Saturday from 9am to 12pm and from 3pm to 7pm. Nestled at the foot of the protected Gardiole mountain, in a magical place called the «Collines de la Moure», this estate exploits 56 acres of vineyards grouped around the nineteenth century castle. It was one of the first in the 60's to plant cabernet – sauvignon and syrah. L'Hymne à la Moure, a white wine, blending the flavours of flowers, toast and dried fruits is to be enjoyed at the aperitif. Le rosé, G'la Moure, has a small sweet side which gives it all the charms of a fruit. To be discovered; Vertige de la Moure, exceptional red wine, to be booked for special occasions. For the varietal wines, the flavours of the viognier, merlot and cabernet – sauvignon will delight your taste buds. Upon booking, the estate can also accommodate banquets

■ CHATEAU DE L'ENGARRAN
Route de Juvignac - LAVÉRUNE
✆ + 33 (0) 4 67 47 00 02
www.chateau-engarran.com

Open every day from 10am to 1pm and from 3pm to 7pm. Organization of group tours by appointment. Participation: €15. On the outskirts of Montpellier, this wine is an issue for women. Two girls of the family, Diane Losfelt and Constance Rerolle exploit as well as possible, as part of a sustainable agriculture, a land representative of this name. Reflection of their wines, the castle – a folly -, its gardens and a wine museum are visited in introduction of a presentation of the production. The AOC was born from syrah, grenache, carignan and cinsault. Always noticeable, the Quetton-Saint-Georges vintage is the fruit of old syrah. Symbols of their land and its potential, some wines are raised in cask, others fruitier in tanks. The estate produces the rosé wines – in AOC and VDP -, two white of pays d'oc, all remarkable.

WINES & SPIRITS - Vineyards

■ DOMAINE GUIZARD
La Ménagerie
12, boulevard de la Mairie - LAVÉRUNE
✆ + 33 (0) 4 67 27 86 59
www.domaine-guizard.com
Open Monday to Friday from 5pm to 7pm. Or by appointment.
In the old village, on the old outbuildings of the castle that adjoins the Lavérune town hall, the Guizard estate has the originality of being run by the same family since 1580, with documents as proof. The vineyards are grown in AOC over 45 acres of rational culture, mainly on the Saint-Georges-d'Orques and the Grès de Montpellier lands. From the top of the range with vintage 400 (20 months on 24 in barrels of oak, new barrels) with the very characteristic and persistent notes of plum, smoked and spices. A vintage with powerful tannins, but very fine, rich in the nose as in the mouth. First-class still: the Cuvée Prestige (Syrah and mourvèdre over poor output, breeding 24 months in barrels and still 24 months after assembly), very successful, of purple dress, spiced up, with complex nose (cherry, spices), rich and round at the same time, closed in the mouth. Ideal for a saddle of lamb. For the white wine, the estate is in organic (Chardonnay) and also offers a traditional approach (white of sparkling white). Finally, the vintage Grès De Montpellier (syrah and grenache) with the subtle nose dominated by prune and humus. The house also offers some new: the whole organic olive oil and a beautiful range of local product.

■ DOMAINE SAINT JEAN DU NOVICIAT
Mas du Novi - D 5
Route de Villeveyrac
MONTAGNAC
✆ + 33 (0) 4 67 24 07 32
www.masdunovi.com

Open every day and public holidays from 10 am to 7 pm. Open on Sunday. Visit and free tasting.
«Siste et ora, viator», sit and pray, traveller, such is the motto of Mas du Novi, former outbuilding of the abbey of Valmagne. A variation of the occitan cross signs the finest productions of this 100 acre estate, on different floors. A small chapel of the twelfth century is to be visited. Since 1994, full-bodied and long; that of slope-of- Languedoc red (typical grape varieties), presented in three wines including a «Prestigi» in oak, brilliant, which gives to the nose and taste flavours of red fruits and woody fondue, a remarkable complexity. For the traveller, who will have abandoned prayer, the facilities will lead to the presentation of a unique case in France, a sparkling red, assembly of Alicante, cinsault and carignan, which the winemakers recommend chilled on a dessert to chocolate or red fruits... If you visit the tent, you can also discover the famous Rove goats in the property.

■ DOMAINE DE LA PROSE
Route de Saint-Georges d'Orques - PIGNAN
✆ + 33 (0) 4 67 03 08 30 / + 33 (0) 6 11 03 80 24 /
+ 33 (0) 6 10 32 77 46
www.domaine-de-la-prose.fr
Open on Wednesday and Friday from 10am to 12.30pm and from 3pm to 6pm. Saturday morning from 10am to 12.30pm. Or by appointment.
The Domaine de la Prose above the abbey of Vignogoul plays with the colours of nature, the blue of the sea that takes shape on the horizon and a whole range of the scrubland which surrounds the Estate. The Mortillet family chose the Saint-Georges land to add to their expertise, the magic of the ground. Their great vintage, enjoyed in its earliest youth, has all the characteristics of a vin de garde, intense beauty of its dress, and already the advanced spice flavours and stewed fruit.

■ FRANCOIS HENRY
2, Avenue d'Occitanie
SAINT-GEORGES-D'ORQUES
✆ + 33 (0) 4 67 45 57 74
www.domainehenry.fr
Open Monday to Friday from 3pm to 7pm; Saturday from 9am to 12pm. Take appointment for tastings.
From a family of winemakers, Laurence and François Henry settled in Saint-Georges-d'Orques, attracted by the beauty and the potentials of the vineyard. They also studied the history of this soil and were immersed to produce wines in the purest qualitative tradition. To continue with the beautiful red, pink and white wine range, the Mailhol vintage, entirely from ancient grape varieties now forgotten like black aspiran, the morastel, the illade, gives a remarkably fruity and gourmet wine. You should also taste at the Henry, the beautiful red passerillé, a rich wine of great gastronomy sold in bottle of 50 Cl. Range from 7.50 € to 45 €.

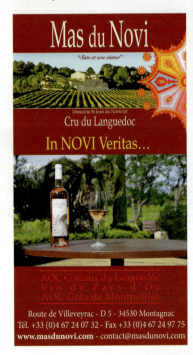

Beauty & Wellness

Hairdressers → 80
Relaxation & Body Shape → 81

Hairdressers

Hair Salons

■ **ATELIER DE COIFFURE VALERIE HEBDA**
467, rue de la Roqueturière
C. Commercial
✆ + 33 (0) 4 67 79 14 04
www.atelier-coiffure-montpellier.com
Cut (from): woman €43.90, man €21.50. Color: from €30. Rate teenager until 15 years: 17,90€.
This is more than twenty years that Valérie Hebda created his salon. With her team of top hairdressers of the latest trends, she welcomes you in her contemporary salon workshop. And there you go for a moment of relaxation. Because here we take care of you well especially of your hair. Before the hair cut, each hairdresser offers his advice. So you can get the hair style that best fits your personality. In a word, at Valérie Hebda, your hair is cut, but your needs and profile especially are taken into account, we analyze your face to give you the best. A VIP service based on relaxation will be offered to you at the beginning of the week. They are treatments for men and women with a special range of products and a cranial massage.

■ **CLAUDE MICHEL COIFFURE**
1, place Rondelet
✆ + 33 (0) 4 67 58 78 08
www.coiffure-claude-michel-34.fr
claudemichelcoiffure@sfr.fr
Open Tuesday to Friday from 9am to 6pm; Saturday from 9am to 2.30pm. Cut (from): woman €38, man €19, child (less than 12 years) €15. Color: from €23. -10% for the students.
Opposite the Rondelet post, Fabienne and her husband, the talented Claude Michel, welcome you in a lounge atmosphere. The decoration was renovated with taste. The hair is pampered as it should be. For the treatments and the shampoos, we use the Phytosolba products made with (90%) plants. Whether you want a modern or trendy cut, wicks or a colour, the couple knows what perfectly suits us. Recommended for all those seeking the cut at the forefront.

■ **MONSIEUR LAURENT GARCIA.................Men**
30, rue Foch
✆ + 33 (0) 4 67 66 04 04
laurentgarcialbc@gmail.com
Open on Tuesday and Thursday to Saturday from 9am to 12.30pm and from 2pm to 7pm. Cut: man €25.
Laurent Garcia is craftsman in the field since he has done male haute coiffure in Montpellier for over a decade, as he likes to say it. He moved in 2013 his barber shop, 30 metres away. It is the reference in Montpellier. The amenities are varied: beautician, cuts, barber and manicures. The atmosphere is relaxed, regular and visiting guests exchange in a good mood some words on everyday life. Here, high range hairstyles are made. Benedicte is here to assist him with discretion and efficiency. One comes out of it with impeccable cut.

■ **STUDIO 54**
10, rue Saint-Denis
✆ + 33 (0) 4 67 92 70 34
www.studio54coiffure.com
studio54coiffure@gmail.com
Open Tuesday to Saturday from 9am to 8pm. With or without prior appointment. Cut (from): woman €35, man €21, child (less than 14 years) €14. Color: from €25. Permanent €48, rates teenager (14 to 18 years) from €17.
In this beautiful lounge, where the decor cleverly combines the hairdressers original and modern touch, Eddy and Guillaume offer advice to find the cut that will enhance your face. Whether you want to try something classic or more daring, Eddy can switch! The address, very friendly, also organises exhibitions and thematic evenings (clairvoyance, lingerie, etc.). A hair salon recommended for its

---

studio 54

HAIRDRESSING & RELOOKING COACH

10 rue Saint-Denis
34000 Montpellier
Tel. +33 (0)4 67 92 70 34
www.studio54coiffure.com

Tuesday to Saturday from 9 am to 20 pm
by appointment

Massage – Relaxation - **RELAXATION & BODY SHAPE** 81

reasonable prices and its professionalism, with the added bonus of a warm welcome! You should know that Eddy is also a make-up artist and an image consultant; he works on shooting fashion with various photographers.

Hair complement – Wig

■ **SENEGAL BEAUTY**
11, rue Maguelone
✆ + 33 (0) 4 67 42 88 08 / + 33 (0) 6 65 50 67 57

www.senegalbeauty.com
neworac@yahoo.fr
Open Monday to Saturday from 10am to 7.30pm.
Between station and comedy, Racky and his small team welcome you with a smile in this temple of African hair beauty: wigs, hairpiece, hair extensions (hot or cold), cleaning products for the growth and beauty of the hair. And also, cosmetics, make-up, cream for the body, Shea butter, (in the second shop, behind the station). The choice is impressive on the hair; natural, semi-natural or synthetic and in all colours and in the most famous brands. Note that Racky offers the putting of extensions in weaving.

Relaxation & Body Shape

Fitness Centres

■ **LES ARCADES**
1756, avenue de l'Europe
CASTELNAU-LE-LEZ
✆ + 33 (0) 4 67 72 80 87
www.mjc-castelnau.fr
Open every day from 8am to 10pm. Open on Sunday (9.30am – 12.30pm). From 220/year.
Five hundred thousand members in this club, 16 qualified state instructors, bodybuilding, cardio training... Adapted gym lessons from 3 to 99 years old. Group lessons, zumba, sterching, pilates, urban dance... A room that can vary with the trends. Crossfit soon.

■ **MJC DE CASTELNAU**
Centre André Malraux
10, avenue de la Moutte
CASTELNAU-LE-LEZ
✆ + 33 (0) 4 67 02 99 40
www.mjc-castelnau.fr
Open Monday to Friday from 9am to 12pm and from 2pm to 7pm.
For over 40 years, the MJC or Centre André Malraux has given to children and the adults several leisure, cultural and sports activities. The castelnauviens and people from the surrounding villages are welcome. This year 120 activities, from the very classic hike to the more original activities like; Chinese, flip-flops or harp classes. The MJC also offers rich cultural program, exhibitions, concerts, conferences, theatre and the evening trips to the library of the five continents, one of the highlights of this centre among others. Themed events «around...». The innovation in 2013/14 is around the offer of music school, trumpets, violoncello, and guitar.

Massage – Relaxation

■ **KEEP IN TOUCH**
Le Clos du Pin - 481, rue Fra Angelico
✆ + 33 (0) 6 28 77 72 94
www.keepin-touch.fr
celine@keepin-touch.fr
Open Monday to Saturday from 10am to 8pm. Twinned with a osthéopathe. Approved FFMBE. Single rate of €1 the minute. Happy hour from 4pm to 5pm Monday to Friday -20%.
Céline welcomes you in this relaxation salon opened some time ago, hoping for one thing: bring relaxation and well-being. Qualified expert in body educational techniques and aromatology, she has managed to create an atmosphere and a practice of care as she knows. Listening is one of the highlights of this centre, and the holding of the sessions is agreed during a conversation before massage, in order to offer the care that you need. Based on the relationship between oils and massage, we will struggle to find here a synergy of essential oils and vegetable oils that suits you. A beautiful harmony as for the approach, far from the centre where massages are done in chain. The prices are reasonable, and you are even offered a drink in harmony with the session!

■ **ESPRIT D'AILLEURS**
40, rue Colombiers - RN 113
BAILLARGUES
✆ + 33 (0) 4 67 52 92 27
www.espritdailleurs.fr
contact@espritdailleurs.fr
Open Monday to Saturday from 10am to 7pm.
Set in a charming stone house with exposed beams, vaulted ceilings and bathed in greenery, Esprit d'Ailleurs extends on over 250 m² dedicated to peace and relaxation. Here, overwork, stress and anxiety are banned.

BEAUTY & WELLNESS

They are replaced by massages of stunning variety: dance of the soul (foot reflexology, Tao massage, massage with taï ladles (compresses with Thai herbs) or through body care that can make you dream: the Thai rice wrap, the oriental scrub, bioclimatic energy wrap, the ritual with flowers on skin (Turkish bath, the putting of black soap with orange blossom, hydrating scrub with marine salt Dead sea, moisturising massage with orange blossom melting balm). If you are hesitating over one of the treatments, ask Guy and his team. They can meet your waiting. Another peculiarity of this outstanding place: the practice of treatments that takes place outside, by the pool for example. The outdoor treatments include; hair treatments, cranial massages and Chi nei tsang, a traditional body massage to untie the belly. In a smart approach, Esprit d'Ailleurs also offers the future brides to bury their single life with their friends in this paradise. How can these moments of well-being be refused?

Hydrotherapy

■ O'BALIA
Allée des Sources
BALARUC-LES-BAINS
✆ + 33 (0) 4 67 18 52 05
www.obalia.fr
contact@obalia.fr

Open every day from 10am to 8pm. High season: Friday from 10am to 11pm. Admission: €16.50 (€16.50 Monday to Thursday. €18.50 the 2am consecutive ones and Friday to Sunday). Child as from 8 years: €10.50 Wednesday and Sunday afternoon. Massages from €49 to €108 depending on duration and set of themes. Facials from €49 to €85. Treatments for man from €37 to €77. Aquagym: €12.50 45 minutes. (Rates 2014).

Ideally located on the banks of the Thau Lake, the O'Balia thermal spa opened in spring 2010. Located next to the Hesperides Thermal Baths, this is the first thermal spa of the Mediterranean. It enjoys thermal water from Balaruc-Les-Bains, famous since ancient times for its beneficial properties. Natural noise, aroma of essential oils, relaxing drinks and even a tropical garden, all immerses you in a bath of serenity. Water is declined here in all its forms: mist, fountains, ponds, steam… in a playful spirit. In short, a heavenly setting with a range of treatments and various massages to discover! The Magie de l'Eau area welcomes you in a large fun sensory pool, with bubbling sofas, a river walk, counter-current swimming, geysers and swan necks. This area surrounded by lush Mediterranean vegetation has an onsen, Japanese spa baths, a caldarium and sauna. You can practice sports such as aerobics, but also Zumba, cardio-fitness on latin-american rhythms… O'Balia also sells its own cosmetics products, Thermaliv, made with thermal waters of Balaruc-les-Bains. So, make your choice among all these delights… delightful perfumes, heating mattresses and fairy fingers will make you spend a moment of dreams…

Home – Decor – Garden

Outdoor arrangements → 84
Tableware → 84
Antique Dealers → 84
Arts & Crafts → 85
Do-It-Yourself – Gardening → 85
Decoration → 86

Outdoor Arrangements

■ **SECURIT WERKE** ...... Security – Alarm system
9, avenue Georges-Clemenceau
✆ + 33 (0) 4 67 58 78 00
www.werke.fr
mpl@werke.fr
Open Monday to Friday from 8am to 12pm and from 2pm to 6.45pm.
Desire for well sleeping, leaving your home with doubt on holiday? Securit Werke, the workshop of security, takes care of your accommodation. Specialist in security since 1976, this company offers a range of products like video surveillance and access control. The team has the best products on the market: Bricard (locks), Daitem (alarms), Faac (automatisms), Forestier (deposit), Picardie (locks)... For all budgets and all needs, the name is a reference. On-site parking is available for guests.

Tableware

■ **COUTELLERIE PRADEL-GOLEO**
26, rue de la Loge
✆ + 33 (0) 4 67 60 56 90
www.coutellerie-pradel-goleo.fr
Open on Monday from 2pm to 6.30pm; Tuesday to Saturday from 9am to 12.30pm and from 2pm to 6.45pm. Checks are not accepted.
Small in size, but large by choice, the Pradel cutlery industry is an institution in Montpellier! For nearly 100 years, the passion of the cutlery is passed from generation to generation. Specialist in the knives for professionals and individuals, sharpening and repair, the brand has a crockery and gifts shelf. You can choose among the carafes, pepper mills, porcelain, the trays... Without forgetting the shaving articles, rare on Montpellier.

Antique Dealers

■ **MARCHÉ AUX PUCES ET À LA BROCANTE**
Espace Mosson
✆ + 33 (0) 4 67 75 40 45
Every Sunday from 6am to 1pm.
If the Marché de Broc'Art from the city centre of Montpellier is rather intimate by its size, its big brother of the Mosson, which combines flea market and garage sale, is really big. Hundreds of exhibitors and guests meet every Sunday mornings on this large waste land which remember; welcomes the florists and the nursery gardeners every Tuesday. This place offers a real show: below the scene, markets of the past, where to buy pottery, antique objects from the Mediterranean and the modern amenities for the house and garden. If the paths are more and more reserved for the flea market and the entry for professionals (textiles and beauty or maintenance products at discount prices in particular) a majority of the area is reserved for individuals, who offer their collection of attic or dressing for 1, 2 or 3 €. You will also find several Lorries with terrace where you can have coffee or eat a hot or cold sandwich or chips and which in spring, are full. The advice of Petit Futé: the adjacent car parks often crowded from 8 am; do not hesitate to get there by tram (Mosson from line 1, 200 metres from the market).

■ **TERRES ANCIENNES**
11, rue du Palais des Guilhem
✆ + 33 (0) 4 67 66 11 19
www.terresanciennes.com
terresanciennes@numericable.fr

Open Tuesday to Saturday from 10am to 7pm.
Set in a beautiful vaulted room, the house specialities are; ancient pottery, small kitchen or garden furniture and glassware. Each object exhibited here has transcended time, carries a particular history and even a revealer of popular arts of the nineteenth century. In the rooms of our ancestors are associated more recent decorative objects, but with as much charm. You will find zinc stools, desks and metal chairs, coat rack... A wide choice to give the interior of your house, a little industrial junk shop aspect.

Arts & Crafts

■ ATELIER MYRIAM A
6, rue Alexandre-Cabanel
✆ + 33 (0) 6 10 51 97 23
arras.myriam@gmail.com
Open Tuesday to Saturday from 2pm to 6pm. The morning by appointment.
This studio is full of surprises. As passionate of glass and ground, Myriam designs, draws and gives life to decorative objects. Everything that is sold in this shop is made by Myriam according to traditional manufacturing processes. Colourful jewellery, vases, mirrors, clocks and glass lamps, ceramics... The objects are original, but especially, they are unique. If you want to take part in Myriam's work, she would happily let you enter her back-store.

■ ATELIERS DES MÉTIERS D'ART
53, boulevard Bonne-Nouvelle
✆ + 33 (0) 4 67 59 68 06 / + 33 (0) 6 09 54 21 58
fenma@wanadoo.fr
Created and subsidised by the Montpellier Town Hall, the Ateliers des Métiers d'Art literally are a showcase for local crafts. Opposite the potters' garden, 7 types of crafts are represented in windows: the earthenware from Montpellier and ceramics, jewellery shop, crafts of wood, upholstery, the lute-making, glass, stained glass and fashion. Place of creation and sale, Atelier des Métiers d'Art also has the role to welcome and train young people and future craftsmen. An address to be discovered urgently for the beauty of rooms and the excellence of know-how.

■ DUNES
18, rue de l'Ancien-Courrier
✆ + 33 (0) 4 67 66 49 37
Open Tuesday to Saturday from 11am to 7pm.
Art and tradition combine to provide a journey into the heart of North Africa.
Nicole opens the doors of her shop for an exploration of decorative objects from Burkina-Faso, Morocco, Niger and Mauritania. A trip to discover masks, statuettes and real objects of original creations by local craftsmen. Open to all those who wish to discover new colourful landscapes for a new interior decorated with foreign furniture. Bon voyage!

Do-It-Yourself – Gardening

■ LEROY MERLIN
Ecoparc départemental St-Aunes
avenue de la Saladelle
SAINT-AUNÈS
✆ + 33 (0) 4 67 40 95 00
www.leroymerlin.fr
Open Monday to Saturday from 8am to 8pm. Possible delivery (rental of vans, deliveries from €45).
In Saint-Aunès, east of Montpellier, the shop is a real world that is full of tools and products to answer all of your needs. The sign-posting is explicit there and the layout impeccable. From tools to lighting via decoration, this establishment offers you a wide range of products and amenities especially dedicated to the inside and outside of the house. Professionals are available to meet your expectations and demands for any kind and provide useful recommendations for all your activities of DIY and gardening.
Leroy Merlin also puts you in touch with partner craftsmen for any renovation project in your house. From the apprentice to the experienced handyman, everyone will find all the tools and materials needed for the creation of your project. Leroy Merlin also offers many courses to learn how to hold tinker smart.

Decoration

■ IMAGES DE DEMAIN ....Framing – Painting
10, rue de la Vieille
✆ + 33 (0) 4 67 66 23 45
Open Monday to Saturday from 9.30am to 7.30pm.
Images De Demain stretches out its vast collection of menus in a narrow street in the historic centre of Montpellier, between rue Saint-Guilhem and rue de la Loge. The irreducible ones of the post mail will love it! We find a wide choice of pretty original menus there, for all occasions, at all prices and tastes. It is also a good place to find a souvenir or charming decoration objects: after reviewing the menu in the street, do not hesitate to visit the shop. At the back, a choice of standard or custom-made frames awaits the amateur photographers.

■ MAISON DE BLANC .... Household linen
8, boulevard du Jeu-de-Paume
✆ + 33 (0) 4 67 92 44 59
www.maison-de-blanc.fr
maisondeblanc.piera@gmail.com
Open on Monday from 2.30pm to 7pm; Tuesday to Saturday from 9am to 7pm.
This house is a delight for lovers of beautiful fabrics and fine linens. Here, the linen is available for all tastes, in all colours and pretty prints. There is household linen for each season. In summer, you will be presented a collection that showcases the tables of Provence with warm colours of the South. This collection offers table linen, fabric bag storage and dresses for children. That will make you want to eat under the olive trees in a Provence farmhouse. La Maison also offers a wide choice of net curtains and upholstery that she fashions in her workshop to decorate your interior: curtains, tablecloths, bedspreads, cushions... custom made, according to your desires! For your curtains and net curtains, measurements can be taken on site and the curtain-rods provided and installed.

■ LE QUARTIER DES TISSUS.. Curtains – Hangings
65, rue de la Restanque
✆ + 33 (0) 4 67 92 87 26
www.lequartierdestissus.com
Open on Monday from 2pm to 7pm; Tuesday to Saturday from 9am to 12pm and from 2pm to 7pm.
The designers with golden fingers have found their temple. In this large room hundreds of pebbles of all possible fabrics are displayed indeed. Denim, cotton, silk, lace, synthetic fur, each article is used for making clothes or decoration. Tablecloths, curtains, upholstery, there is really enough choice. The accessories multiply: buttons of all shapes, ribbons and threads of all colours. With all this, it is impossible to stay with your old curtains! Especially with the opening of the new haberdashery shelf and sewing classes given to the learners. It is sure that your interior will appreciate it!

Services

Administrations – Public Services	→ 88
Banks – Insurances	→ 88
Culture	→ 90
Teaching	→ 90
Information – Media	→ 91
Real Estate	→ 93
Wedding & Receptions	→ 95
Business Services	→ 95

©Florian Villesèche - Fotolia

Administrations – Public Services

■ **CHAMBRE DES METIERS DE L'HERAULT**
44, avenue Saint-Lazare
✆ + 33 (0) 4 67 72 72 00
www.cma-herault.fr
chambredemetiers@cma-herault.fr
Open Monday to Friday from 9am to 12: 30 pm and from 1: 30 pm to 5 pm.
La Chambre des métiers is an establishment run by the craftsmen themselves. It has as objective to represent the general interests of crafts to the public authorities. For this reason, this consular room works in close collaboration with the professional organisations in charge of the defence of the private interests of the various trades. The CMA also offers training to the Hérault craftsmen, and advises them when they want to take the route of the training. It organises since 2001, each March, the National week of Crafts.

■ **CONSEIL GENERAL DE L'HERAULT**
1000, rue d'Alco
✆ + 33 (0) 4 67 67 67 67
www.herault.fr
Open Monday to Friday from 8.30am to 12.30pm and from 1.30pm to 5.30pm.
Located in the district of Alco, the General Council of Hérault is now on line 3 of the tram. This is where the Department manages its great missions (regional planning, education, environment, culture, defend the coast) without forgetting all panel of social security (RMI and RSA in particular) which make it one of the social main actors of the Hérault. The General Council provides general public services: weather, archives, transportation, research and consultation of public contracts, maps of the departmental sites, bank of job offers and course (the Bus Information Young People). The Departement also regularly organises competitions to integrate the civil service. The welcome that will make you will be good, and with a little luck you can see an elected!

■ **HÔTEL DE VILLE DE MONTPELLIER**
1, place Georges Frêche
✆ + 33 (0) 4 67 34 70 00 / 0800 34 07 07
www.montpellier.fr
Open Monday to Wednesday and Friday from 8.30am to 5.30pm. Thursday from 10am to 7pm.
Open to the public since November 14th, 2011, the new city hall of Montpellier is a huge nave designed by the architects Jean Nouvel and François Fontès. On the banks of the river Lez, accessible by line 1 from the tramway, the building shaped like a cube is a modern structure in steel and in glass, dressed in blue, black and grey colours. Inaugurated by Hélène Mandroux, it is impressive: 90 metres by 50, for 12 levels on 41 feet high. A thousand agents work here! Although the whole thing is beautiful, its distance from the city centre is regrettable, fortunately it is possible to go to one of the 7 city halls annexes to withdraw a document or make your papers! Also note that certain procedures and requests can be made *via* the website and the answers are often as fast. In May 2013, it was the venue for the celebration of the first gay marriage.

Banks – Insurances

■ **MONTPELLIER ASSURANCES**
1, place Faulquier
✆ + 33 (0) 4 99 13 71 50
www.montpellier-assurances.fr
Open Monday to Friday from 9am to 12pm and from 2pm to 5pm.
GAN ASSURANCES agency and broker, the Montpellier Insurances group run by Achille Amet is specialized in the insurance companies with more than a thousand regional references. Its strength: a multidisciplinary team at your service intervening as well in the domain of property insurance as in the personal insurance. Note that some specialties like Bati-Assur (the insurance construction), Ordi-Assur (the assurance of the laptops), Anilife (the health insurance dogs and cats), Music-Assur (the insurance concert grands). Montpellier Insurances also offers to individuals a wide range of contracts: home, car, leisure, Social Security, health etc.

■ **SOCIETE GENERALE**
11 Boulevard Sarrail
✆ + 33 (0) 4 67 66 57 00
www.societegenerale.fr
Open Tuesday to Friday. External automatic teller machine.

Award-winning products in Montpellier and its surroundings

PELARDON MARBLED CAKE WITH CANDIED ZUCCHINI

€ 5 each

Yarek Konopnicki et Christophe Histe
ARTS ET SAVEURS
134 montée des Picadous
MONTFERRIER-SUR-LEZ
+33 (0)4 67 55 67 32
www.arts-et-saveurs.fr

POULTRY MEAT FRICASSEE WITH FRONTIGNAN MUSCAT

5 € for 200g

FESTIVE

€ 1 each

Lucien Goudard
LO MONACO
8 rue Jean-Jacques Rousseau
MONTPELLIER
+33 (0)4 67 60 76 07

AUTUMN THICK SLICE

€ 1.50 each

BLACK PUDDING WITH ONION

€ 14.90/kg

BOUCHERIE CHARCUTERIE TRAITEUR RIBERA
4 bis route de Montpellier
RESTINCLIERES
+33 (0)4 67 86 94 80

Jean-François Graff
L'ATELIER DES BLES
404 rue Saint Exupéry
MAUGUIO
+33 (0)4 99 54 60 11

LEAVENED ORGANIC HAZELNUTS RAISIN BREAD

€ 4 each (400g)
€ 6.90 each (700g)

The best of Hérault traditional gourmet products

Request the Hérault Gourmand brochure at CMA34
By mail: chambredemetiers@cma-herault.fr
By fax: +33 (0)4 67 72 72 14
Website: www.cma-herault.fr

Culture

■ **PIERRES VIVES**
907, avenue du Professeur Blayac
✆ + 33 (0) 4 67 67 30 00
pierresvives.herault.fr
Open Tuesday to Saturday. See depending on service. Annual closing in August. Closed exceptional public holidays during the year.
The Pierre-Vives building inspired by Rabelais and designed by Zaha Hadid, prize winner of the Pritzker prize in 2004, was born at the end of 2012. His contemporary architecture with pure lines and the bold geometry illustrates the challenge of the Iraqi architect: «to get beautiful views from all possible angles». This City of knowledge and sports for all houses a collection of public services including the Departmental Archives of Hérault, the departmental Media Library, Hérault Sports and the Espace Jeunes Citoyens. Guided tours of the building are organised on Wednesdays and Saturdays at 10: 30 am (excluding public holidays). A visit of the scenes of the Departmental Archives is also possible every first Wednesday of the month from 5 pm to 7 pm excluding public holidays. And note, the many exhibitions organised by the hotel.

■ **AFPA** .... Training company
Direction régionale LR
1021, avenue de Toulouse
✆ 3936
www.languedocroussillon.afpa.fr
Bus line 6, towards pas-du-loup, Ronceray stop
The national Association for Vocational Training for adults is the first training qualifying company in Languedoc-Roussillon. It is one of the references for vocational training for wage earners adults and the unemployed. Among the amenities: orientation in vocational training, vocational training, certification and validation of expertise, accompaniment, and consultancy. 65% of the graduates of Afpa reach an employment in the six months following their training. Note that over 100 sectors are offered, the key sectors in Montpellier: building, climatic engineering, trade, car and communication networks. The unemployed can reach some training free of charge. Afpa also facilitates the relationship with some companies. The trainings can be sponsored for the employees, throughout the year, by the individual leave training.

Teaching

Language Lessons

■ **VICTORIA'S ENGLISH CENTER**
470, rue Léon-Blum
✆ + 33 (0) 4 99 74 22 74
www.anglaismontpellier.fr
Open on Monday from 1 pm to 8 pm; Tuesday to Friday from 8: 30 am to 8 pm; Saturday from 9 am to 1 pm. Annual closing the week between Christmas and the new year and the week of August 15th. Credit card not accepted.

This center was created late 2012 in Montpellier for anyone wishing to learn English or to improve their knowledge at Victoria's English Center, in partnership with Cambridge University. The method combines audiovisual multimedia lockers, exercise, classes and small groups run by english-speaking teachers. Teaching is primarily based on oral with many conversation courses. The timetable is adapted to your schedule. Then, according to your level, this centre will offer a custom-made training to you. The course of this institute are accessible to individuals and employees. The school is an examination center the region fo rTOEIC, Bulats, Cambridge . Tip: The institute offers summer promotions.

Find all our best deals and good addresses on our website www.petitfute.uk.com

Your English courses with Cambridge

Victoria's English Center 470 rue Léon Blum 34000 Montpellier
+33 (0)4 99 74 22 74 • www.victorias.fr

Information – Media

Newspapers

■ LES ANNONCES VERTES
Weekly news
15, rue du Faubourg de Nîmes
✆ + 33 (0) 4 67 60 76 76
www.annoncesvertes.com
audrey.azema@annoncesvertes.com
Publication each week. Rate: €2.50 in the newsagents.
When the good ideas are essential...
In a few years, the newspaper has had the lion's share in the classified ads.
Today, more than 14,000 advertisements are published every week in the 80 pages of the newspaper. Its approach, unlike other media, is to publish the advertisements free but to pay the newspaper.

■ SORTIR À MONTPELLIER
Immeuble el Christina
131, cours des Camisards
✆ + 33 (0) 4 67 61 03 50 /
 + 33 (0) 6 71 65 06 56
www.sortiramontpellier.fr
sortir.montpellier@wanadoo.fr
Publication each week. Free. Also consultable on line.
As its name suggests, this small magazine is there to help you to prepare your trips.
Cinema, shows, concerts, and various evenings, this small mag essentially made of advertisement gives you some restaurants, among which one can easily find 3 or 4 of them that are original.
Publishers indicate a print run of 35,000 copies and 1,200 points of circulation (shops, bakeries, cafés, restaurants, etc.)! This is thirty years that it lasts, and Robert the owner is not ready to stop!

INFORMATION – MEDIA - Newspapers

■ **LE TAFEUR** .... Monthly news
48, cours Gambetta
✆ + 33 (0) 9 50 23 37 81
www.letafeur.com
tafeur@gmail.com
Free semi-monthly. 1000 points of distribution.
Le Tafeur, it is the new born of the association is Tout à Fond, which runs on the in Saint-Jean de Védas an elegant concert hall, tributary of a large shaded courtyard (ideal as from the return of fine weather) and several recording rooms well equipped, on the site. And for good measure, the association decided to produce its magazine that presents every two months, all concerts in the south of France, Perpignan to Nice! The magazine also devotes many pages to the cultural events and regularly offers zooms on local groups, release of albums or movies as well as small special folders, including the new Marseille rock generation.

■ **LAYALINA**
125, avenue Alfred-Sauvy
PÉROLS
✆ + 33 (0) 6 99 56 32 00
www.layalina.fr
marc.brun.redac@wanadoo.fr
Born in Dubai fifteen years ago, *Layalina* cut through a path to Montpellier in 2009. This city magazine, dedicated to the lifestyle, is also played in Béziers, Agde, Nimes and on the coastline héraultais. Throughout the kiosks, it keeps you informed of the agenda of the city and addresses. You will also find the portraits of local personalities and everything that makes the region. *Layalina* is also distributed at all doctors, avocado, hairdressers, and other institutes in 7,000 copies per month.

■ **MIDI GOURMAND**
Mas de Grille
SAINT-JEAN-DE-VÉDAS
✆ + 33 (0) 4 67 07 67 07
www.midigourmand.com
dtradux@midilibre.com
Quarterly – 120 pages – 3,90€.
Midi Gourmand is the quarterly gourmet of the Midi Libre group. The magazine with hints of the South (of France) reveals the talents and culinary traditions of the Languedoc-Roussillon region. Skilfully led by Didier Thomas Radux, throughout the numbers and the articles, you go from the desire to go for a crunch of chocolate to that of strolling in an open-air café or to a gourmet interview... Without forgetting the traditional cooking recipes, from Nîmes to the Cathare country: appetisers with peas, with aubergine roulades, skewers of prawns, cherry soufflé...

■ **TERRE DE VINS**
Le Mas de Grille
SAINT-JEAN-DE-VÉDAS
✆ + 33 (0) 4 67 07 69 01 / + 33 (0) 6 85 61 11 16
www.terredevins.com
1 year of subscription (6 numbers + 2 except series): €29.
Wine, an exceptional product, is treated in these pages with all the luxury that it deserves. It is the upscale magazine of the Midi-Libre group and the Sud-Ouest group, dedicated to the vine-growing. Consecrated from its origins to the wines of the Languedoc-Roussillon region, this beautiful magazine places regional wines under the spotlights. But it has been open for two years to the other regions: Bordelais (the editorial is now located partly in Bordeaux), and all the regions of France. Served by beautiful photos, items tell the men and the ground, and all that concerns wine «On the estates, names, specific information, but also column and address book on the cuisine, the wine tourism... A beautiful window of all the wines of the South.

Radio

■ **RMC**
Zac Peyrière
SAINT-JEAN-DE-VÉDAS
✆ + 33 (0) 4 67 69 51 29
www.rmc.fr
104.3.
RMC Info, it is the radio of the FM generation information. Live talk show, permanent interactivity, etc. With Jean-Jacques Bourdin and Brigitte Lahaie. All the RMC Info programs inform you and give you the floor live. RMC Info is also the n° 1 radio on sports with almost 50hrs on air per week, and shows presented by old celebrities of sport, including Luis Fernandez or Rolland Courbis, or Jean-Michel Larqué, «Jean-Mimi» that prevails in the radio without his former accomplice in philosophical developments of high flight, Thierry Rolland.

■ **RTS FM**
49, rue des Cormorans
SÈTE
✆ + 33 (0) 4 99 57 22 22
www.rtsfm.com
info@rtsfm.com
Montpellier, Sète, Lunel: 106.5; Nimes: 106.6; Avignon: 106.7.
First independent radio of Languedoc-Roussillon, created in 1983 by Gerard and Madeleine Delacoux. The news and the weather are focused on the region. You can listen to it everywhere in the Languedoc-Roussillon region, Vaucluse, and on the Internet of course. Find tips, and music programming mainly facing an audience of young adults. Daily games and gain gifts, listen to the news, and play back many programs thanks to the podcasts.

**Find all our best deals and good addresses
on our website www.petitfute.uk.com**

Real Estate

Real Estate Agencies

■ **AGENCE CORUM IMMOBILIER**
15, rue du Faubourg de Nîmes
✆ + 33 (0) 4 67 79 39 40
www.corum-immobilier-montpellier.fr

The Corum Immobilier Agency has been part of these agencies of regional identity for over thirty years; it offers its services in the fields of the purchase, sale and the rental management of the real estates, to individuals, companies including the sales persons. Thanks to their technical, financial, tax and judicial skills, the team of the Agence Corum Immobilier represents the qualified professionals to conclude your project. Their advices are customised and they take care of all types of rentals and real estate management.

Added to Montpellier, the agency exclusively covers the geographical areas of Frontignan, Grabels and Le Crès. In one word, it is the assurance to find happiness in Languedoc-Roussillon.

■ **IMMOBIS**
7, boulevard Sarrail
✆ + 33 (0) 4 67 60 31 60
www.immobis.com
immobis@immobis.fr

Immobis, which has several locations in Montpellier, was to become one of the leading real estate transaction and rental since 1981.

The main agency in place de la Comédie covers the Montpellier area and also the department. The catalog of transactions and leasing is particularly well supplied: studios, apartments, town and countryside houses. The highlights of the agency: a welcoming real estate agents working in true professionalism and know of the sector perfectly. Immobis ensures both the management of your property and the search for tenants.

REAL ESTATE - Real Estate Agencies

MANAGEMENT - SALES - RENTALS

YORICK AND GEORGINA
WELCOME YOU AT

Tel.	+33 (0)4 34 66 69 08
Port.	+33 (0)6 61 15 69 08
	+33 (0)6 65 18 19 29
Fax.	+33 (0)4 67 67 14 58

Résidence Parc Domitia
166, rue Jean Thuile
34090 MONTPELLIER
www.yorickimmo.com

■ **GALERIE GREGOIRE**
15, rue Foch
✆ + 33 (0) 4 67 66 00 79
www.galerie-immobilier.com
Open Monday to Friday from 9am to 12.15pm and from 2pm to 6.30pm.
Galerie Grégoire is the oldest of the real estate agencies of the city of Montpellier. It opened in the Foch Street in 1926. Its manager, Patrick Boyer, offers a fine selection of apartments in downtown, especially in the Ecusson. It must be said that the speciality of the agency goes from the bourgeois apartment to the accommodation in mansions. The Galerie Grégoire also covers the area of faculties and the northern Montpellier district with goods from studios to prestigious apartments.

■ **YORICK IMMOBILIER**
166, rue Jean-Thuile
Résidence Parc Domitia
✆ + 33 (0) 4 34 66 69 08 / + 33 (0) 6 61 15 69 08 / + 33 (0) 6 65 18 19 29
www.yorickimmo.com
contact@yorickimmo.com
The specialist in Montpellier city and villages, the agency run by Yorick Rotombe is located in the Aiguelongue district. After having taken an appointment, you will enjoy the experience of this Fnaim certified real estate agent for lease, the sale or the purchase of group and individual houses. He will be able to find in Montpellier the rare gem, but also in the towns of the centre and the east of Herault. For business people, no worries, he will find the required premises and leasehold. You can also leave your good to this agency ensuring its management from the car park to the villa.

General Manager

■ **CORUM IMMOBILIER**
15, rue du Faubourg de Nîmes
✆ + 33 (0) 4 67 79 39 40
www.corumimmobilier.com
montpellier@corumimmobilier.com
Open Monday to Thursday from 9 am to 12 pm and from 2 pm to 5: 30 pm; Friday from 9 am to 12 pm and from 2 pm to 5 pm.
Corum Immobilier has been a specialist in the management of properties and leasing for over 30 years now. It is a family business with Dolores Chartier in charge of management and trustees, and her son Roger in charge of transactions. A park of 500 apartments is available each year at the best price. It is a reference address in property business in Montpellier.

Wedding & Receptions

Wedding Receptions

■ **CLOS DE L'HIRONDELLE**
48, rue Ferdinand-Barre
✆ + 33 (0) 4 67 65 48 02
www.cabiron.com
Open all year.
This former cellar with exposed stonework, domaine du traiteur Cabiron turns into a reception room on request. The spacious dining room accommodates up to 140 people, possibly complemented by two others which can hold 70 people also. Le Clos also offers a shaded terrace and a large private parking. Stronghold of the caterer, you will have his services for the reception.

Equipment Rental

■ **AD SUD RECEPTION**
1, ZA Les Baronnes - PRADES-LE-LEZ
✆ + 33 (0) 4 67 59 71 26 / + 33 (0) 6 09 24 00 98
www.adsudreception.com
With 30 years of experience, just know that AD Sud Réception knows much on the installation of tents. The choice is huge, the company offers about ten tents and different roofs, to what it should added the wall and floor panelling. Once the structure chosen, you must furnish the interior with a dance floor, shrubs, tables, chairs... All these takes much time, but the result is wonderful. AD Sud Reception takes care of everything, from assembling to the disassembling of the structures. And all this with quality and good mood.

Animation – Show

■ **INNO VENTS**
4, rue des Tamaris
CASTELNAU-LE-LEZ
✆ + 33 (0) 6 63 64 24 96
www.innov-ents.com
philippe.fabre@innov-ents.com
Rates in function, on request.
Open communication with a touch of originality and spontaneity; that is the simple principle of Inno vents. It is a matter of immortalizing an event of great importance through snapping your hosts and integrating them into an original communication support, DVD or interactive map, so that you can be remembered! A good idea to remember a wedding!

■ **ARTISHOW**
8, rue du Couchant
LE CRÈS
✆ + 33 (0) 4 67 72 53 88
www.artishow.biz
compagnie.artishow@yahoo.fr
For more than ten years, Bruno Fit organises shows for individuals and professionals, adults and children. Artishow organises great entertainment of 10 to 5000 people. Between shows, performances and writings of sketches, Bruno plays with humour that will make children and adults roll around the floor laughing.
Its services are just as different as one another: clown, Père Noël (father christmas) evening, puppets, magic, fakir... An original place for your children's birthday party.

Business Services

■ **COPIDOC**
56, avenue Charles-Flahault
✆ + 33 (0) 4 67 63 53 00
www.copidoc.net
Open Monday to Thursday from 9am to 7pm; Friday from 9am to 6pm.
The brand has two shops and offers a range of services. Photocopies and scanning of course, but also run print of maps, of posters, creations of posters, of inserts and flyers, and even shaping and binding. The teams are dynamic and friendly and the equipment of good quality. Y ou will also be able to connect to the Internet and send faxes. The shops are of easy access and car park reserved for guests awaits you opposite each entrance.

BUSINESS SERVICES

■ NET OFFICE
9, rue de Verdun
✆ + 33 (0) 4 67 06 90 21
Open all year. Monday to Saturday from 10am to 11pm; Sunday from 2pm to 11pm.
Much more than a simple Internet cafe, the shop located steps from the Comedy is a real secretarial with all its facilities – computer, binder, printing, scanner -, and also phone booths. More: keyboards «qwerty», in English for tourists from across the channel!

■ REPAR-ORDI
25, avenue Georges Clemenceau
✆ + 33 (0) 9 65 22 17 66
Open Monday to Saturday from 9.30am to 1.30pm. Quotation: €25, offered if repair.
If the screen of your Iphone is broken, your computer becomes slow, you have trown coffee on your laptop... No panic Repar-ordi is there for you! Recently on Montpellier, this new computer towing service (that is mobile) gives a second life to your computer equipment and very quickly. It takes 2 hours to change the screen of your mobile phone. Repar'ordi also offers the recovery of your data on USB key and even the «white room» protection! In the shop, you will find second-handed equipment for sale

■ STYLOGRAF
34 bis, rue de l'Université
✆ + 33 (0) 4 67 60 91 60
www.stylograf.fr
info@stylograf.fr
Open Monday to Friday from 9am to 6.30pm; Saturday from 9am to 12.30pm and from 2pm to 6pm. Copy black and white: average price enters €0.03 and from €0.10; laser copy color: from €0.14 to €1.20; 1000 flyers n& B, €14.16.
It is now 22 years that Stylograf deals with copying, printing and binding your documents.
It stock was recently renewed and the latest printers will allow you to enjoy an optimum level of quality. After the latter acquisitions, the printing capacity is now more than 12,000 pages/hr for black and white and 7,000 pages/hr for the colour... Suffice to say that you will not wait long. Other amenities: production of flyers, posters, scanners and printing on t-shirts. Note: there are computers to print yourself.

Tours – Points of Interest

Tourist Offices ➔	98
Guided Tours ➔	98
Monuments & Buildings ➔	102
Religious Buildings ➔	104
Museums ➔	105
Urban Sites ➔	107
Parks & Gardens ➔	108
Nature Sites ➔	110
Discovery Sites ➔	112
Theme Parks ➔	113
Animal Parks – Aquariums ➔	113

Tourist Offices

■ **TOURISM OF CARNON**
Rue du Levant
CARNON
✆ +33 (0) 4 67 50 51 15
www.carnontourisme.com
tourisme@mauguio-carnon.com
Low season: open Monday to Friday from 9 am to 12: 30 pm and from 1: 30 pm to 5 pm; Saturday from 9 am to 1 pm. High season: every day from 9 am to 6: 30 pm.
In addition to the usual amenities, this office offers many tourist services. Some are free of charge, by the way: guided walks on the banks of the Or pond to explore the fauna and flora of the lagoon, every thursday; also, for children, young discoverers game, a hunting for treasures in the city, on wednesdays morning.
Charged activities: Stand up paddle (€10 per hour of initiation), bike rental (€6 half – day), walks in gastropod (€35 per hour); the new feature includes the possibility of hiring a catamaran for a day, for big game fishing or balades.

Guided Tours

■ **TOURS OF THE TOURIST OFFICE**
30, allée de Lattre de Tassigny
✆ +33 (0) 4 67 60 60 60
www.ot-montpellier.fr
contact@ot-montpellier.fr
From €8. To consult the list of the visits, go on the site: www.ot-montpellier.fr.
As for guided tours, the tourist office of Montpellier offers an impressive range of circuits that address a range of varied themes. Apart from the quality of the explanations, the advantage is to visit mansions or inaccessible unaccompanied tourist attractions. This is particularly the case of Fessiers medieval. There is also a pell-mell, a vineyard tour in the municipalities of the metropolitan area, the discovery of medicine in Montpellier, mansions, the historic development of Montpellier through its city center, the Jardin des Plantes, Saint-Pierre Cathedral, Montpellier «music lover» Lez bike tours ... The list is long and everyone is benefiting. The number of participants at each visit is limited and it is advisable to book, especially in high season.

■ **HISTORIC HEART TO THE MODERN DISTRICTS – GUIDED TOUR OF MONTPELLIER**
Office de tourisme de Montpellier
30, allée Jean-De-Lattre-de-Tassigny
✆ +33 (0) 4 67 60 60 60

Montpellier & Street Art

The *Street art* or urban art is the artistic movement that climbs. It came from Gaffiti; it takes very different forms now (collages, stencils, drawings and installations) and invites even the most sophisticated New York art centers, Paris or Berlin.
Montpellier has always been ahead of this and now poses as the capital of this small French discipline, with a national reputation. There have even been ephemeral projects of houses Customised from floor to ceiling by artists («Parcour» and in January 2014, «The FMR Project «), which attracted thousands of visitors and of which even the national press has repeated. If the city has galleries (Montana, At Down, The Mat ...) entirely dedicated to this discipline, the urban art also remains there in its place of origin, namely the street. There are indeed hundreds small creations in the city center. Collages, paintings, you just have to look up in the badge to discover and be surprised! Jonny Style Zoulette by passing through AI or BMX, many local and anonymous artists, regularly cover the walls of varied works, funny, surprising, sometimes involved. Residents and the municipality, aware of this added artistic value, let go with a smile. Walking through the old stone mansion, we can discover another Montpellier, that of the twenty-first century, full of color and life! You just take the time to look around you and it is really worth it.

GUIDED TOURS

www.ot-montpellier.fr
contact@ot-montpellier.fr
From November 1st, 2013 to January 1st, 2016.
To combine business with pleasure, here is an urban promenade, as well as contribute to your daily physical training, invites you to enrich your knowledge about Montpellier. Thus, after passing through the Arc de Triomphe, the mikvah and mansions during the historic center, your tour guide takes you successively to Antigone district of neoclassical and Port Marianne. Depending on your stride, neighborhoods with modern and futuristic architecture reflect the ambition of developing the gifted one.
▶ **Price:** at €12 per adult, at €10 discounted rates (6 years old children for 18 years, pupils, students, retirees and more than 60 years, the unemployed and owners of a disabilty card).
▶ **Duration:** 2hours.
▶ **difficulty:** easy.
▶ **Other practical information:** reservations are required from the Tourist Office of Montpellier, in front of which you can visit 10 minutes before departure (comedy square). minimum 8 participants.

■ **A TREASURE HUNT «DISCOVERING MONTPELLIER»**
Office de tourisme de Montpellier
30, allée Jean-De-Lattre-de-Tassigny
✆ **+33 (0) 4 67 60 60 60**
www.ot-montpellier.fr
contact@ot-montpellier.fr
From November 1st, 2013 to January 1st, 2016.
Who says city walks tires children? If you feared to a cretain point that your little wolves are bored to visit monuments and listen to the explanations of a guide, that's undoubtedly the activity you need: the hunt! Provided their discovery is book and accompanied by a guide from the tourist office, children workout for two hours as a historical investigator. Traditional urban tour then takes a different turn ... Both sporty, fun and educational, track games definitely good for perfect family outing!
▶ **Single price:** €15 package for 1 or 2 children + 1 accompanying adult.
▶ **Duration:** 2hours.
▶ **Difficulty:** easy.
▶ **Other practical information:** a treasure hunt for children from 7 to 11 years; reservations are required from the Tourist Office of Montpellier, in front of which you have an appointment 10 minutes before departure (place de la Comédie). At the beginning of the visit, the brochure *Jeu de piste (Game track)* will be given to children. minimum 8 participants.

■ **MONTPELLIER BY BIKE**
Office de tourisme de Montpellier
30, allée Jean-De-Lattre-de-Tassigny
✆ **+33 (0) 4 67 60 60 60**
www.ot-montpellier.fr
contact@ot-montpellier.fr
From November 1st, 2013 to January 1st, 2016.
Guests who move daily by car or public transportation, did you know that Montpellier had a cycling network of almost 150 km?

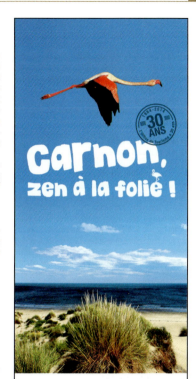

Seven kilometers of beaches, dunes and fine sand which are streched towards the sea between the vast Etang de l'Or and the Mediterranee.
Ideal for family holidays.
Welcome to Mauguio Carnon by the sea!

Information at the Tourist Office:
+33 (0)4 67 50 51 15
www.carnontourisme.com

Forget the old customs and get started! Cheaper, less pollutant, quicker during rush hours and especially very pleasant under this beautiful mediterranean sunshine, cycling is an activity of many benefits. You do not have your own bike? Go to one of the 49 automatic Vélomagg' stations and serve yourself: it will cost you only fifty centimetres per hour!
- **Price:** free; Vélomagg': 0.50 €/h.
- **Distance:** cycling network of 150 km.
- **Difficulty:** easy.

■ MONTPELLIER WINE TOURS
92, rue Mathieu Laurens
✆ +33 (0) 6 95 16 25 61
www.montpellierwinetours.com
info@montpellierwinetours.com

Montpellier Wine Tours is a wine tourism agency to discover the wines and vineyards around Montpellier. From this city, the circuits of Montpellier Wine Tours are by the day or half-day and always in small groups of 2 to 8 people for a pleasant and friendly visit. During these tours, visitors can sample wines of selected areas but also meet the winemakers, learn almost everything about the management of vineyards, tasting process and wine making. They are welcomed by winemakers and can visit the cellars of winemaking and aging and walk in the vineyards before moving to vault and tasting. Every day from Monday to Saturday. Rates per person: €65 half day - €95 day, meal option: € 22/ person, transportation, tour and tasting included..

■ «PETIT TRAIN» OF MONTPELLIER
8, rue du Tibidabo
✆ +33 (0) 4 67 66 24 38
www.petit-train-de-montpellier.com
trainmontpellier@aol.com
In front of the florists of the Esplanade

Closed from December to January. Low season: open every day from 11am to 4pm. High season: every day from 10.30am to 6pm. Adult: €7. Child (up to 12 years): €4.

This white train offers a guided tour of the historic center of Montpellier, available in 8 languages. Departure from place de la comedie every 30 minutes in july-august. In 40 minutes, the train crosses comedy square, a few streets from the L'Écusson and marks a stop on the pretty place de la Canourgue. For lovers! Note that the course is very pleasant unless you have difficulties moving, the Ecusson is not very wide.

■ FROM PORT MARIANNE THE «MAISON DE LA NATURE»
www.portmarianne.montpellier.fr

Are you ready to discover the fauna and wild flora of Petite Camargue? Petit Futé offers a really easy bike ride – there are only flat ones – that will lead you in the middle of ponds, to explore the Camargue birds. To make this little excursion, it is preferable that it has not rained the day before. The starting point is the path that follows the river, at the Jacques -Coeur basin in the district of Port Marianne. Heading south along the river to the end of the path. In front of you stands the Marina Port Ariane and its colorful buildings. Take the road on the right, then first one on the left – a driveway lined with palm trees. Cross the bridge over the canal which connects the port and the leisure pool. Continue straight between buildings and go under a wide avenue – Avenue de l' Europe – to arrive at the Jacques – d'Aragon shopping centre. From here, take the direction «Collège Georges Brassens» from which the Maison la Nature is signposted. To get there, it passes through a residential area, then you walk along a canal. Once at the Maison de la Nature, take the bridge – on foot or by bicycle – and follow the path of around 7 kilometers that runs between ponds: it will take you back to the same gateway – authorized access from 9:

The Works Of Art Tour

The Contemporary art lovers will be charmed by this circuit, over the first tram line…
- **Train Station.** The Journey of Sarkis. On the theme of travel, the artist set thirty-two seats on both sides of the palm trees, planted along the way from the tram. Every seat is refered to one of the cultural wonders of the world: Taj Mahal, Sainte-Sophie… The distance from here and Elsewhere is engraved on the seats.
- **Corum station.** Les Allégories d'Allan McCollum. To Admire these sculptures, you will need to get out of the tram and take the monumental staircase leading to the Esplanade. According to the words of the artist, these works are allegories «de la dissolution et de la Renaissance, de la résurrection par la technologie moderne «. For the record, these five damaged statues with farting colours are mouldings of works used by the time and which formerly adorned the gardens of Domaine de la Mosson, one of the most impressive follies, built in Montpellier and of which it remain today almost nothing.
- **Université-des-Sciences station.** Hommage à Confucius, a work of Alain Jacquet. To admire this sculpture called by students and locals la Grande Saucisse or le Donuts, you will have to get around on foot to the faculty of arts and Sciences and the university canteen. This very showy work, a creation of the French sculptor, installed in New York in the years 1960, is a part of the current pop art. Far from the gourmet allusion, it draws its inspiration from the binary system whose father is none other than the famous Confucius.
- **Mosson station.** La Constellation de Chen Zen. This work is relatively far from the others since it is located at the end of the tram, in Mosson. It was designed by the artist for this multicultural neighbourhood. It symbolises the modern «les champs modernes du dialogue et de l'échange fraternel entre les peuples» It is composed of two spherical big plates around which, are arranged seventy chairs of aluminium alloy, copied from the models that were lent by the locals.

GUIDED TOURS

Discovering The River Lez

Duration: 2 hours. Walks are easy. It's impracticable by bike. From the Saint-Lazare station, on the tramway line 2, go down the avenue de la Justice towards Lez. The Walk starts on rue de Ferran, just before the pont de la Concorde that is the connection between Montpellier and Castelnau. You cross the bottom of the park Méric, formerly owned by the family of the painter Frédéric Bazille. After a few hundred meters, take the path on stilts which begins on the right of an imposing plane tree. The view of the old village of Castelnau is worth a look and then you cross an ancient well. Continue by the path along the river and enjoy the pontoons which are installed on the river to take a short break – with a little luck, you will see a cormorant, a kingfisher or a heron. Then A staircase will allows you to reach a panoramic viewpoint on rue de Ferran. Continue on the main road in the same direction, Wood posts shows that the road becomes again accessible to cars, but traffic is low. For a few hundred meters, walk on a paved road, then you cross rue de la Combe-Caude, without taking it, you cross the Domaine de Bergemont on your left. The road climbs up to the Domaine municipal de la Valette. To the left of a large green gate, a door gives access to the Réserve Naturelle du Lez. The path is marked, so it is impossible to get lost! You end up on a large clearing below zoo de Lunaret. Here Le Lez offers some beautiful waterfalls and beautiful lakes. Continuing, the path takes up. You overlook the river by moving on a wooden path on stilts. Then you reach the Domaine d'Agropolis. Continue under a century-old plane trees alley that leads to a former mill, now turned into a canoe base. On your right, you can take a break on the large pebbles beach. Bypass the mill to a gate – which is usually half-opened; enter the park of an old orphanage. Be on your way to the marked path. Tables are set up for a picnic. Still walk a few tens of meters, and you arrive at the end of this walk, on the parking of Agropolis. Just Above, several buses will allow you to return to the city centre.

00 to 16: 30. Here you can enter a protected area, breeding many species of birds. The greatest respect is called for! If you still have time, the Maison de Nature is a permanent exhibition on the site, the observation of a stork's nest filmed live and an observatory.

■ VISITING THE MEDIEVAL CITY
Office de tourisme de Montpellier
30, allée Jean-De-Lattre-de-Tassigny
✆ **+33 (0) 4 67 60 60 60**
www.ot-montpellier.fr
contact@ot-montpellier.fr
From November 1st, 2013 to January 1st, 2016.
The medieval past of Montpellier is difficult at first: no castle, no walls, no moat or remains of drawbridge. However, while digging a little deeper and linger on some architectural details dotted here and there, the doubt disappears. Accompanied by a lecturer guide, you will walk for two hours along the streets and the inner courtyards of the old town, and will soon find traces of medieval hostal and its occupants...
▶ **Price:** €9 per adult, €7 at discounted rates (6 years old children for 18 years, students, students, retirees and more than 60 years, the unemployed and owner of a disabilty card).
▶ **Duration:** 2: 00.
▶ **Difficulty:** easy.
▶ **Other practical information:** reservations are required from the Tourist Office of Montpellier; rendezvous in front of the potters, near the Corum tram station. minimum 8 participants.

■ GUIDED TOUR IN THE HISTORIC CENTER OF MONTPELLIER
Office de tourisme de Montpellier
30, allée Jean-De-Lattre-de-Tassigny
✆ **+33 (0) 4 67 60 60 60**
www.ot-montpellier.fr
contact@ot-montpellier.fr
From November 1st, 2013 to January 1st, 2016.
Two hours of walking and a journey through time, here is a summary of what awaits you in this guided tour of the historic center of Montpellier. Accompanied by an approved lecturer/guide, discover the secrets of the lighthouses monuments in the neighbourhood, usually inaccessible to the public. On the programme of course: Mikvé (Jewish ritual bath), the Arc De Triomphe or mansion classes, all on based on stories and anecdotes that marked the city. In other words, how to exercise while gaining informing!
▶ **Price:** €9 per adult, €7 at discounted rates (6 years old children for 18 years, pupils, students, retirees and more than 60 years, the unemployed and owners of a disabilty card).
▶ **Duration:** 2hours.
▶ **Difficulty:** easy.
▶ **Other practical information:** reservations are required from the Tourist Office of Montpellier, in front of which you take an appointment 10 minutes before departure (place de la Comédie). minimum 8 participants.

■ GUIDED TOUR OF THE MANSIONS OF MONTPELLIER
Office de tourisme de Montpellier
30, allée Jean-De-Lattre-de-Tassigny
✆ **+33 (0) 4 67 60 60 60**
www.ot-montpellier.fr
contact@ot-montpellier.fr
From November 1st, 2013 to January 1st, 2016.
If you live in Montpellier, probably you pass daily in front of these buildings, without taking note of their luxurious façades. Dating from the seventeenth, eighteenth and nineteenth centuries, the mansions bear witness to the architectural evolution and the progressive growth of the city. Today, to tell you their history, to sharpen your look and make you discover their nuances, the Tourist Office offers an interesting program of guided tours. The two hours of walking that await you will be very rewarding...

Monuments & buildings

■ ANCIEN PALAIS DE JUSTICE
Rue Foch
On the site of the former courthouse, the highest point of the city, was in the Middle Ages, the castle of the lords of Montpellier: the Guilhems. It is already on this site that the latter exercised their power at the time. The fortress was destroyed in 1206 to leave room for the royal palace of Aragon that will be completed in 1250. The royal palace underwent important deteriorations during the religious wars. It was partly rebuilt in the seventeenth century to become one of the most beautiful kingdoms. Still rebuilt and enlarged in the middle of the nineteenth century, it has not changed since. Its architecture is characterised by its well-balanced proportions and its main façade with triangular roof, supported by columns with Corinthian capitals. You can admire a fresco of Romus the sculptor here representing «Justice protecting the innocent one and revealing the crime». Its peristyle is decorated with statues of Cambacérès, famous magistrate in Montpellier, and the cardinal of Fleury, minister of Louis XV and native of the region. The new law courts, where the Montpellier magistrates now exercise, is located a few steps away, below the Peyrou promenade: place Pierre-Flotte.

■ AQUEDUC SAINT-CLÉMENT
The Saint-Clément aqueduct was built in the seventeenth century on the plans of engineer H. Pitot in order to facilitate water supply of the city. It stretches over 14 km from the town of Saint-Clément-de-Rivière, north of the town, to the water tower designed by Jean-Antoine Giral at the end of the Peyrou promenade. The last 800 metres that cross the Arcades (below Peyrou) are the most impressive of the structure and are reminiscent of – all things considered – the outline of its Roman ancestor, Pont du Gard. Thanks to this new source of water supply, many fountains, now disappeared were installed at the time (the Pyla Saint-Gély, Faubourg de Lattes, or la Putanelle fountains on the banks of Verdanson). You can also see other parts of this aqueduct in the Croix-Verte neighbourhood in the north (rue de La Croix de Lavit) and the town of Saint-Clément-de-Rivière (boulevard de la Lironde).

■ ARC DE TRIOMPHE
Rue Foch
Free access 24/7 h.
This gate, symbol of power, was built by a Roi Soleil anxious to show his power, at the end of the seventeenth century. It was made as the first of Montpellier in the big national campaign of beautification work in the cities. Designed by the architect François d'Orbay, a pupil of Mansart, this triumphal arch, imitation of Parisian gateway was built on the site of one of the gates of the ancient wall. Some medallions show Louis XIV slaying an eagle (Empire) and a lion (England). More peaceful, a trio of characters symbolises the canal du midi joining the Mediterranean and the Atlantic Ocean. Virgin marble plaques still await the name of the consuls who were unobtrusive during the revolution. At the end of 2003, restoration works returned to the arch all its prestige. The brave, curious, or the sports lovers, can after climbing the 130 steps (in guided tour with the Tourist Office), discover a majestic view of Montpellier and its surroundings.

■ CHÂTEAU DE FLAUGERGUES
1744, avenue Albert-Einstein
✆ +33 (0) 4 99 52 66 37
www.flaugergues.com
visiter@flaugergues.com
Gardens open every day Monday to Saturday from 9 am to 12:30 pm and from 2:30 pm to 7 pm (Sunday and public holidays from June to September). Castle (interior) June, July and September from 2:30 pm to 6:30 pm, except Monday, the rest of the year by appointment. Adult: €9.50 (visit gardens only: €7). Reduced rate: €7. School rate: €4.
Built in the late seventeenth century, Flaugergues is one of the houses called «follies» built in the countryside of montpellier with Grammont cable. Passed down from generation to generation, Flaugergues today bears witness to the life of the montpelliérains notable of the time. The gardens, around the castle, restored by M. and Mme Colbert, stretch over five acres. They are five places: the terrace in front of the castle which has a unique, bare and classic look, on the floor terrace which is very symbolic of this place and was a model in the 18th century with many other floors of the region, the large alley, the said olive trees alley, along the house to the west, is a beautiful view of 400 m surrounded by boxwood and olive trees, in the south-west of the castle is the English garden, a botanical garden, and finally, the vineyards in the east. See, touch, feel, such are the priorities in a stunning garden of 5 senses. A restaurant was recently opened in this exceptional settings, le Folia (menu €17 to €19.70).

MONUMENTS & BUILDINGS

■ LE CORUM
Esplanade Charles-De-Gaulle
✆ +33 (0) 4 67 61 67 61
www.enjoy-montpellier.com
corum@enjoy-montpellier.com
Tram lines 1 and 2. Le Corum stop

The entrance to the Corum conference centre and opera is done from the charles-de-gaulle Esplanade. However, it is from the road of Nîmes, below, that this building of about fifty metres high with bunker look, dressed with pink granite, has to be admired or at least observed, according to the taste of each. Opened in 1990, it is the work of the architect Claude Vasconi. If its external appearance is contested, the interior architecture is generally quite popular, especially for work on the remarkable light and an opera room of rare acoustic quality. When you enter the depths, you have the impression to enter a maze inspired by the Cretan architecture of Knossos or Phaestos. Its roof accessible to tourists from the Esplanade offers stunning views of the north of the city and the hinterland.

■ FACULTE DE MEDECINE
Rue de l'Ecole-de-Médecine

The building that houses the faculty of medicine today was built in 1364 on the request of pope Urbain V, to accommodate the Saint-Benoît and Saint-Germain monastery. It belonged to the same complex as the Saint-Pierre cathedral. It is only since 1795 the the faculty occupies these buildings. However, the lesson in medicine and law begun much earlier; as from the twelfth century. They were held then in an informal way. Pope Nicholas IV awarded the Masters and students of the city the title of university in canon and civil law, medicine and arts, on October 26th, 1289. The University of Montpellier is therefore one of the oldest in the western world. The base of science was then the reading and the comments of Canon d'Avicenne, philosophical doctor of the tenth Century. The classes were sometimes of theology, astrology and even magic! It is the first university in France to have had the authorisation, in 1366, to dissect corpses. It had among its students, personalities as famous as Nostradamus or Rabelais, which you can admire the signature in a register.

■ HOTEL HAGUENOT
3, rue Clapiès
✆ +33 (0) 4 67 92 25 62 / +33 (0) 6 19 07 27 58
www.hotelhaguenot.fr
hotelhaguenot@orange.fr

Open all year. For the individual ones: from January to July included, and from September to December included (by appointment). Groups: all year by appointment. Free for under 18-year-olds (and for the disabled people). Adult: €7. Rental of the hotel for receptions between €1000 and €4000. Guided tour (from 45 to 60 minutes – house and garden).

Built by Jean-Antoine Giral for Professor Henri Haguenot (1760), this madness (include house in the woods, in the leaves) is in a garden with fountains, a real haven of greenery and freshness, some steps away from the Ecusson. The house on one level testifies a classic architecture decorated with plasterwork (plasterer figures) typical of the eighteenth century. The hotel welcomes 20 to 120 people inside, in three rooms of 34.36 and 50 m ^{2}; and more than 300 outside, in the more than 2,000 m ^{2} garden. If you are not too many, ask to visit the astronomical terrace, the panorama is exceptional! The place can be entirely or partly rented for a reception in all seasons. An exceptional setting to celebrate a wedding, organise a cocktail evening, a meal or other festivity! Note however that the owners, concerned with not disturbing the neighbours and that the place does not get deteriorated, remain very selective for accepted events. Given the beauty of the place, you can only understand them.

■ MANSIONS

The Ecusson has an impressive number of mansions and sumptuous classic residences, built for the most between the seventeenth and eighteenth century. Hôtel des Trésoriers de la Bourse, Hôtel de Manse, Hôtel de Varennes, Hôtel Sabatier-d'Espeyran, Hôtel de la Vieille Intendance, Saint-Côme Hotel... The list is long. Each of these small palaces is organized around one or several courtyards that often hide magnificent examples of the architecture of the time – stairs, ornaments, colonnades... Some are accessible to the public all year round, others are open only during the Heritage Days or tours organised by the tourist Office.

■ MIKVE MEDIEVAL
1, rue de la Barralerie

The mansion houses in the cellars, important relics of a Hebrew religious complex of the twelfth and thirteenth centuries. The Jewish community of Montpellier, made of thousands of people, was, at the time, particularly important. It included property owners, craftsmen, traders and doctors. The only element worth visiting at this Hebrew complex is Mikvé. This Jewish ritual bath allowed ablutions of purification, especially before the Jewish Easter. It is naturally fed by an underground tablecloth. It is composed of a bay with gemeled columns, the capitals decorated with plant that connects to changing cabin and the bath. You can also admire magnificent semi-circular vaults. The synagogue and adjoining rooms, from the same period, make this place a unique heritage in Europe. Owned by the city of Montpellier, Mikvé is visited exclusively for a tour of the Tourist Office.

■ LES TROIS GRACES
Place de la Comédie

Certainly the most symbolic monument of the city, the Trois Graces were carved by Etienne Antoine in 1776. These pretty Montpellier statues, a little round with eyes of our contemporary but canons of beauty in their time, are the gods of Joy, Charm and Beauty, daughters of Zeus. Initially housed at the place de la Canourgue, then place du Marché-aux-Fleurs, it is in 1797 that the setting of place de la Comedie was chosen to them. Those you can admire outside today are actually only moulding. The original ones are preserved in the theatre to protect them from bad weather and unpatriotic degradation. The Trois Grâces are not climbed!

■ FORTIFICATIONS

The Pins tower, the tower of Babote and the porte de Blanquière are the unique testimonies of the fortifications that protected the town from the twelfth century.

The Pins tower, opposite the jardin des plantes, rises 23 metres high. It owes its name to the two pines which grew at its summit. It was used as a refuge for Protestants during the sixteenth century, then a prison during the French Revolution. It welcomes archives of the city today. At the end of boulevard du Jeu-de-Paume, the tower of Babote was one of the gates to enter the city.
Only the ground floor is original. An observatory was installed in the eighteenth century by the royal Academy of Sciences. This is where Lenormand would have flown away with an umbrella. Finally, you can admire below rue de l'Université, right next to the Ursulines convent, the Blanquerie portal, or Vieille Porte. Built in the first decade of the thirteenth century, it enabled the city to communicate with the outside and the suburbs.

■ **CHÂTEAU DE CASTRIES**
Rue du Château
CASTRIES
http://www.chateaudecastries.com
The first castle of this very fine estate was built in the eleventh century. The successive buildings will be in the Castries family until the revolution. The castle was bought in the nineteenth century by the second duke of Castries that will restore its glory to it. In 1985, at the death of the last duke of Castries, the castle was bequeathed to the French Academy and then became the property of the Region. The buildings are arranged in a U-shape, around a courtyard. The main body is preceded by a portico where a bust of Louis XIV is set. The French gardens, designed by Le Nôtre, are packed with water features, boxwood floors and even a cave.

Religious Buildings

■ **CATHÉDRALE SAINT-PIERRE**
Place Saint-Pierre ✆ **+33 (0) 4 67 66 04 12**
www.montpellier.fr
Open Sunday to Friday from 9am to 12pm and from 2.30pm to 11am; Saturday from 9am to 6.15pm. Free.
Former chapel of the Benedictines in 1364 built by pope Urbain V, it became Episcopal headquarters in 1536, when the bishopric was transferred from Maguelone to Montpellier. Destroyed during the wars of religion, it was rebuilt in the seventeenth and nineteenth centuries, in several parts contrasting with its austere façade and its porch of the fourteenth century. La Révolution proclaimed it «Temple de la Raison «, like many other churches, before it became a military warehouse. Despite these changes, it still has a monumental painting, «the miracle of Saint-Pierre», which we owe to the Montpellier painter Sébastien Bourdon (seventeenth century). See absolutely the porch; imposing canopy supported by huge circular batteries that made the arms of Urbain V. In its continuation, the faculty of medicine occupies the buildings of the former Benedictine monastery.

■ **LE COUVENT DES URSULINES**
Boulevard Louis-Blanc
This convent was designed by architect Jean Bonnassier in the mid-seventeenth century on request of the Ursulines. During the Revolution, the building is transformed into a prison for women. Acquired by the municipality in the years 1980, it now houses the national choreographic Centre, as well as many shows during the celebrations in summer. Although most rooms are therefore closed to the public, it is however possible to climb the steps to the raised square and, if you can be discreet and not disturb, take a look at the beautiful lobby.

■ **ÉGLISE SAINTE-ANNE**
Rue Sainte-Anne
This church built in the nineteenth century has the distinction of having the highest bell tower of the city. It stands in the middle of the square of the same name, very nice with its cafes and restaurants in the calm. Converted into a cultural centre since the beginning of the year 1990, it now hosts prestigious exhibitions of contemporary art and international artists, whose program is available on the sites of the Tourist Office and the town hall, on which it depends. The entrance of the exhibitions has the distinction of being free.

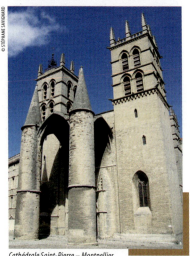
Cathédrale Saint-Pierre – Montpellier.

MUSEUMS

■ **ÉGLISE SAINT-ROCH**
Place Saint-Roch
Open depending on the events (church always in activity). Often open the afternoon.
Built in the nineteenth century in a neo-gothic style, at the Saint-Paul church of which remains the open-air apse, on the same level as the sacristy, the church houses the relics of saint healer of the plague victims, of which it is named. The construction that was to be imposing was financed by a lottery but was never unfinished. The marble statue of the saint who was to decorate the façade stayed at the presbytery.

■ **CATHÉDRALE DE MAGUELONE**
Domaine de Maguelone
VILLENEUVE-LÈS-MAGUELONE
✆ +33 (0) 4 67 50 63 63
www.compagnons-de-maguelone.org
esat@compagnons-de-maguelone.org
Access through Palavas, right bank: off-season free access, in summer, compulsory pay parking. Access through Villeneuve, pay parking in summer.
Open all year. Low season: every day from 9am to 6pm. Parking €4 from beginning of May to mid-September (free in low-season). Guided tour (audio-guide recommended). Shop.
Between the pond of Prévost and the sea, on a small island of vineyards and pine trees, stands the Maguelone cathedral, a Romanesque building that was the seat of the bishopric of Montpellier from the fifth to the eleventh century. The original building was destroyed after the reconquest of Saracens, in the eighth century, and rebuilt at the beginning of the twelfth century. It is from this time that the polygonal apse and the arched apse in half dome originated. From 1158 to 1778, the old nave was replaced by the current barrel vault whose walls are cut into a Shelly limestone. Only embellishments, the tympanum of the western portal is carved in a very pure white marble and represents a Christ in majesty surrounded by the symbols of the evangelists. Recently, the cathedral was decorated with modern stained-glass windows with uncluttered style is suitable for architecture and classical music is experienced there every summin in June. This very calm estate is a protected site and managed by a centre of tour by the work which you will find the shows in the shop (wines) and the shop at the edge of the pond (seafood).

Museums

■ **ESPACE DOMINIQUE BAGOUET**
Esplanade Charles-de-Gaulle
Open Tuesday to Sunday from 10am to 1pm and from 2pm to 6pm.
The square housed the photographic collection reserved since the year 1990 at the popular House. It was renovated in 2012 and is now used to showcase the great regional artistic figures; not shown due to lack of space, the Fabre museum being turned more and more to the international level. The heritage in this area is important and wonderful discoveries are to be made.

■ **INSTITUT DE BOTANIQUE**
163, rue Auguste-Broussonet
✆ +33 (0) 4 99 23 21 82
Visits by appointment.
With its four million samples of rare plants preserved on six floors, this herbarium is unique. The collection began with Charles Flahaut in 1890 and then grew rich. The oldest rooms are perhaps those of the Chirac collection of the seventeenth century, or the famous Delile herbarium brought back during the campaign of Egypt in 1798…
It is true that this place, not really adapted for visit, barely receives a few curious, given that for a few years now, for fire safety reasons, only the small patio is open to the public.

■ **L'HOTEL SABATIER D'ESPEYRAN**
6 bis, rue Montpelliéret
✆ +33 (0) 4 67 14 83 00
www.ot-montpellier.fr
Open Tuesday to Sunday from 2pm to 6pm. Closed on Monday. Open on July 14th and on August 15th. Adult: €4. Reduced rate: €2.50. Family package: €8. Admission tickets to be withdrawn with the Fabre museum.
On the Esplanade, a block from the Fabre museum, the Sabatier d'Espeyran hotel is a museum dedicated to decorative arts of the eighteenth and nineteenth centuries, opened in 2010. Its strong point, the objects and furniture are presented in context in an authentic setting. The mansion, bequeathed by the Sabatier Espeyran family, was restored by the Emmanuel Nebout architecture workshop. Most rooms presented come from the Sabatier Espeyran family; the others are donations of furniture from the antique dealer Jean Pierre Rouayroux. The restoration of the place, faithful, allows you to discover rooms designed like living quarters. The ground floor is devoted to ceramics and silverware, while the first floor reconstructs the apartments of a family in the nineteenth century. As for the second floor, it presents furniture of the eighteenth century such as chests, seats, and baskets. During the visit, a videophone will allow you to get more information on the collection. The tickets are on sale at the reception of the Fabre museum.

MUSÉE ATGER
2, rue de l'Ecole-de-Médecine
✆ +33 (0) 4 34 43 35 81
Closed during school holidays. Open on Monday, Wednesday and Friday from 1.30pm to 5.45pm. Limited schedules, suitable for modification, it is preferable ask for information front. Free.
Hosted by the library of Médecine, this museum is dedicated to the collection of Xavier Atger (1758-1833), passionate of prints and drawings that donated his collection at the university. It has more than a thousand drawings of French, Italian and Flemish schools of the sixteenth, seventeenth, and eighteenth centuries, 5,000 prints and a few paintings. The visit is not of easy access, but deserves some efforts on behalf of lovers of these artistic periods. It is also possible that these huge collections one day join those of the cabinet of drawings of the Fabre museum and the complex has a specific exhibition place, which would make them more reachable.

MUSEE DE L'HISTOIRE DE MONTPELLIER
Place Jean-Jaurès
✆ +33 (0) 4 67 54 33 16
Closed public holidays. Open Tuesday to Sunday from 10.30am to 12pm (last visit at 11: 50) and from 1.30pm to 6pm (last visit at 17: 20). Free for under 26-year-olds. Adult: €3. Group (20 people): €2.
Down the place Jean-Jaures, the Notre-Dame-des-Tables crypt, as old as it is, houses an ultra-modern museum. In the base, the building traces the history of Montpellier through that of the church and uses visual and sound entertainment. Of Romanesque origin, the crypt is made up of the original church Sainte-Marie in the tenth Century. In the twelfth century, a new church was built. It received its name when money changers settled at the foot of its walls. In this small space, where remains only part of the retaining walls and a little pavement, as well as part of the foundations of the tower and the ambulatory of the twelfth and thirteenth centuries, a virtual tour in the past of Montpellier was installed. The vaulted room presents on its part, the recent history of the city and its future evolution. The entire visit is done with the audio helmet, which releases information continuously; it lasts about half an hour.

MUSÉE DU VIEUX MONTPELLIER
Place Pétrarque
✆ +33 (0) 4 67 66 02 94
Open Tuesday to Sunday from 10am to 1pm and from 2pm to 6pm. Free for under 26-year-olds. Adult: €3. Free for over 60-year-olds, unemployed people, etc
Thanks to a single ticket of 3 €, you can visit three museums in Montpellier: the museum of Pharmacie and Chapelle de la Miséricorde, the history museum of Montpellier and the museum of Vieux Montpellier. It contains furniture elements, current objects (currency, clothing, accessories) and decorative arts that recall the history of the town from the middle Ages, birth date of the city, the Empire, via the Renaissance and the Revolution.

MUSÉE FABRE
39, boulevard Bonne-Nouvelle
✆ +33 (0) 4 67 14 83 00
musee.fabre@montpellier-agglo.com
tram
♿ 🧑 🎵 ◆

Closed on January 1st, May 1st, May 8th, November 1st and December 25th. Open Tuesday to Sunday from 10am to 6pm. Free for under 6-year-olds. Adult: €6. Child (from 6 to 18 years old): €4. Ticket family at €12. Tourism label & Disability. Guided tour. Catering facilities. Shop. Activities. Reference library.
The recent renovation and the expansion (800 works over 9,200 m2) of the Fabre museum boosted its visiting. One of the most important collection of France is highlighted here: Flemish, Dutch, Italian, Spanish and French collections represented by the painters of European schools from the sixteenth to the eighteenth century (Zurbaran, Reynolds, Tenier, Veronese...) and French (Greuze, Ingres, Delacroix, Courbet, Bazille...)contemporary ceramics, sculptures, and paintings. The painter Pierre Soulages, who donated part of his work, enjoys a special room. You come regularly to the Museum for the quality of its temporary exhibitions. The Fabre museum is also a modern, pleasant and functional equipment, with new services: reception, bookshop, reference library, changing rooms, cafeteria (entrusted to the Pourcel Brothers)...

MUSÉE LANGUEDOCIEN
7, rue Jacques-Cœur
✆ +33 (0) 4 67 52 93 03
www.musee-languedocien.com
museelanguedocien@wanadoo.fr
Open all year. Low season: Monday to Saturday from 2.30pm to 5.30pm. High season: Monday to Saturday from 3pm to 6pm. High season: From June 15th to September 15th. Adult: €7. Group (30 people): €10. Credit card not accepted. Children welcome. Guided tour (in French and English, €10/pers). Shop. Activities.
The Hotel des Trésoriers de France is set in a former mansion. It has hosted the headquarters of the Société Archéologique de Montpellier (the Archaeological Society of Montpellier) since 1901. The various rich collections present goes from Prehistory to decorative arts of the 19th century and is intended to save the cultural heritage of the town and the region. The magnificent staircase leads the visitor to some twenty period lounges and apartments and to the discovery of popular arts and traditions amongst other features. We therefore feel like walking in the steps of Jacques Coeur who lived in the hotel during the 15th century and in those of Francis I, Henri de Navarre and Louis XIII who apparently also stayed there. Note that there is a «curiosity cabinet» which covers the fundamental influences of Antique civilisations from the Renaissance up to today.

MUSÉE MONTPELLIÉRAIN DE LA PHARMACIE
Faculté de Pharmacie
15, avenue Charles-Flahault
✆ +33 (0) 4 67 54 80 62
Open on Tuesday and Friday from 10am to 12pm. Possibility of guided tour. The restrictive hours leaves little time for the visit. It is a pity for a museum which traces the

history of pharmacy, medicine, surgery and sciences which are listed to it. Numerous objects and documents are exhibited here: pots, herbarium, furniture, models, instruments, and archives, allowing you to imagine this universe in the past. It is the only Pharmacy museum in France of this importance on a university site, ensuring the protection of the pharmaceutical heritage and the memory of its profession.

■ LA PANACEE
14, rue de l'Ecole de Pharmacie
℃ +33 (0) 4 67 34 59 16
Open all year. Free. Children welcome. Guided tour (free). Catering facilities. Shop. Activities.
This place of art and creation commits a dialogue between various disciplines: visual arts, writing and the digital one. Housed in the buildings of the former university of medicine, then alternately the faculty of Pharmacy, the school of Right and the national laboratory of Health in the twentieth century, La Panacée is a real «city of artists», dedicated to contemporary art. In addition to exhibitions, La Panacée organises shows, cycles of conferences, interventions around the visual arts and artistic current practices. The place also hosts artists in residence, and workshops from 28 to 60 m^2.

■ PAVILLON DU MUSÉE FABRE
Esplanade ℃ +33 (0) 4 67 66 13 46
Closed on Monday. Free admission (except exception).
This House with a neo-classical architecture, located between the trees of the Esplanade and the garden of Champ De Mars, has found one of its old names: «Pavillon Populaire», and is now dedicated to photography. It is lively with temporary exhibitions with some coming from the Auer photographic collection; a couple of Swiss patrons, purchased by the City and that makes Montpellier, «the French capital of photography and one of its European capitals».

■ MUSÉE ARCHÉOLOGIQUE HENRI PRADES
390, route de Pérols - LATTES
℃ +33 (0) 4 67 99 77 20
museearcheo.montpellier-agglo.com
Open all year. Monday and Wednesday to Friday from 10am to 12pm and from 1.30pm to 5.30pm; the weekend and public holidays from 2pm to 6pm. closing at 7pm the weekend in the event of exhibition. Adult: €3.50. Child: €2. Group: €3. Temporary exhibitions: €4. Free admission 1st Sunday of each month. Guided tour.
The archaeological museum, located in the former Mas Saint-Sauveur on the edge of the old port, invites you to discover the remains of the Lattara antique. Discovered by Henri Prades in 1963, the Lattes delivered gradually all the civilisations that have succeeded. The museum takes you on a journey through time to research and explore our ancestors. It presents the result of the excavations on 1,000 m^2 divided into three levels: contact with the Etruscan world, a redistribution centre of the Greek trading in Marseillan, the Gallo-Roman conurbation of the city of Nîmes, through a multitude of objects: ceramics, perfectly preserved glass ballot boxes, objects, tools, crockery, jewellery, oil lamps, coins, sculptures, ancient funerary steles... It also allows the public to discover, through its temporary exhibitions, other antique Mediterranean civilisations.

Urban Sites

■ ANTIGONE
Avenue Samuel-de-Champlain
Before the construction of this monumental district, the site was occupied by an important tile factory. Near the current Juvénal bridge, was found the old port of Montpellier was: the Juvénal harbour. Remained in waste for a long time, it is in 1977 that this site was chosen by the city to explore the Antigone operation. On this reserve of 40 acres, the municipality required the Catalan architect Ricardo Bofill to think this area as a real centre, a full-fledged heart, combining accommodation, offices and shops. With its place du Nombre d'Or and its vast perspectives, it was designed in the style of a forum in the neo-classical style. Antigone has several major amenities that is worth a look: the central municipal library of Paul Chemetov and Borja Huidobro and the Olympic pool of Ricardo Bofill.

■ LA PLACE DE LA COMEDIE
Place de la Comédie
Free access 24/7 H (public place).
Ah, the famous place de la comedie! Iconic place of the Montpellier life! Always busy, it is tread by the original Montpellier inhabitants, the newcomers, French and foreign tourists. Wherever you walk in the Ecusson, you will always end up crossing it. La Fontaine des Trois-Grâces is a standard meeting place, at the Œuf – but if, by lowering the eyes, you will notice the oval shape layout that gives it its name. Lined with majestic buildings mostly built in the nineteenth century, it overlooks the beautiful opera in town (hence its name, obviously).
The square is ideal to sit at the terrace of a café during the beautiful days of winter, but can become a real furnace during the summer season. Throughout the year, activities, concerts, markets or even beach volley-ball tournaments hold there! Many street artists from all Europe also go there. One does not guarantee the quality of creations that is more irregular. This place is a place of life and incomparable expression, and that is the most important!

LA RUE DES SŒURS-NOIRES
Free access, 7 days a week.
This small street adjacent to the place Saint-Roch has become an obligatory and fun passage of the pedestrian centre. Its peculiarity, fifty bollards, originally intended to prevent the vehicles from parking that the inhabitants painted with varied and multicoloured patterns. Originally, it was a wild appropriation of public area by the residents. Each person therefore took his bombs and egrets and decorated a bollard according to his inspiration. The municipality, aware of the originality of the concept, decided to keep them. After ten years of good and faithful service, the drawings of the first edition were covered in January 2014 to make way for new patterns, created by local professional artists or by the learners. Between popular, naive or art works, you can see among others pumps on a black background with white peas, faces, abstract patterns, and even a tribute to General Alcazar, a local singer who died in 2013.

LA RUE DU BRAS-DE-FER
Rue du Bras-de-Fer
Many are the steep streets in the heart of the Ecusson. The rue du Bras-de-Fer, which connects the place Castellane and the rue de l'Ancien-Courrier, owes its name to an ancient still visible brand. What it is exceptional about it is that you can admire an arch of the fourteenth century linking the buildings on each side of the street. By carrying on your way to the Grand-Rue, rue Voltaire on the right – towards Saint-Roch – has a similar arch.

Parks & Gardens

DOMAINE DE GRAMMONT
Avenue Albert-Einstein
90 acres of oak forest, copses and flowery meadows make this area one of the biggest in Montpellier. Designed by the city, the Estate is the centre of several activities: theatre of the Treize Vents, festivals, sports complex – football, tennis, fitness trail, skateboard track… -, municipal horticultural centre, equestrian centre, outdoor and leisure centres, etc. In The middle of the park, ideal for family picnics, under the several times centenary cedar, the former monastery of the twelfth century avoids even festival clothes on Saturday, by offering its very capitulary dining area for the marriages of the Montpellier inhabitants. It is also here that took place the biggest open air concerts of Montpellier, with big groups like U2 for example.

DOMAINE DE LAVALETTE
Rue Jean-François-Breton
The territory of this old property is mainly occupied today by the Agropolis centre and its researchers. Some parts of Lavalette are nevertheless open to the public. The visit of this site lasts about good half an hour. The easiest way is to leave your car at the car park, at the avenue d'Agropolis, whose entrance is located opposite the museum of the same name. At the end of the car park, in the opposite direction of the road, is located a path along a tributary of the Lez to the main waterway. Following the path, you cross a thick forest planted with centenary plane trees, cypress bald and holm oaks of imposing sizes. Just before reaching the buildings of an old orphanage, you can admire a beautiful magnolia whose branches of an impressive size fall down on the floor. By skirting round the building, you reach a vast sandy beach which runs along the waterfalls formed by the Lez. The vegetation and the river here are beautiful.

DOMAINE DE MERIC
Rue de Ferran
Open all year. From March 1st to May 31st and from September 1st to October 31st, open from 8am to 8pm. From June 1st to August 31st, open from 8am to 9.30pm. From November 1st to February 28th, open from 8am to 6pm.
Within walking distance of avenue de la Justice-de-Castelnau, this park and its residence, resembling a Tuscan villa, were owned by the family of the Montpellier painter Frédéric Bazille. This estate inspired him of some of the most famous works including La Robe rose, Réunion de famille or the Vue de Castelnau-le-Lez. Today, this green area charms by the quietness that reigns there. At its entrance, the beautiful meadow flowers in spring, the orchard and the proximity of Lez have something which reminds the poppy Fields of Monet… A children play area, an area for dogs and vast areas for the ball games – except in spring, obligatory respect of the meadow -: there really is something for everyone here!

ESPLANADE CHARLES-DE-GAULE
Esplanade Charles-de-Gaulle
Planted with centenary plane trees and with fountains, it hosts during the summer, passers-by seeking a little freshness. Between snack bars and public benches, the Montpellier inhabitants picnic there! Not far from the Fabre museum, a small square of games with extravagant shapes for children, free exhibitions are to be seen in the popular House and the Espace Bagouet and a park with a pond allows you to be at the green for a nap! At the end, the view encompasses the northern districts of the city. Contemporary art enthusiasts will appreciate Les Allégories d'Allan McCollum. This colourful work of art reproduces five life-size mutilated statues, found in the Domaine de la Mosson, the mutilated work itself was covered with silver painting. Smart plan: climb on the roof of Corum

PARKS & GARDENS

to enjoy an exceptional view of the Saint-Loup peak and the Hortus. In summer, it is also the venue of the Estivales every Friday evening. If the place is beautiful and full of life, it unfortunately remains to be avoided after 1 or 2 am: despite the considerable efforts of the municipality, the drug dealers and the homeless persons are numerous there and not always in good shape. But you can get there without any problem during the day and evening, the place is charming.

■ LE JARDIN DE LA REINE
This very beautiful tree-lined garden of 4400 m2, in the extension of the jardin des plantes, had stayed in wildland and was forbidden to the public since too many years. It was bought back from the State by the Montpellier Town Hall at the end of 2013 in order to be more open to the public again. It includes among-others an artificial mountain created in the sixteenth century by Richer de Belleval. Eventually, it is planned to setup a shared vegetable garden as well as disabled access. It is given in state, as it is for the moment only occasionally reachable, but you can find the opening days on the town hall's website and that of the association that fought for its renovation, on www.sauvonslejardindelareine.wordpress.com.

■ JARDIN DES PLANTES
1, boulevard Henri IV
ⓒ +33 (0) 4 67 63 43 22
Open all year. Low season: Tuesday to Sunday from 12pm to 6pm. High season: Tuesday to Sunday from 12pm to 8pm. Visit kitchen garden Tuesday and Thursday, at 1.30pm. Free admission. Guided tour (in French and English for groups of 15 to 30 people, on request written, at least 1 month before the desired date).
It is in a desire to promote health with plants that Henry IV in 1593 entrusted to Pierre Richer de Belleval, teacher in botany and anatomy, the creation of a royal Garden. At the time of its foundation, the jardin des plantes of Montpellier was intended for the cultivation of the simple ones. Throughout times, the garden extended. Boissier of Sauvage built the first tropical greenhouses there and Broussonnet created an orangery there in 1804. On 4.5 acres in size, other facilities allowed the making of an English garden with swimming pools and a botanical institute, a systematic school and a forest school, reserved for students and the researchers. Along the alleys, magic operates between secular trees (Holm oaks of four centuries or the oldest; ginkgo biloba of the hexagon), bamboo forest, or vegetable garden (visit Tuesday and Thursday at 1: 30 pm). Recent works enabled the integration of new trees in this garden: brunge pine, maple with obier flowers, oak of the Canary Islands, palm tree of Mexico...

■ JARDIN DES POTIERS
Rue du Faubourg-de-Nîmes
Free admission.
Just beside Corum, this small planted garden with exotic species – palm trees, pink laurels and cypress – welcomes the remains discovered during the construction of the first tram line. The most important of them, the door of Pila-Saint-Gély, marked the royal entrance of the city during the medieval period, and also the entry point for pilgrims on their way to Saint-Jacques-de-Compostelle. On the ground, the caladons way reproduces the authentic look of Cami Romieu. You will also find in the garden, the foundations of the church of the hospital enclosure around Saint-Esprit founded at the end of the twelfth century. This site was once occupied by workshops of potters, whose ovens were unearthed and whose rooms are exhibited in the column of lifts, giving access to the Esplanade. However, avoid in the evening, the places that are not particularly visited much.

■ JARDIN DU CHAMP-DE-MARS
Boulevard Sarail
Free admission.
Just behind the Charles-De-Gaulle esplanade, the parade ground of the city has given way at the beginning of the twentieth century to a English public park. Designed by Edouard André, also designer of the Buttes-Chaumont in Paris, the Champ-de-Mars garden has in its centre a swimming pool with curved lines in which a plethora of ducks and swans wade. The range of plants represented is extensive and characteristic of the species in vogue at the beginning of the year 1900. Podocarpus, ginkgo, orange trees of Osages, magnolias, cedars, nettle trees and palm trees decorate the blue vast lawns, overcrowded by the Montpellier inhabitants as the first rays of sun show up. The atmosphere is relaxed here, with the students playing the guitar, the workers granting themselves a siesta during their lunch picnic or families strolling. If the place is very pleasant during the day, the Montpellier inhabitants will not advise you to go there in the evening because, despite the efforts of the municipality, this garden is «the hunting ground» of a good number of small drug dealers and the sleeping area of a good number of homeless persons, especially during summer. The atmosphere in the day is fortunately much nicer.

■ JARDIN MEDIEVAL
Rue de l'Aigrefeuille
Free admission.
In addition to the untouched green area that it offers to the residents of the neighbourhood, this nice garden of 740 m² has the distinction of being made up of patches of medicinal plants. It was designed in tribute to private gardens of herbs that existed in the Ecusson, and with the tradition of the teaching of plants at the University of Montpellier from the fifteenth century. The many fragrant and medicinal plants are arranged according to the sun and remote regions, and are surrounded by small boxwood banks. The garden offers a high terrace to relax, and a fine example of medieval renovated vaults.

■ JARDINS DU PEYROU
Boulevard Louis-Valleton
Free admission.
This promenade of 3 acres at the gates of the old town is one of the symbolic monuments of Montpellier. Built starting from 1689 and especially from 1766 to 1777 per J.- A. Giral and J. Donnat, the Jardins du Peyrou are characterised by their perspectives and their straight routes, highlighted by plantations of trees, initially elms, now replaced by plane trees. At its centre, the square has an equestrian statue of Louis XIV. The hexagonal water tower, built at the end of the esplanade, is the point of arrival from the Saint-Clément aqueduct.

Below, there are long shaded paths with pools and magnolias, close to where the Montpellier inhabitants like to sit immediately the sunny days arrive. The royal edicts of 1775 and 1779 have limited the height of buildings around the square, thus maintaining a breathtaking view of the surroundings, the Saint-Loup peak in the massif of la Gardiole. You can also walk without twisting your ankles since the paths were covered with sand. Since September 2012, a market with antique is also held there on Sundays from 7: 30 am to 2: 30 pm (see section « Dimanches du Peyrou «).

■ SQUARE PLANCHON
Rue de la République
Free admission.

This small park facing the Saint-Roch station was in 1858 designed by the Bühler brothers, and was restored during the construction of the first tram line. It is a pleasant place to refresh in summer while waiting for your train, your bus or tram. It is planted with exotic essences, including the ginkgo biloba, the chestnut tree, the maple, the liquidambar, the Lebanon cedar, there are even a few palm trees and some bamboos.

The curiosity of this garden is the imposing mossy island that adorns the pond. It was in its creation a small rock of about fifty inches, which in the course of time was enriched with limestone and moss, to give this huge aggregate. As for the rue Maguelone, the park welcomes the bust of the scholar Emile Planchon – 1823-1888 -, in tribute to part that he played in the fight against phylloxera, by the introduction of American vines in the nineteenth century.

On the way, note that the character, at the foot of the bust that pays tribute to Jules Planchon, is represented in the features of the famous Montpellier painter Frédéric Bazille, who was a model to the sculptor. Do not come however to wander at night, the station is not of good reputation.

■ DOMAINE DE RESTINCLIERES
Maison Départementale de l'Environnement
RD17
PRADES-LE-LEZ
✆ +33 (0) 4 99 62 09 40
mde34@cg34.fr

The estate is open 24/24 and 7 days a week. House of the biodiversity open Monday to Sunday, from 2pm to 5.30pm in winter, from 2.30pm to 6pm in summer. Free admission. Closed public holidays.

This beautiful and large park of 215 hectares, located between Prades and Saint-Mathieu-de-Tréviers, houses a lovely southern residence and its French gardens, seat of the Maison départementale de l'Environnement. This year, it offers fun exhibitions on the biodiversity, and what is done on the international level to protect it (second half of 2013). The originality of the garden of Restinclières lies in its setting in several terraces due to the slope of the land. About fifty species of trees are present, including the magnolia or the bald cypress. The surrounding area is ideal for walks – on foot, on horseback or mountain bike – or for a picnic between the Lez and the Lirou course. Playgrounds, a discovery path and marked out hiking trails complete the amenities.

■ PARC DU TERRAL
Domaine du Terral
SAINT-JEAN-DE-VÉDAS
✆ +33 (0) 4 67 13 82 31
www.saintjeandevedas.fr

Closed in August. From March 1st to October 31st, open Wednesday, public holidays and school holidays, from 1.30pm to 5.30pm (weekend from 1.30pm to 6pm). From November 1st to February 28th, open Wednesday, weekend, public holidays and school holidays, from 1pm to 5pm.

Nature Sites

■ BOIS DE MONTMAUR
Chemin du Réservoir-de-Barre
Closed grids the night. Free admission.

Not far from the Lunaret zoo , the Montmaur woods is a 30 acre park crossed by a network of paths that go up and down, under a Mediterranean vegetation mainly planted with pines, cypress trees and oleanders. The site, particularly popular with joggers and lovers of its health course, is also a nice place to relax and walk.

The park is equipped with tables to picnic and a bowling alley. Our advice if you are with the family: avoid however the too remote little pathways, which provide a pull area known by the local gay population, and where sometimes you are likely to certainly come across fun activities but very hot...

■ GROTTE DES DEMOISELLES
RD986/108e
SAINT-BAUZILLE-DE-PUTOIS
✆ +33 (0) 4 67 73 70 02
www.demoiselles.com

Open all year. Flexible schedule depending on the seasons. Free for under 3-year-olds. Adult: €9.50. Child (from 3 to

5 years old): €1.50 (6 to 11 years: €6.50; from 12 to 17 years old: €7.50). Reduced: €8. Guided tour (almost every hour. Audioguides in three languages). Catering facilities (salads, sandwiches, pizzas, ices, etc). Shop.
These «fairies» which peasants believed to see when they dared to approach the chasm were none other than the draped white calcite stalactites. You will appreciate the beauty and the grandeur of the reception building, perfectly integrated into the cliff and the ascent by funicular. During a visit of 1 hour 10 minutes, you happily discover a decor sculpted by water in this cave of the Demoiselles. In the heart of the «great organ», under a «canopy», the centrepiece is an incomparable stalagmite named «la Vierge et l'Enfant», because of its ghostly figure and its whiteness. Thanks to a clever tracking balcony, you can explore and enjoy it in all its aspects. Its dimensions are impressive: 52 m high, 80 m wide and 120 m in length! In order not to shiver, come along with your wool: the cave maintains a temperature of 14 degrees whether summer or winter.

■ **GROTTE DE CLAMOUSE**
Route de Saint-Guilhem-le-Désert
SAINT-JEAN-DE-FOS
✆ **+33 (0) 4 67 57 71 05**
www.grottedeclamouse.com
clamouse@gmail.com
Closed from November 15th to February 8th. Low season: open every day 10.30am to 16: 20. High season: every day of 10.30am at 17: 20. In July and August, until 18: 20. Free for under 4-year-olds. Adult: €9.50. Child (from 4 to 12 years old): €5.50. Group 30 people: €5.70. Teenager (15 to 18 years) and reduced rates (students, unemployed): €8. Holiday voucher. Guided tour. Catering facilities. Shop. Entertainment. Games for children. Wifi access.

Twenty minutes away from Montpellier, in the heart of Grand Site de France «St Guilhem-le-Désert/Gorges de l'Hérault», Clamouse is located beside the road, not far from Aniane. The cave owes its fame to the richness and diversity of its concretions: white corridor, wonderful aragonite crystals similar to sea urchins, majestic organ cases and gigantic meduse occupy this underground world. Halfway, a surprise awaits you, the new show «, Magnificat poem of Clamouse,» sung by the big Italian soloists «Sei Voci» accompanied by the organ and a harp. These true drops of water opera will delight you. Before entering this cave with wonders, a 7 minutes film will give you the keys to understand the geological history of the cave and its old stalactites of over a million years. Since 2005, Clamouse is classified «scientific and picturesque site» by the ministry of Ecology and Sustainable Development. To protect this natural heritage, Clamouse in 2010 became an eco-responsible site: it is the first tourist cave fully equipped with LED lamps, a pioneer operation! Tip: to avoid the queue and enjoy a discount of about 1 € per ticket, book your place on their website. Cover up, because the tour lasts 1hr15, and underground, the temperature ranges between 16 and 17 degrees …

Discovery Sites

■ LE MIKVE
1, rue de la Barralerie
✆ +33 (0) 4 67 60 60 60
Possible visit in the setting of the guided tours organized by the Tourist Office (days and flexible schedules, on request. The mikveh, Jewish ritual bath dating from the thirteenth century is powered by a groundwater and rainwater; it was frequented by women. Rediscovered in 1980, it shows the presence of the Jewish community, based in Montpellier in the twelfth century. Jews have also been among the most illustrious teachers of the Faculty of Medicine of Montpellier in the Middle Ages, and have contributed to its development. The visit leads in this underground place, a quiet area, which is important for its originality and the story it recalls.

■ PLANETARIUM GALILÉE
100, allée Ulysse
Odysseum
✆ +33 (0) 4 67 13 26 26
www.planetarium-galilee.com
planetarium@montpellier-agglo.com

Open all year. Wednesday, Saturday and Sunday from 1.30pm to 6.30pm. Open during school holidays Monday to Sunday from 1.30pm to 6.30pm and until at 9pm Saturday. Free for under 12-year-olds. Adult: €6.30. Child (from 12 to 18 years old): €5.30. Tourism label & Disability. Guided tour. Located in the heart of Odysseum, the Galilée planetarium is a theatre of stars where one can dream, observe and understand the stellar world. Behind its curved glass facade that invites to an intersidereal trip, you will discover the mysterious stones, the giant cross word of stars, the wall of the constellations, the solar system, the asteroids floating in space, a scale of the moon, meteorites beached on the floor... The shows, that last for about 45 minutes are fun and educational with beautiful images and you can even ask questions to a scientific mediator.
Don't hesitate to renew the experience, the shows are renewed regularly, in an elegant room show of 156 seats topped by a screen in the shape of half sphere that looks strange but pleasant with a feeling of being immersed in the image.

■ SERRE AMAZONIENNE
✆ +33 (0) 4 67 54 45 23
www.zoo.montpellier.fr

Low season: open Tuesday to Sunday from 9am to 5pm. High season: Tuesday to Sunday from 10am to 6.30pm. Free for under 6-year-olds. Adult: €6.50. Child (from 6 to 12 years old): €3. Disabled access. Guided tour (audio-guide: €1). Montpellier got itself a corner of the Amazon, with the greenhouse, located inside the Lunaret Zoo (which remains open access). Now the public can, starting from the mouth of the Amazon, explore the mangrove where caimans, anacondas and piranhas live, the flooded forest with monkeys tamarins and sakis, the dense forest that contains the anteater and ocelot, forest mountain and its permanent fog (remarkably restored). During an artificial storm, the visitor takes refuge in a cave which houses bats, armadillos and sloths, and then fly over the treetops (canopy) on a bridge before heading down to the marshy plain with its colorful birds.

■ MAISON DE LA NATURE
Chemin des Etangs
LATTES
✆ +33 (0) 4 67 22 12 44
www.ville-lattes.fr/nature.html
nature@ville-lattes.fr

Low season: open on Tuesday, Wednesday and Friday to Sunday from 2pm to 6pm. High season: Tuesday, Wednesday and Friday to Sunday from 9am to 12pm and from 4pm to 8pm. Free. Dogs prohibited in certain sectors of the reserve. On the Lattes, the Maison de la nature is at the entrance of the Méjean reserve. It offers exhibitions and information on the biodiversity. Here, you can stroll through 465 acres of untouched nature, around the Étang du Méjean. The opportunity to observe flamingos fishing shrimp in the lagoon behind a furnished observation point. Various types of waders also live here: storks, nestled without fear of walkers and clap above your heads, the crest or herons. The maison de la nature organises guided tours on request, as well as activities for children occasionally. Part of the trails, open 9 am to 6 pm, was designed so that the physically disabled can reach the reserve. Admission is free. Caution: some days, bicycles are prohibited, in favour of horses.

Find all our best deals and good addresses on our website www.petitfute.uk.com

Theme parks

■ **LASER QUEST**
130, rue Emile Julien
✆ +33 (0) 9 72 43 24 96
www.laserquest34.com
Open all year. Tuesday to Sunday from 2pm to 10pm. Adult: €8. Children welcome. Catering facilities.

In the darkness of a large maze, armed with a laser gun come to challenge friends for a fight.
On 400 m² and three levels, many places to hide and watch for your opponent in order to draw him above. It is harmless. At the end a passport will be given to you with the result of your shots.

Animal Parks – Aquariums

■ **AQUARIUM MARE NOSTRUM**
Odysseum
Allée Ulysse
✆ +33 (0) 4 67 13 05 50
www.aquariummarenostrum.fr
contact@aquariummarenostrum.fr
Low season: open every day from 10am to 7pm. High season: every day and public holidays from 10am to 8pm. Cash desks closing 1.30am before closing. Free for under 5-year-olds. Adult: €15.50. Child (from 5 to 12 years old): €10.50. Group (20 people): €12.50. Reduced rate: €12.50. Ticket family: €48. Catering facilities. Shop.

The aim of this new generation aquarium, which already recorded two million visitors, is to discover the marine biodiversity and houses more than 300 species from the four corners of the world. Each sector is showcased with its species. Therefore follows; Californian fish, jellyfish, Mediterranean fauna, crowded in the 40th howling in the cabin of a cargo, landscape of ice and its penguins, the abyssal zone in the submarine of captain Némo, the scientific observation of the seabed, to end in the Tropics, at the edge of a lagoon and its multicoloured fish. At the exit, a well-stocked shop offers original gifts and souvenirs: decorative objects, cuddly toys, puzzles, books, CD and DVD player, and hundreds of gadgets... The success is such that 1,000 m² extra were added to complete the visit with an area dedicated to those alive, 7 new aquariums on the theme of the islands, a 180 seat auditorium broadcasting 3D film, documentaries, hosting conferences, seminars..., 3 educational rooms to develop the environmental education part, a simulation of hurricane, a new shop, and a new area dedicated to temporary exhibitions. Still new in 2013 on the first floor is the South African area. You embark for a dive into the heart of the south-African landscapes to meet the penguins of Cape Town, the only species of penguins present in the African continent.

direct access to the beach	visually impaired disability	take away
bar	mental handicap	room service
laundry	motor disability	fitness room
air conditioning	garden or park	playroom / tv
nightclub	games	modern sanitary
cash machine	washing machine / laundry	water sports
drinking water	bicycle rental	tennis
horse riding	grocery store	archery
smoking area	airport shuttle	waterslide
non-smoking	fishing	fan
fitness	indoor swimming pool	toilet drain
miniature golf	outdoor heated pool	sailing
hard of hearing disability	outdoor pool	

ANIMAL PARKS – AQUARIUMS

■ LE PETIT PARADIS
Route de Castries
RN110
VENDARGUES
✆ +33 (0) 4 67 91 99 33
www.petitparadis.com
contact@petitparadis.com

Low season: open on Wednesday, Saturday, Sunday and public holidays from 10am to 7pm. High season: every day and public holidays from 10am to 7pm. Open from 10am to 7pm during school holidays and from 2pm to 7pm the days of school from March 1st to October 25th. Free for under 2-year-olds. Adult: €6 (high season rate adults €7). Child (from 2 to 18 years old): €5. Group: €4 (group rate reserved the nurseries, to pupils… by reservation). Notebook of 10 child entries: €39. Holiday voucher. Children welcome.

Between Castries and Montpellier, a small paradise strives to delight children. A large botanical park of 1.5 acres has been planted in its centre a refreshing oasis of greenery. The whole is animated by a herd of miniature animals in semi-freedom: horses, cows, ponies… with the height of a toddler. Children scream of joy when discovering the pigs village or the island of goats! The most timid have some apprehensions in front of the geese or the bleating sheep… But they all love rabbits! Several playgrounds and picnic grounds were laid out in the park. An artificial lake also allows children to discover the aquatic environment and especially beautiful Japanese carp specimens. You can take a tour in the boat on the lake. A mini-golf course completes the wonderful offers of this park! A paradise for adults too.

■ PARC ZOOLOGIQUE DU LUNARET
50, avenue Agropolis
✆ +33 (0) 4 67 54 45 23
www.zoo-montpellier.fr

Open from 9.30am to 6.30pm from April 1st to September 30th, from 10am to 6pm from February 1st to March 31st and in October, de10h at 5pm from November 1st to January 31st. Closed weekly Monday. Free. Except Amazonian greenhouse. Children welcome.

It is undoubtedly one of the most popular attractions in public places of the city. In the morning, the joggers stride along the sand paths, strollers arriving later, then families (possibility to picnic) who come to get lost on the nine kilometres of pedestrian paths or take a small train. This large hill with its 80 acres of scrubland, forest of green oaks and Alep pines, the greenest public area of the city, houses many animals in partial release. The population of the zoo is enriched from year to year. The lion of the Atlas saw itself joined by two new lionesses while the powerful rhinoceros is now accompanied by two females. Two cheetahs, a maned wolf, Iberian wolf and Bongo antelopes joined the 150 species already present on the site. Since March 2010, a large enclosure housing four giraffes of Rotschild came to enrich all the species in the park. A walk is necessary to make for all the Montpellier inhabitants and the tourists.

Travel – Tourism – Transport

Travel Agencies → 116
Transport → 116
Vehicle Rentals → 120

Travel Agencies

■ **EUROMER ET CIEL VOYAGES**
5 et 7, quai de sauvages
✆ +33 (0)4 67 65 95 11
www.euromer.com
info@euromer.net
Open Monday to Friday from 9am to 7pm; Saturday from 9am to 6pm.
When the ferries travel specialist, well-known by camping-caravaning drivers creates a business aviation agency, of air cargo and airlines representation (GSA) that gives Euromer & Ciel Voyages. This agency, or rather this group, ably led by Philippe Sala for nearly 20 years has a full range of the travel products: charter flights & regular, train tickets, tours, trips, cruises, hotel booking, organised visits trip… There is everything. The future traveller is greeted by a smiling staff and always of good advice. Note that the website is particularly clear and easy to use. Even the less geeks among you should be able to prepare their trip there in peace.

Transport

■ **TAXI TRAM**
1, place de Strasbourg
✆ +33 (0)4 67 58 10 10 / +33 (0)4 67 92 04 55
www.taxi-tram.fr
taxi.tram@wanadoo.fr
Taxis available 7 days a week, 24/24.
Group of Independent craftsmen, Taxi Tram has about fifty air-conditioned cars, from 4 to 6 seats (trucks, breaks, minivans). Drivers are at your service throughout the year for the classic tours, but also for school transport, the tourist routes, and the exits of hospital…

Bus – Coach

■ **EUROLINES**
8, rue de Verdun
✆ 08 92 89 90 91
www.eurolines.fr
montpellier@vt-eurolines.eu
Open Monday to Saturday from 10am to 12pm and from 2pm to 6pm.
The most well-known truck operators companies carries the Montpellier inhabitants in search of travelling over five hundred destinations in Europe (the main ones are: Barcelona, Milan, Madrid), and offers them many attractive promotions throughout the year. Enough to satisfy the enemies of plane and the small wallets!

■ **HERAULT TRANSPORT**
148, avenue du Professeur-Viala
Parc Euromédecine II
✆ +33 (0)4 34 88 89 99
www.herault-transport.fr
info@herault-transport.fr
Open Monday to Friday from 8.30am to 12.30pm and from 1.15pm to 5pm.
This organization elected by the general council controls the departmental transport companies. It provides information on the various lines and publishes time sheets, found in the bus stations, Tourist Offices and the town halls. The time sheets and rates are also available on the site.

Train

■ **GARE DE MONTPELLIER-SAINT-ROCH**
Place Auguste-Gibert
✆ 36 35
www.sncf.com
The Montpellier train station, open from 4: 30 pm to midnight during the week, with variations on the weekend, is crossed by the TER and TGV. The TGV makes the junction twelve times a day from Paris (in 3 hours 30), plus a night trip at slow speed. It is possible to buy your ticket at one of the machines of the station, to order online or by telephone – delivery of the ticket at home -, or go to one of the SNCF shops. Ask for information there comfortably on the rates and the hours, but take your dignified suffering as it may be quite long. The advide of Petit Futé: if you are in the historic centre, choose the small SNCF shop rue Saint-Guilhem to prepare your trip or buy tickets. It is much nicer and above all, the wait is less long!

■ **IDTGV**
www.idtgv.com
IDTGV is a service erected exclusively on the Internet. Reservations are open every 3 months for the next 6 months. You can start the day with iDTGV from 19 €, the prices of the attractive tickets are open to all and without restraint: it is needless to spend the weekend on site or take a shuttle to enjoy it. The prices are valid for all ages and all periods of the year. Booking is made exclusively on Internet and tickets must be printed or embedded on a Smartphone via the iDTGV application. If you wish to change your departure days and/or travel time, you will have to pay 12 € expenses for a change in line and 17 € by telephone with the help of an advisor per passenger and trip, as well as possible price difference between the old and the new ticket. The iDTGV ticket is only exchangeable against another iDTGV ticket, other than any other ticket, especially the SNCF tickets (TGV, Corail…). You can also choose your atmosphere: iDZen (quiet) or iDZap (you can make telephone calls). iDZinc, the bar car offers a variety of activities: concerts, touchpad, nibbling… A «door to door» service thanks to the Navendis mini-shuttles is bookable until 12 hours before the departure of train and available from the idtgv.com site. This service is offered at the departure or the arrival of the Parisian stations. With Navendi, the price of the trip is known from reservation, the prices are fixed and car sharing is rewarded by a 4 € voucher to needed on a next booking.

Urban Transport

■ **HERAULT-TRANSPORT**
148, avenue du Professeur-Viala
Parc Euromédecine II
✆ +33 (0)4 34 88 89 99
www.herault-transport.fr
info@herault-transport.fr
Open Monday to Friday from 8.30am to 12.30pm and from 1.15pm to 5pm.
With a ticket, a network of bus is at your disposal! Hérault-Transport provides bus connections by coach to the hinterland, the other regions and the towns and villages of the urban area of Montpellier.
Every day, several lines connect Montpellier to Palavas, Carnon, La Grande-Motte, Sète, Agde, Béziers… In all, nearly 70 lines take you anywhere you want. Some intermodal titles allow you to also travel on the urban network of Montpellier.

■ **TAM**
6, rue Jules-Ferry
✆ +33 (0)4 67 22 87 87
www.tam-way.com
contact@tam-way.com
Open Monday to Saturday from 7am to 7pm. Second antenna: 27, rue Maguelone (Monday to Saturday of 9am to 12 and from 2pm to 5pm).

Opposite the station, the TAM offices will provide information on their rates, or if you do not have the courage to queue, you will find hours and maps of the network on leaflets. Montpellier is well served by the TAM, its four trams and its colourful fleet of blue buses: 30 lines link the cities of the urban area.

■ VELOMAGG'
27, rue Maguelone
✆ +33 (0)4 67 22 87 87
www.velomagg.com
contact@montpellier-agglo.com
Open Monday to Saturday from 7am to 7pm. 0.50 €/h, from 3 to 12 months: €50 with the card Pass' Agglo, €80 without.
Following the example of Paris, Montpellier Agglomération created in 2007 its system of bicycle rental at low cost. Thousand bikes are now open to residents and tourists in fifty bike stations- Tam agency, Saint-Roch station, Tam car parks in the city centre, bike parks of the tram car parks, Maisons de l'Agglomération, pools, media libraries, Maisons pour Tous, Tourist Office, Crous, etc. The rentals are noted down for durations ranging from a few hours to a year. The Tam subscribers benefit from the free payment on the short stay rentals.

Plane

■ AÉROPORT MONTPELLIER-MÉDITERRANÉE
Mauguio
✆ +33 (0)4 67 20 85 00
www.montpellier.aeroport.com
rh@montpellier.aeroport.fr
Open from 5.30am to 11pm. A shuttle makes it possible to join Montpellier (Place de l'Europe, stop served by trams 1 and 4) in 15 minutes, every day from 8.30am to 11pm approximately. Schedule on www.herault-transport.fr.
The Montpellier airport leads to regular companies: Air France, Ryanair, Easy Jet and Air Arabia. Possible destinations in France: Lille, Nantes, Lyon, Paris, Strasbourg. In Europe, Rotterdam, Munich, London, Frankfurt, Brussels, and, in season: Ajaccio! (2 weekly flights from the end of April to the beginning of October), and various Moroccan towns, and exceptionally the Madeira (only on March 27th and May 12th, 2014). New: Alitalia opened a line to Rome from Montpellier, since March 2013, with 3 flights and the planes also go and come from Copenhagen (seasonal), with Norwegian at a rate of 4 weekly flights from June 23rd to August 9th, 2014. And if you do not find your happiness here, take a look at the flights served from Marseille-Provence, in just 1hr30 by car via the A9. Guests can go far and for unbeatable prices.

Parking – Car Parks

■ TAM STATIONNEMENT
5, rue Frédéric-Fabrèges
✆ +33 (0)4 67 58 55 25
www.montpellier-agglo.com
Open on Monday of 8.30am at 18: 50; Tuesday to Friday of 8.30am at 17: 50; Saturday from 9.30am to 12.30pm and from 1pm to 4pm.
In addition to public transport, Tam manages seven car parks in the city centre (that is; 4,000 places). The car parks (Arceaux, Comédie, Corum, Europa, Gambetta, Laissac and Antigone) each have different rates, but offer resident rates. As for the places on highways, there are 3 parking areas: short (yellow area), average (orange area) and long life (green area). The guests can (and must) get the Oxygène card which allows you to pay much cheaper your parking. Since parking is expensive in Montpellier, we recommend the tram!

Taxis

■ TAXI BLEU DU MIDI
148, rue Marius-Carrieu
✆ +33 (0)4 67 03 20 00 / +33 (0)4 67 10 00 00 / +33 (0)4 67 70 36 21
www.taxisbleudumidi.fr
contact@taxibleudumidi.fr
Open every day. 24/24. 7 days a week, 24/24.
A simple call, 24hrs/24 and 7days/7, and a blue taxi from the South comes for your outing in Hérault, in a radius of 40 km around Montpellier. In addition to the standard tours, from the airport or train station for example, officially agreed medical transport, the tourist routes, the Taxis Bleus also offer services for companies organising conferences, and can also take care of the delivery of an urgent package! A VIP service for great events where the prestigious guests also exist...

■ TAXI TRAM
1, place de Strasbourg
✆ +33 (0)4 67 58 10 10 / +33 (0)4 67 92 04 55
www.taxi-tram.fr
taxi.tram@wanadoo.fr
Taxis available 7 days a week, 24/24.
Association of independent craftsmen, «Taxis Radio Artisans Montpellier», based in front of the Saint-Roch station is at your service throughout the year. They have a fleet of fifty air-conditioned taxis, from 4 to 6 seats, for the classic tours, but also for school transport, the tourist routes, the hospital exits...

Find all our best deals and good addresses on our website www.petitfute.uk.com

Vehicle Rentals

Car

■ ADA
58 bis, avenue Clemenceau
✆ +33 (0)4 67 58 34 35 - www.ada.fr
Open Monday to Friday from 8am to 7pm; Saturday from 9am to 12.30pm and from 3.30pm to 7pm. Car rental week or weekend: from €0.25 the km.
Ada's rates are among the lowest of the market. They offer packages of all kinds to adapt to request. Possibility of car rental for a day, for the weekend or a week, and commercial vehicles from 3 to 23 m³. Good service, and professionalism: vehicles are inspected before departure and very well maintained. The vehicles must be returned to the agency where they were recovered.
Other agencies: at the Fréjorgues Montpellier airport ✆ +33 (0)4 67 20 02 12 or opposite the station, 12 bis rue Jules-Ferry (tel) +33 (0)4 67 92 78 77.

■ AUTO HANDICAP 34
226, rue de la Jasse-de-Maurin
✆ +33 (0)4 67 69 35 50
www.auto-handicap34.fr
Open Monday to Friday from 9am to 12pm and from 2pm to 6pm. Rental day from €79, the week at €377 and the month at €944. Vehicle adapted to the transport of the people in wheel chair: from €99 per day.
Auto Handicap offers two distinct types of services to disabled people: for drivers and passengers. For the first, the establishment offers the installation of helping equipment for the driving adapted to handicap; for the second, it equips the vehicle with the helping equipment to transport, designed for people with disabilities in armchair (TPMR). Auto Handicap also rents cars of category A (Modus Twingo) or B (Peugeot 307, Clio) in adapted automatic version, as well as more imposing vehicles (Renault Kangoo or Traffic, Peugeot Partner). A very professional address where reception and the council are particularly efficient.

■ AUTO LOCATION 34
754, avenue du Marché de la Gare
✆ +33 (0)4 67 34 00 22
www.autolocation34.fr
Open Monday to Friday from 7.30am to 12pm and from 2pm to 6.30pm; Saturday from 9am to 12pm and from 6pm to 7pm. Located next to the highway, this independent company created by Laurent Fort in 1990 combines speed and efficiency. The range is wide whether you want to buy a sofa and reserve a van (from 38 € 1/2 a day), or whether you want a vehicle for a week (Ford party 35 €/day for 150 km), finally minivan (for a weekend 170 €) and minibus of 9 seats with a large safe (from 109 €).

■ BSP AUTO
✆ +33 (0)1 43 46 20 74 - www.bsp-auto.com
Open every day from 9am to 10pm. Free estimate. From 28 € per day for a 7 days duration in a category A.
The greatest selection of large car-hirers in the train stations, airports and city centres with the most competitive rates in the market. The rates always include unlimited mileage and insurances. Bonus BSP: book now and pay only 5 days before taking your vehicle, no application fee nor cancellation fees, the cheapest zero deductible services around. Special discount for the readers of this guide with the code «petit futé».

Bicycles

■ VELOMAGG'
27, rue Maguelone ✆ +33 (0)4 67 22 87 87
www.velomagg.com
Accessible service 24/24 and 7 days a week. Rental tourist: €0.50 per hour. Creating Vélomagg', the city of Montpellier did not suspect the success of such an operation. The bicycles are available in 49 stations in the city. A practical and cheap way of transport when you leave the pedestrian and steep Ecusson! To enjoy these bikes, there are several possibilities: the annual subscription card, use your credit card in a point of reception or add the Velomagg extension to your subscription for public transport from the TAM. Caution: only the points of the main stations function with a credit card: take a bike in a spontaneous way could run you to this problem. It is better to learn about the site in advance. Recent and quite unknown service: electric bikes can be tried, for 5 € /day. Information at the Velomagg agency of the Saint-Roch station.

Boat

■ LOCABOAT PLAISANCE
LATTES
✆ +33 (0)4 67 20 24 12 - www.locaboat.com
No the rental from November 8th to March 25th. Open the starting days from 2pm. Rental-week of a pénichette classical 3-5 people: €847 off-season, €1,547 in summer.
Renter of barges, Locaboat Plaisance allows you to spend peaceful holidays, while sailing quietly away from the noise (on the rivers and canals, no jet skis) to the rhythm of canal du midi and the bassin de Thau. The renter offers 3 types of small barges: the classic one, on the terrace or flying bridge. Whether you are two or twelve, you will find the boat that you need! As for your apprehensions for sailing, no worries: Locaboat offers an introduction to you before departure (it is generally held at Lattes) to familiarize you with the passages of locks. Then, good sailing!